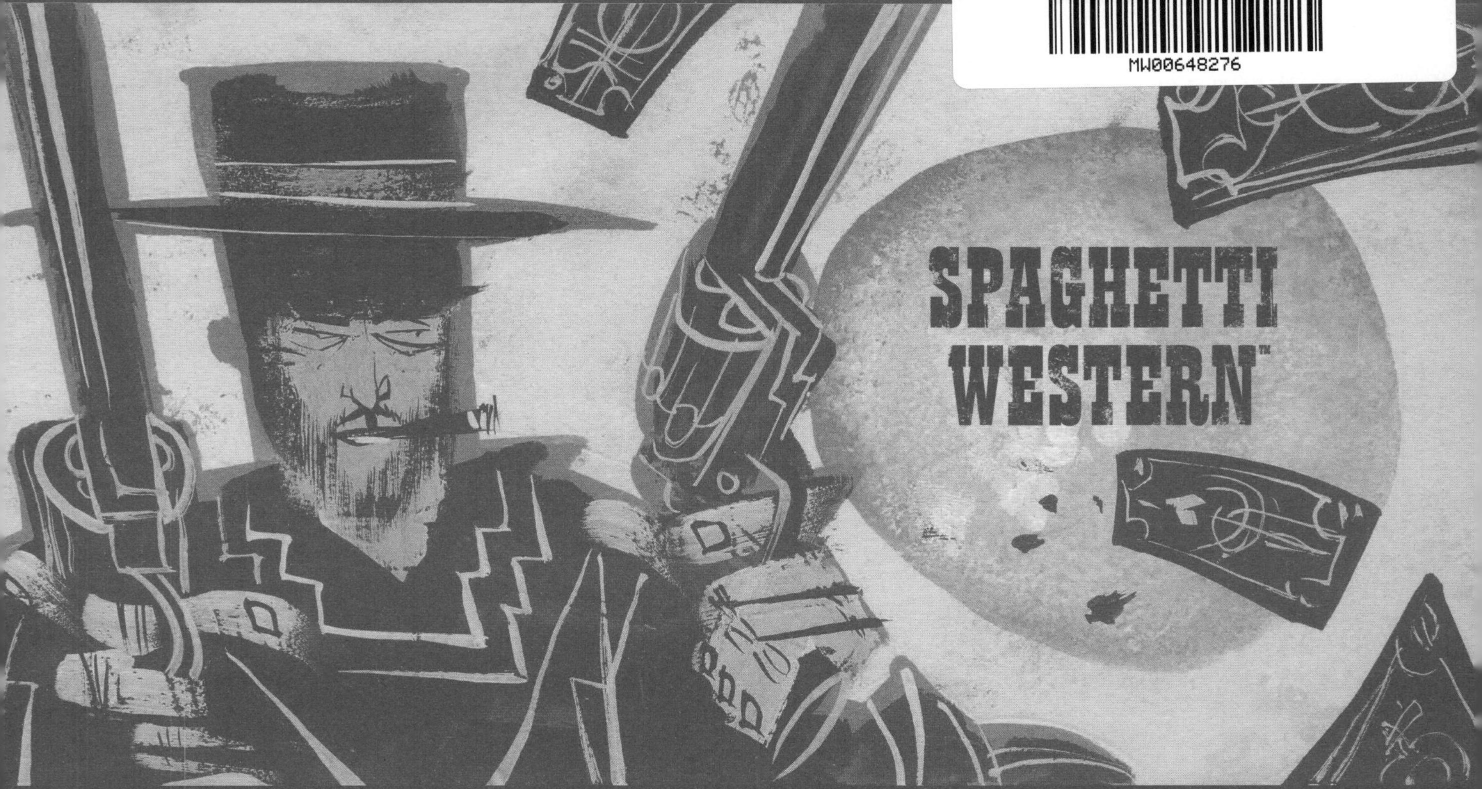
SPAGHETTI
WESTERN™

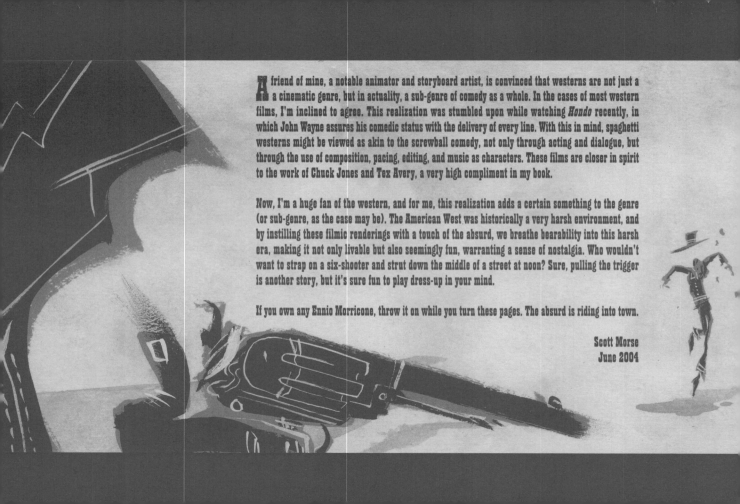

A friend of mine, a notable animator and storyboard artist, is convinced that westerns are not just a cinematic genre, but in actuality, a sub-genre of comedy as a whole. In the cases of most western films, I'm inclined to agree. This realization was stumbled upon while watching *Hondo* recently, in which John Wayne assures his comedic status with the delivery of every line. With this in mind, spaghetti westerns might be viewed as akin to the screwball comedy, not only through acting and dialogue, but through the use of composition, pacing, editing, and music as characters. These films are closer in spirit to the work of Chuck Jones and Tex Avery, a very high compliment in my book.

Now, I'm a huge fan of the western, and for me, this realization adds a certain something to the genre (or sub-genre, as the case may be). The American West was historically a very harsh environment, and by instilling these filmic renderings with a touch of the absurd, we breathe bearability into this harsh era, making it not only livable but also seemingly fun, warranting a sense of nostalgia. Who wouldn't want to strap on a six-shooter and strut down the middle of a street at noon? Sure, pulling the trigger is another story, but it's sure fun to play dress-up in your mind.

If you own any Ennio Morricone, throw it on while you turn these pages. The absurd is riding into town.

Scott Morse
June 2004

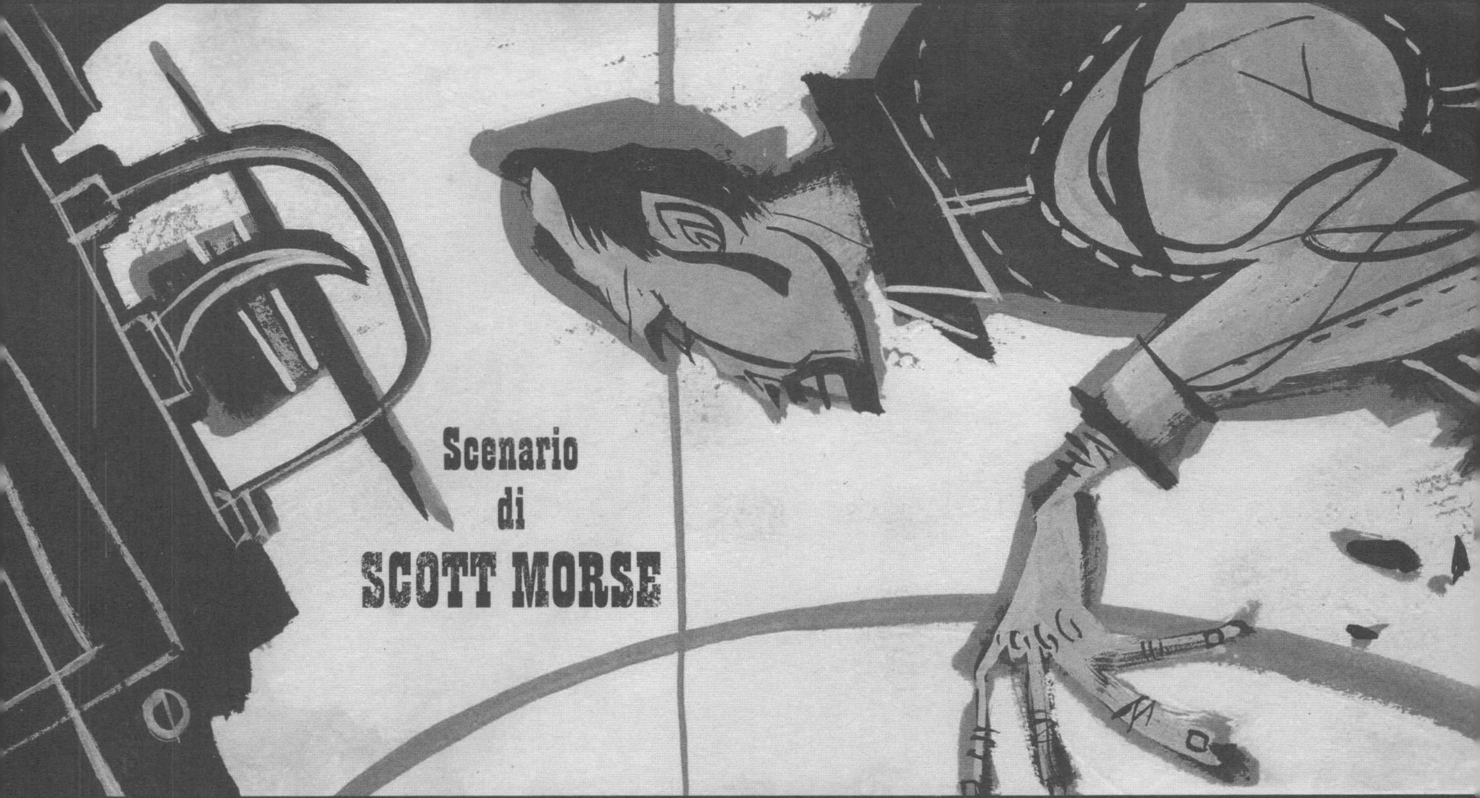
Scenario
di
SCOTT MORSE

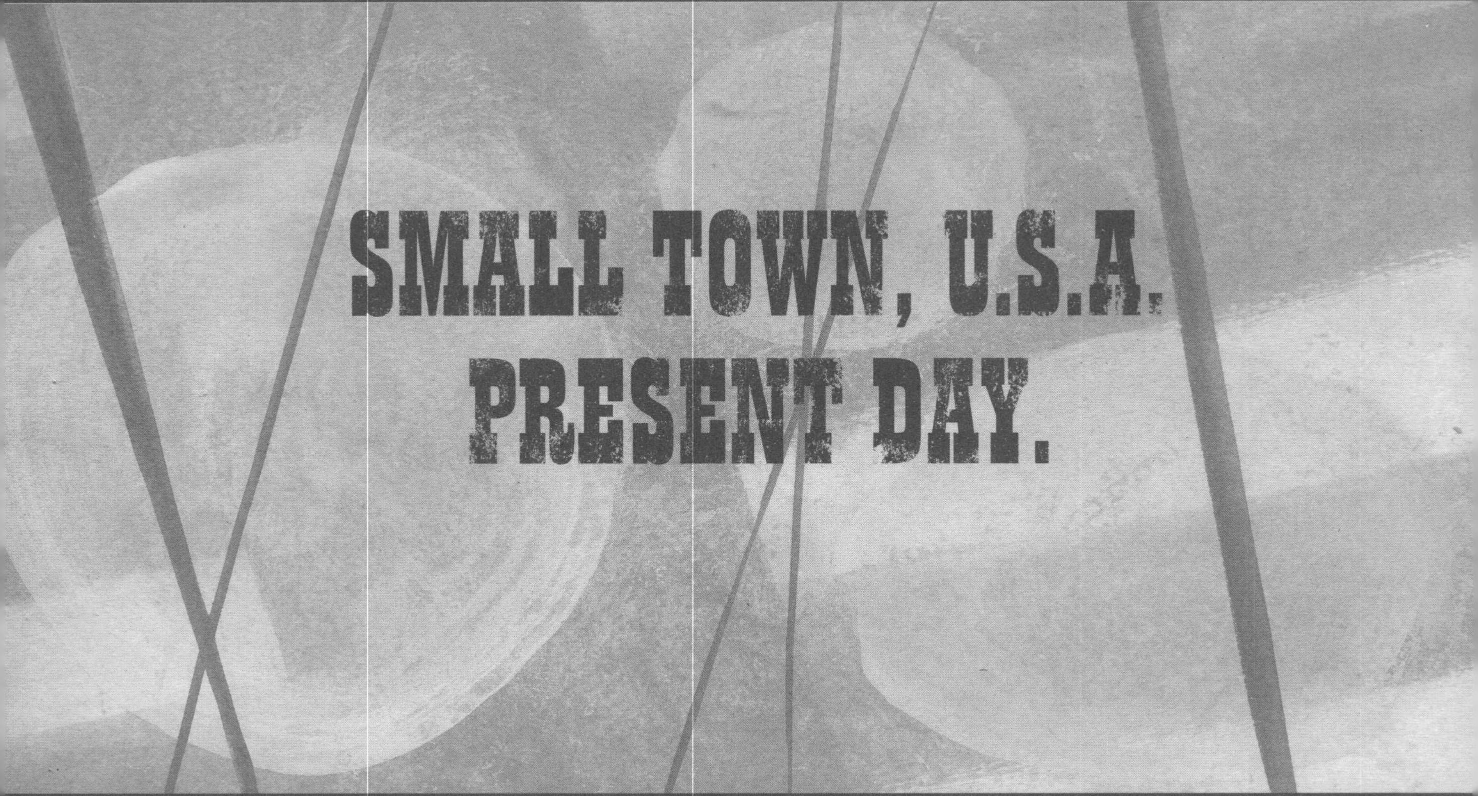
SMALL TOWN, U.S.A.
PRESENT DAY.

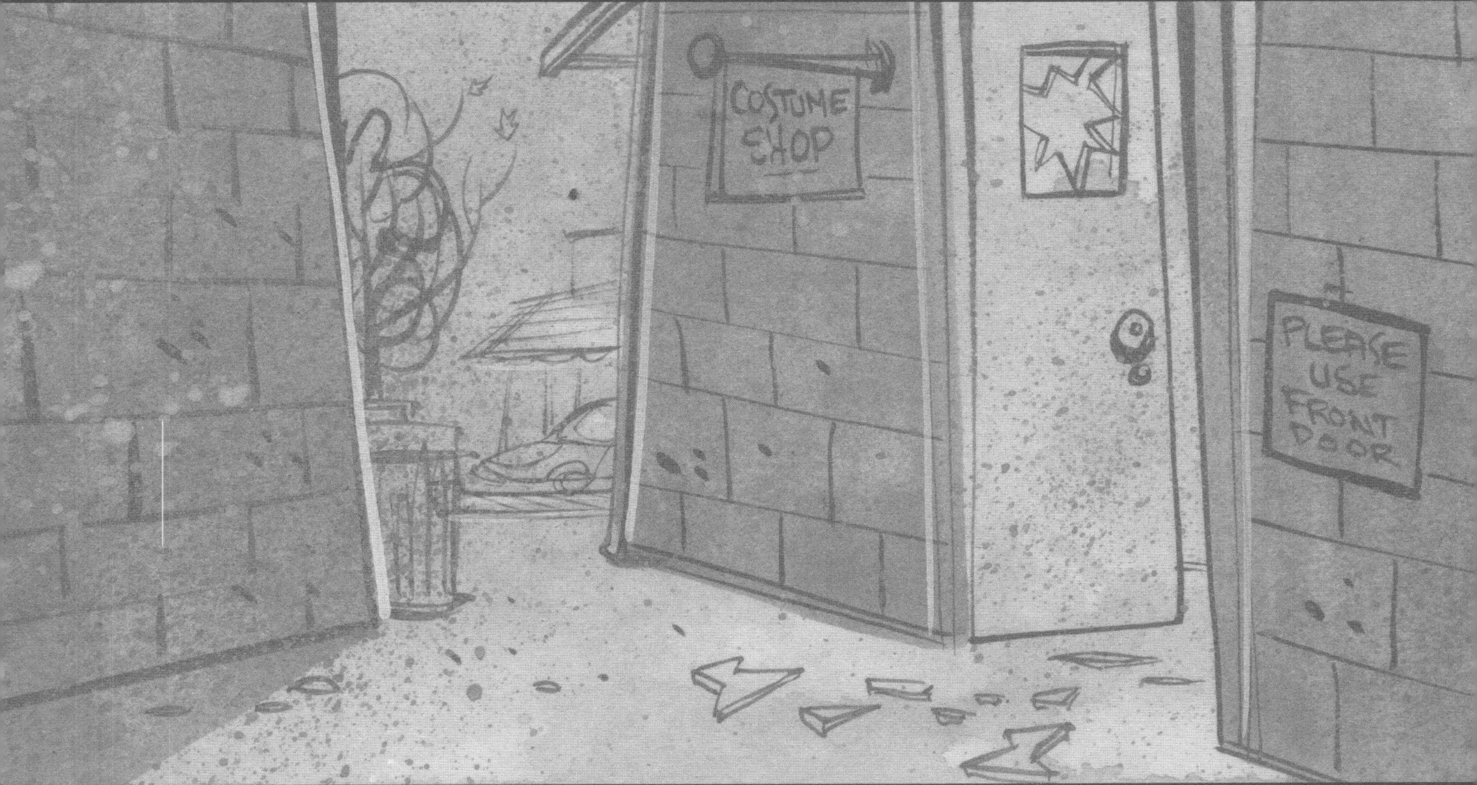
COSTUME SHOP
PLEASE USE FRONT DOOR

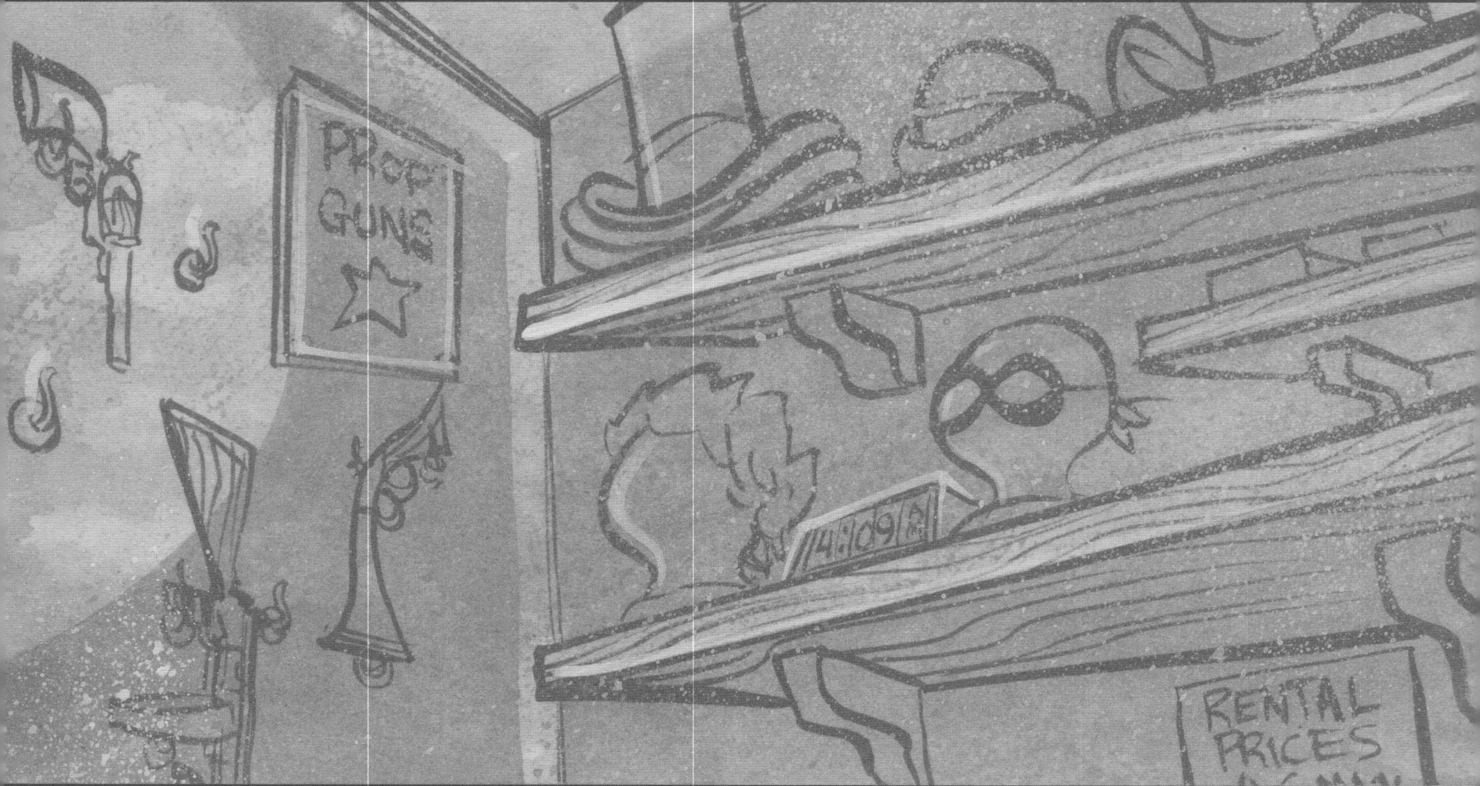
PROP GUNS
4:09 AM
RENTAL PRICES

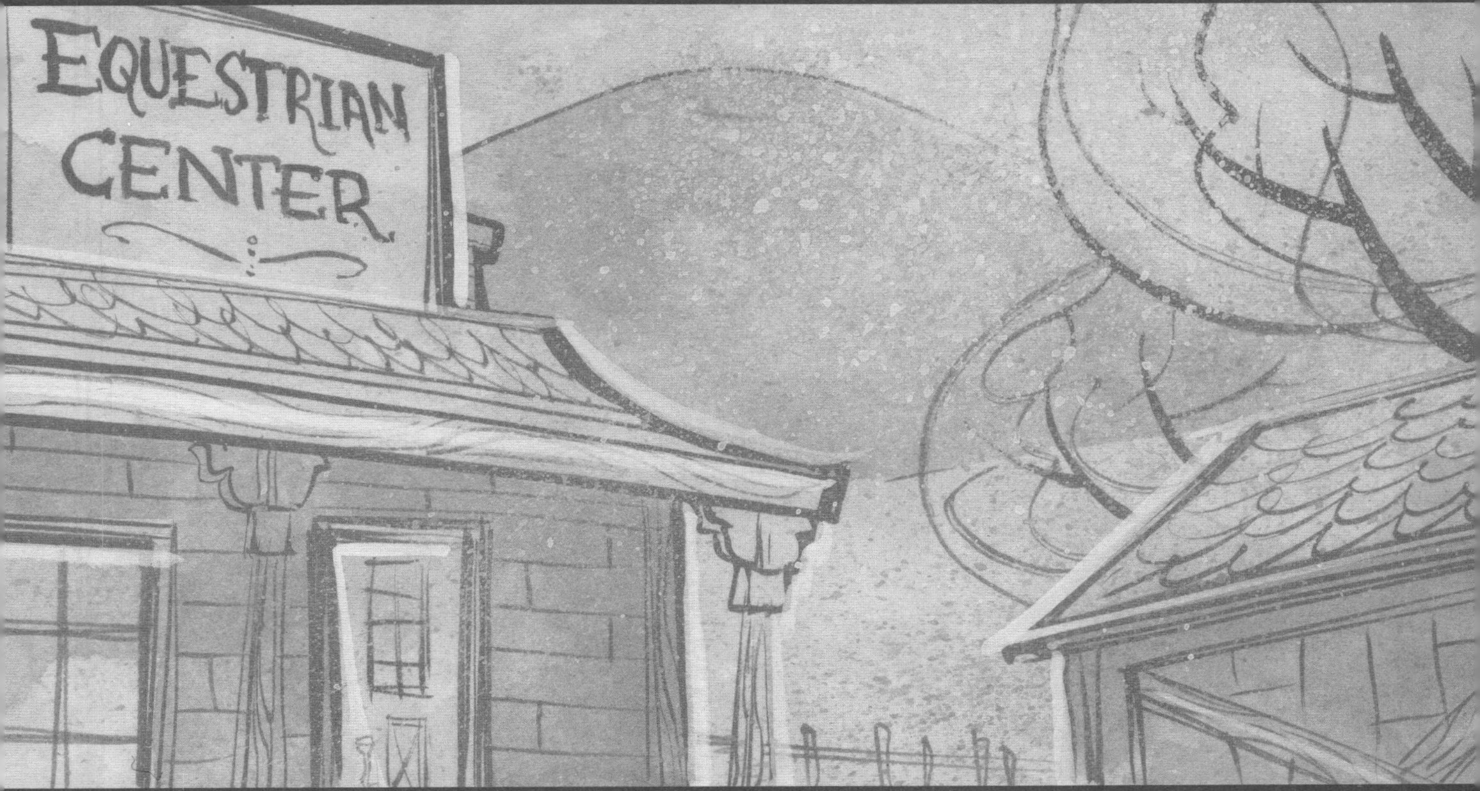
EQUESTRIAN
CENTER

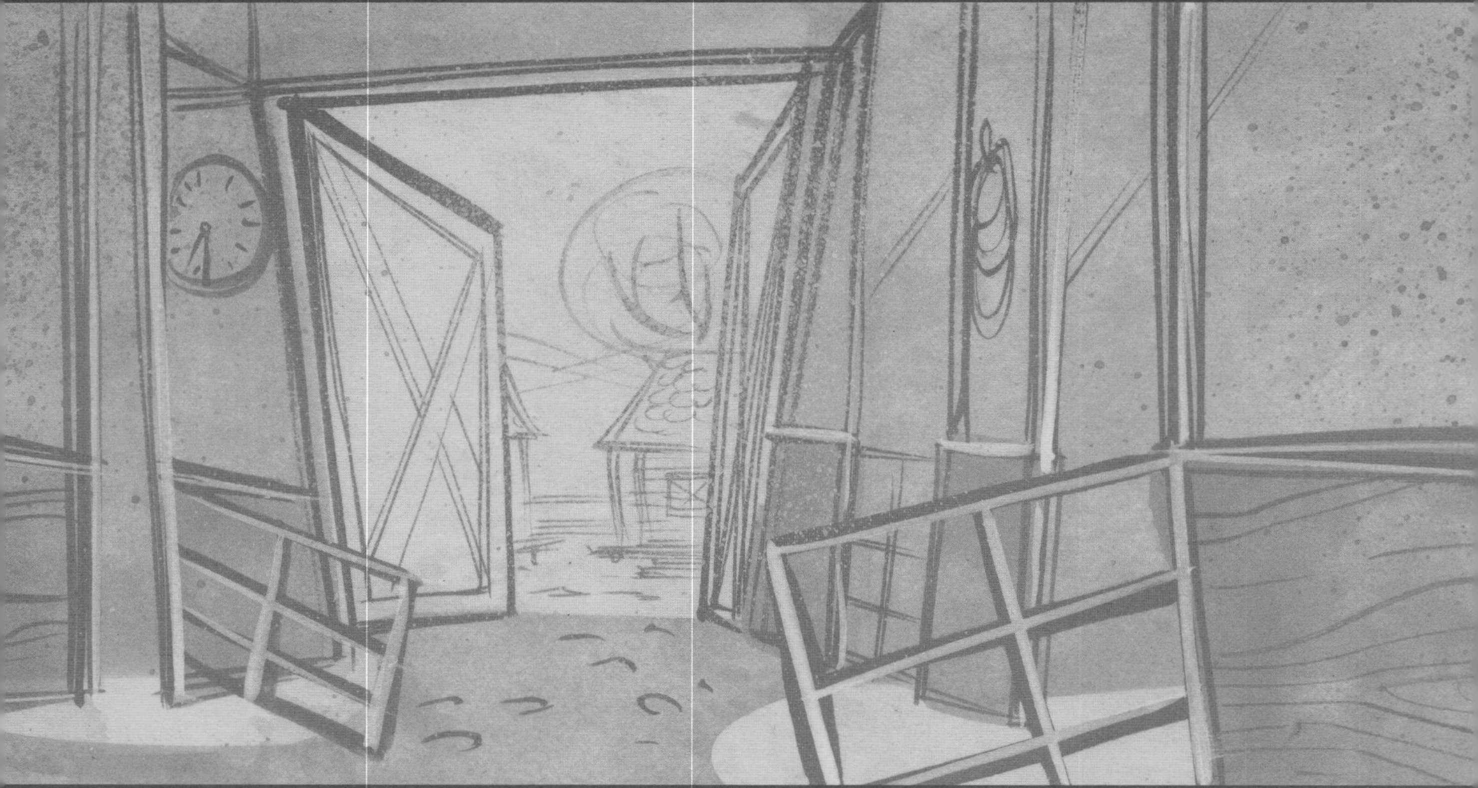

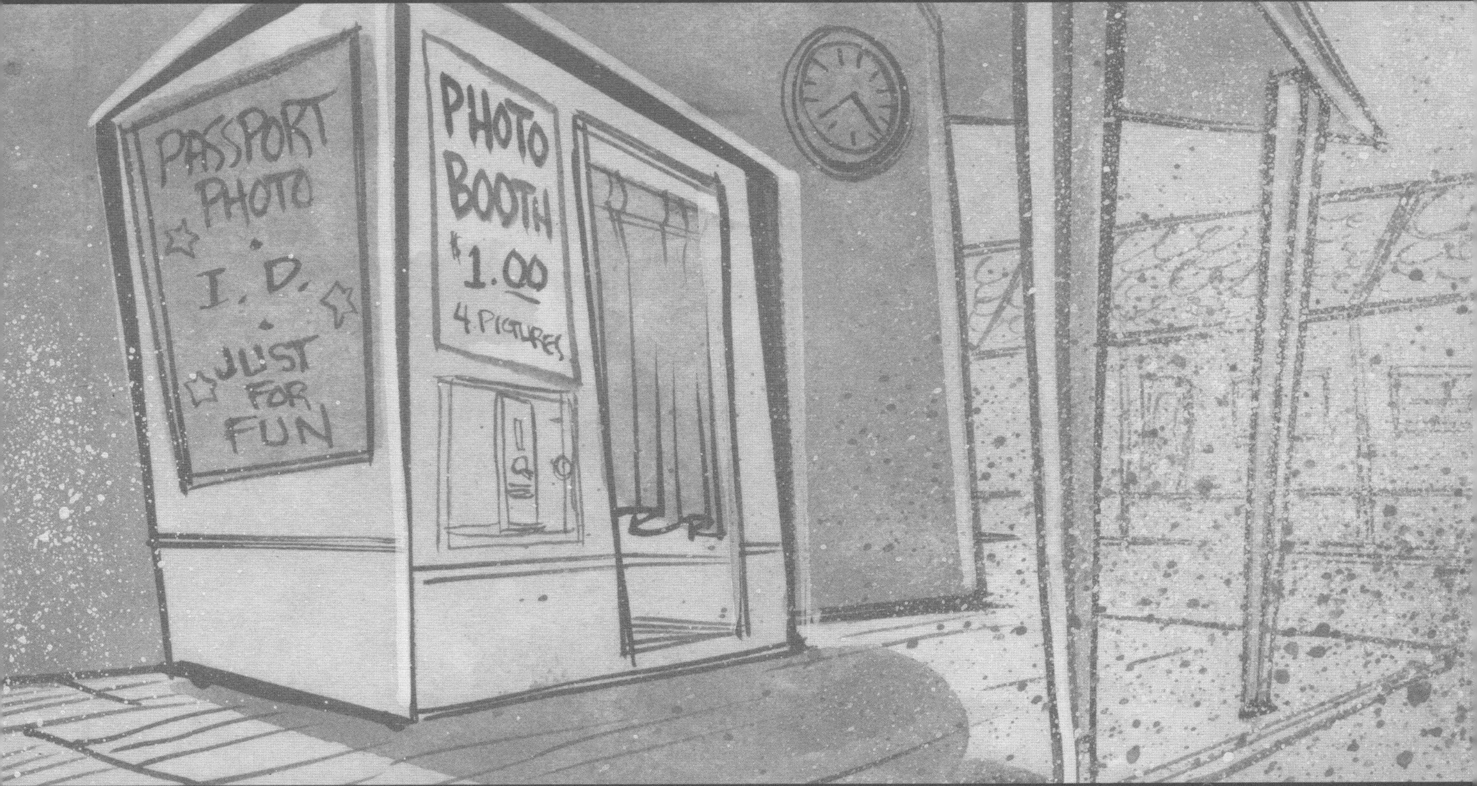
PASSPORT PHOTO
I. D.
JUST FOR FUN
PHOTO BOOTH
$1.00
4 PICTURES

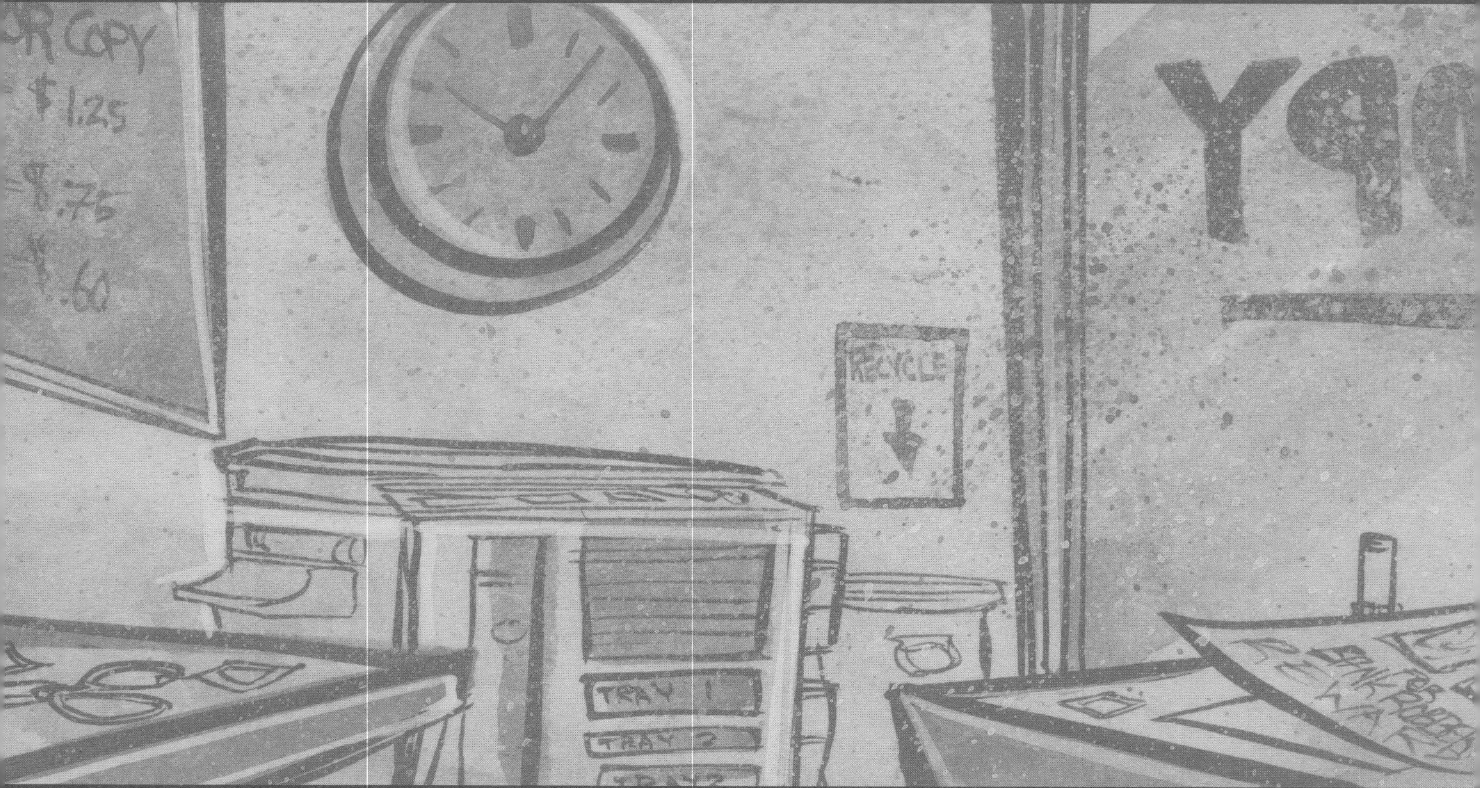
OR COPY
$1.25
$.75
$.60
RECYCLE
TRAY 1
TRAY 2

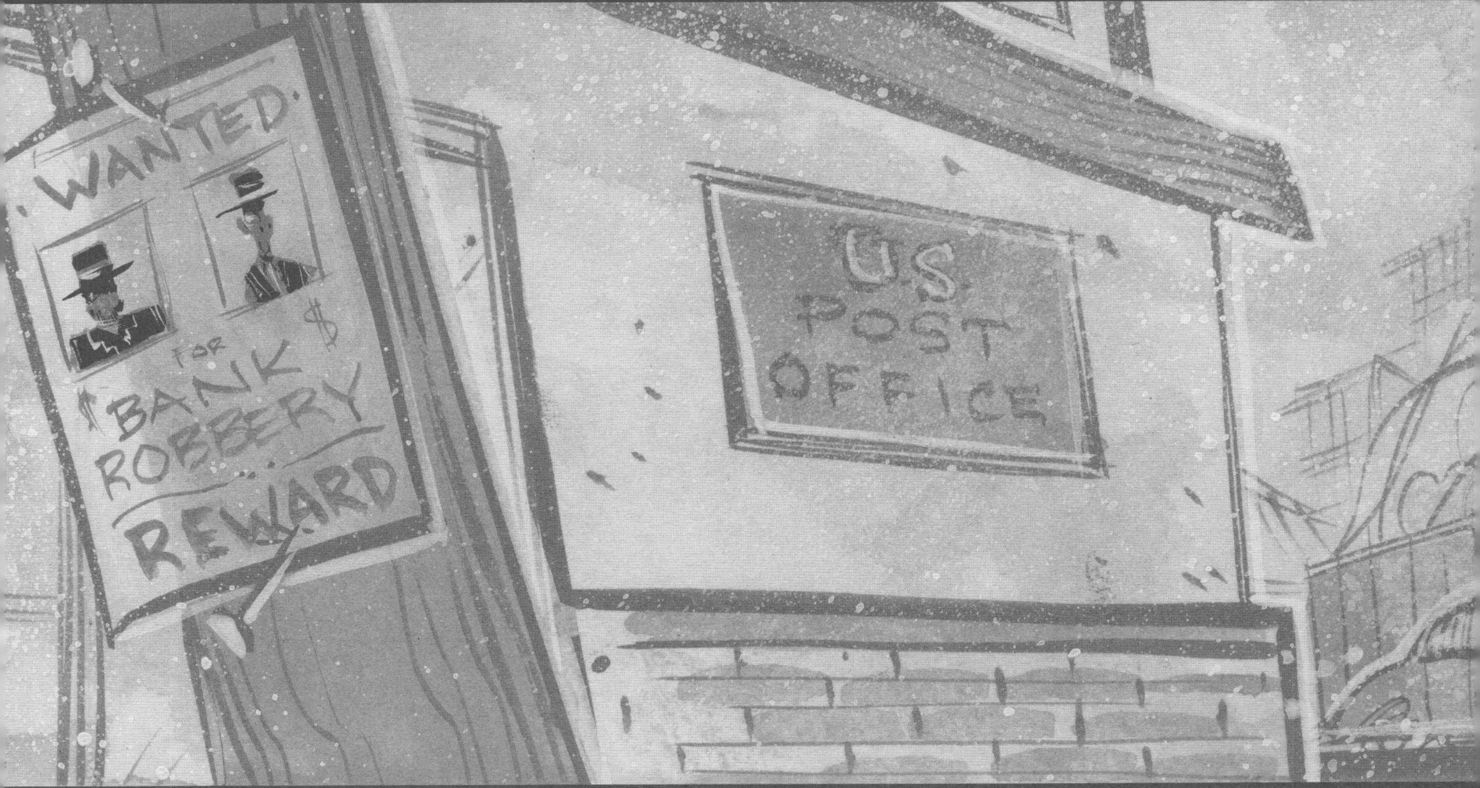
WANTED
$
FOR
BANK
ROBBERY
REWARD
U.S.
POST
OFFICE

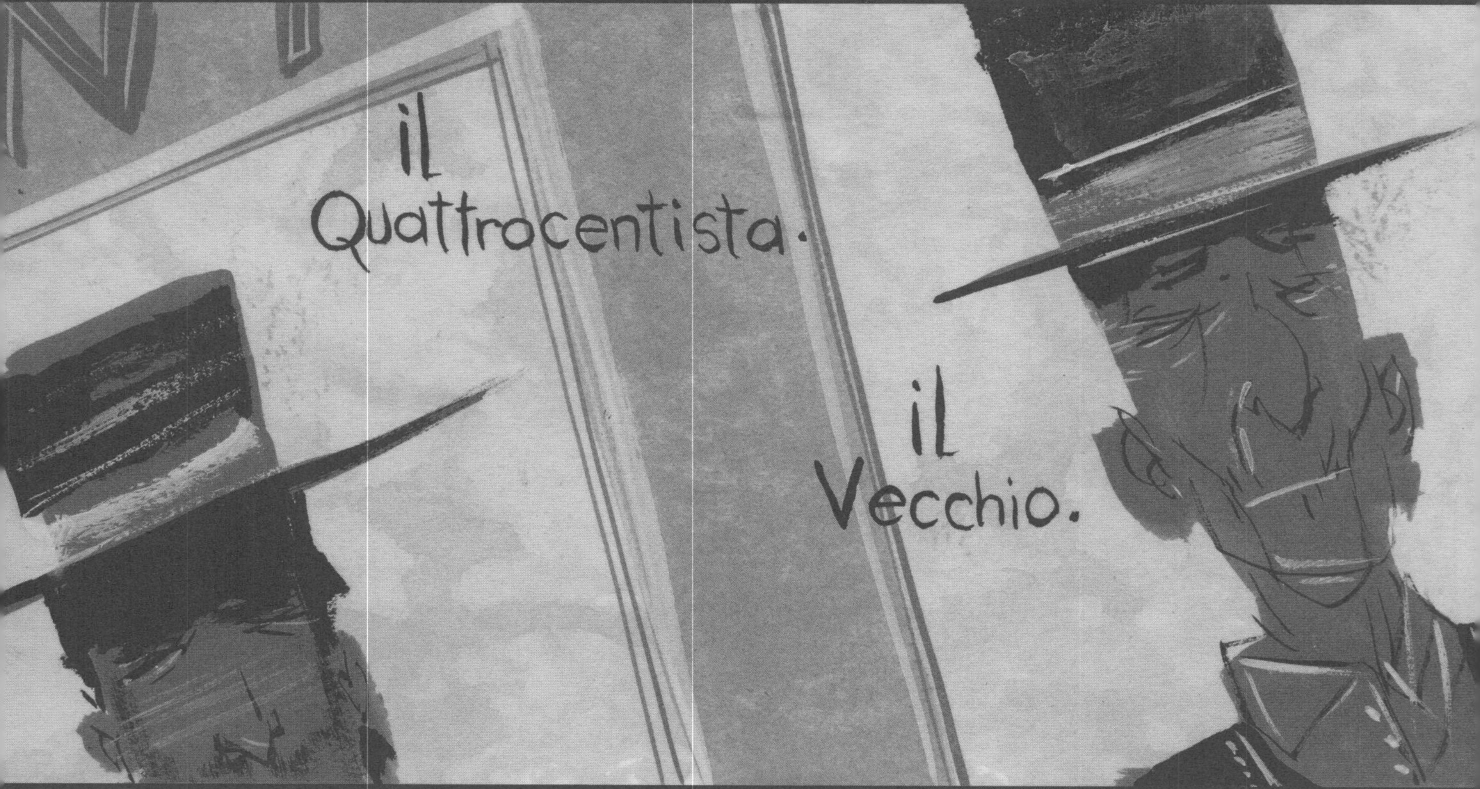
il Quattrocentista.
il Vecchio.

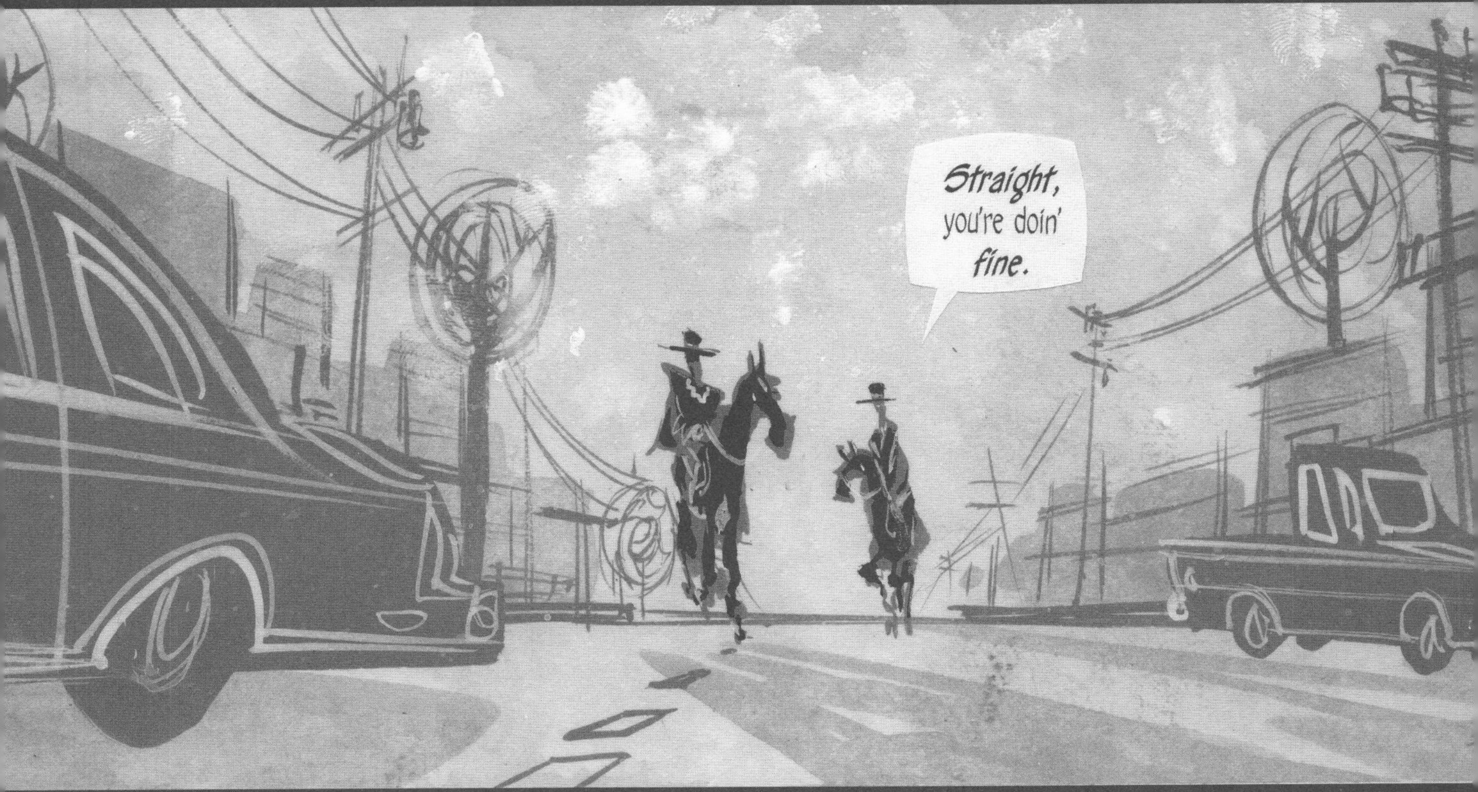
Straight, you're doin' fine.

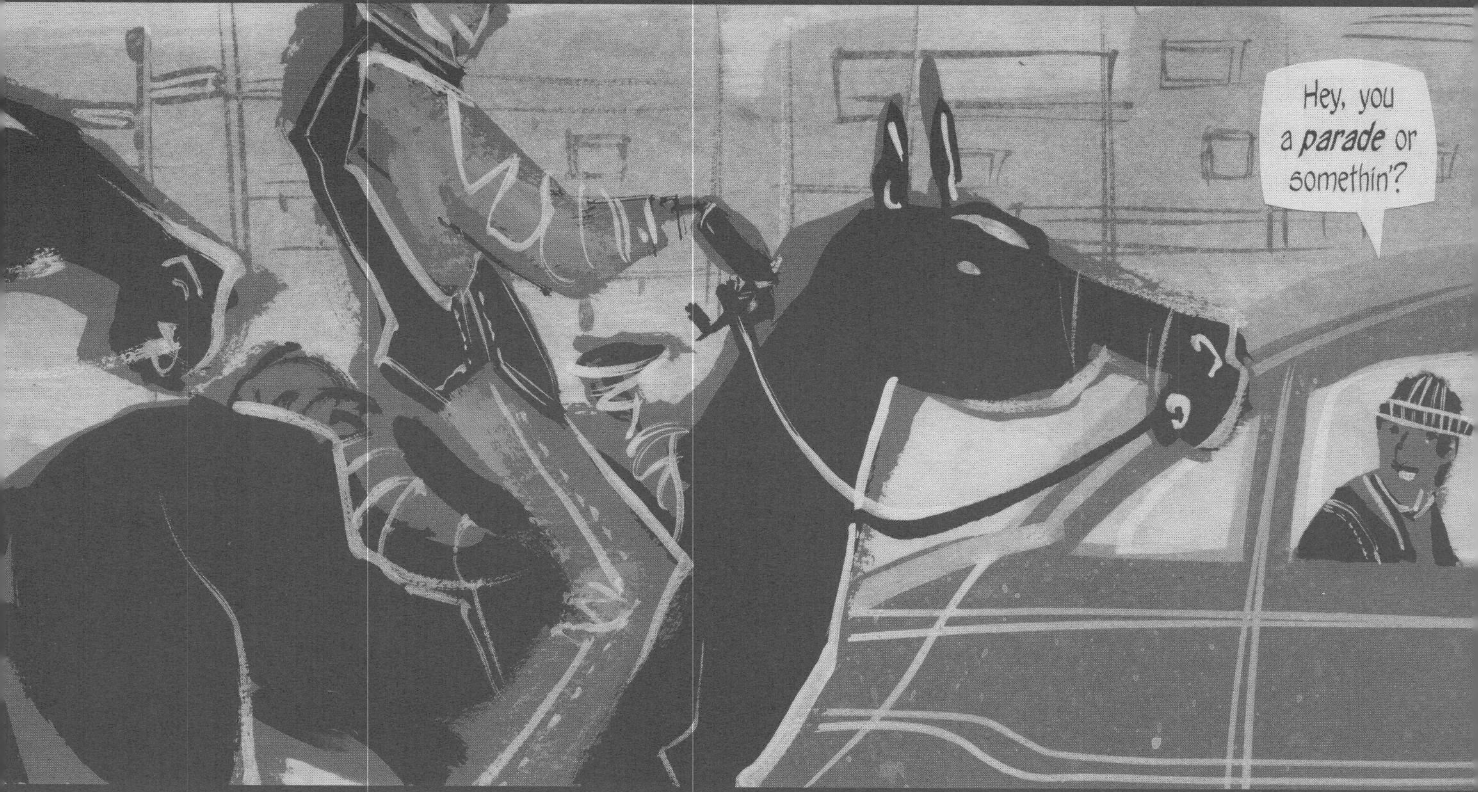
Hey, you a *parade* or somethin'?

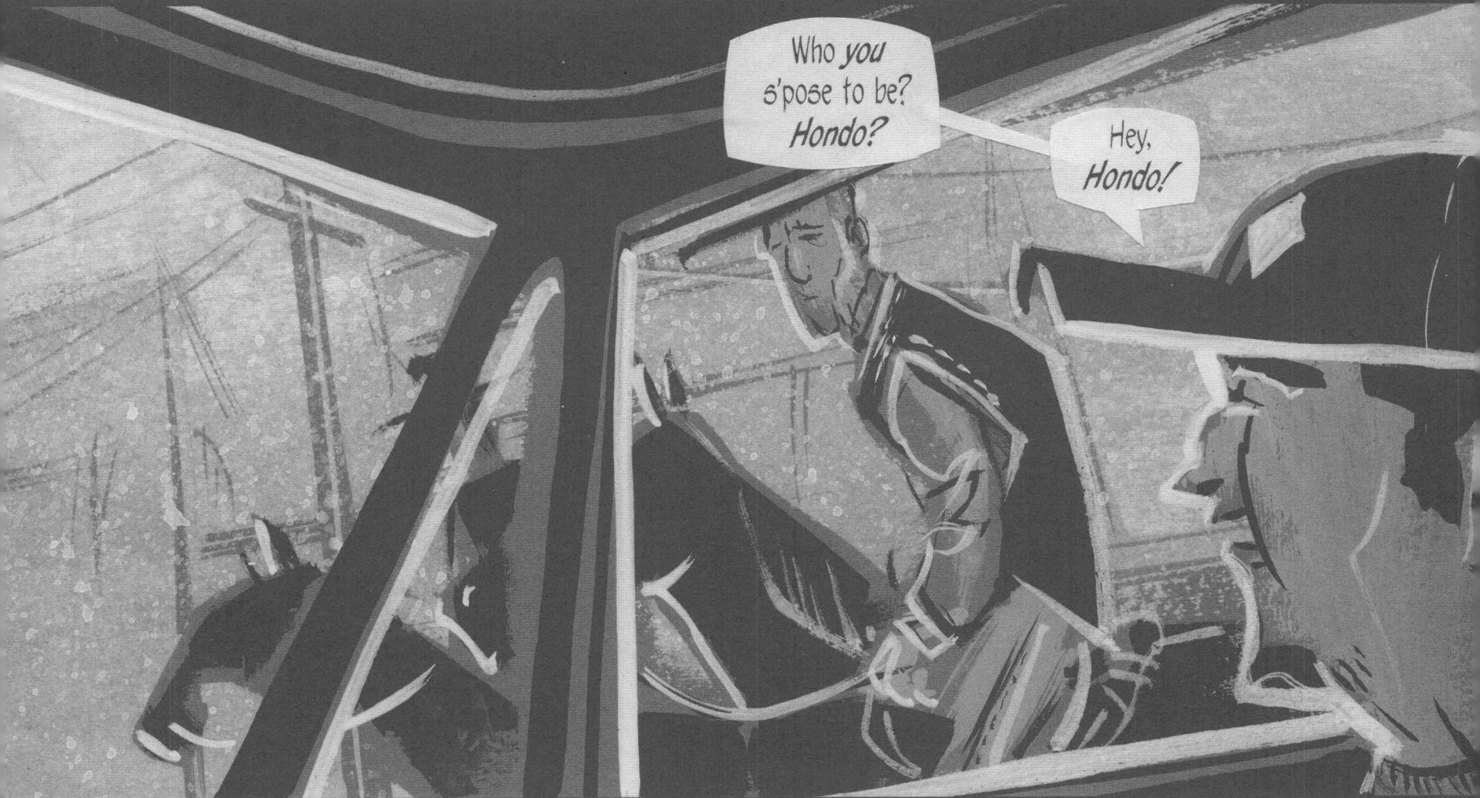
Hey, Hondo!
Who you s'pose to be? Hondo?

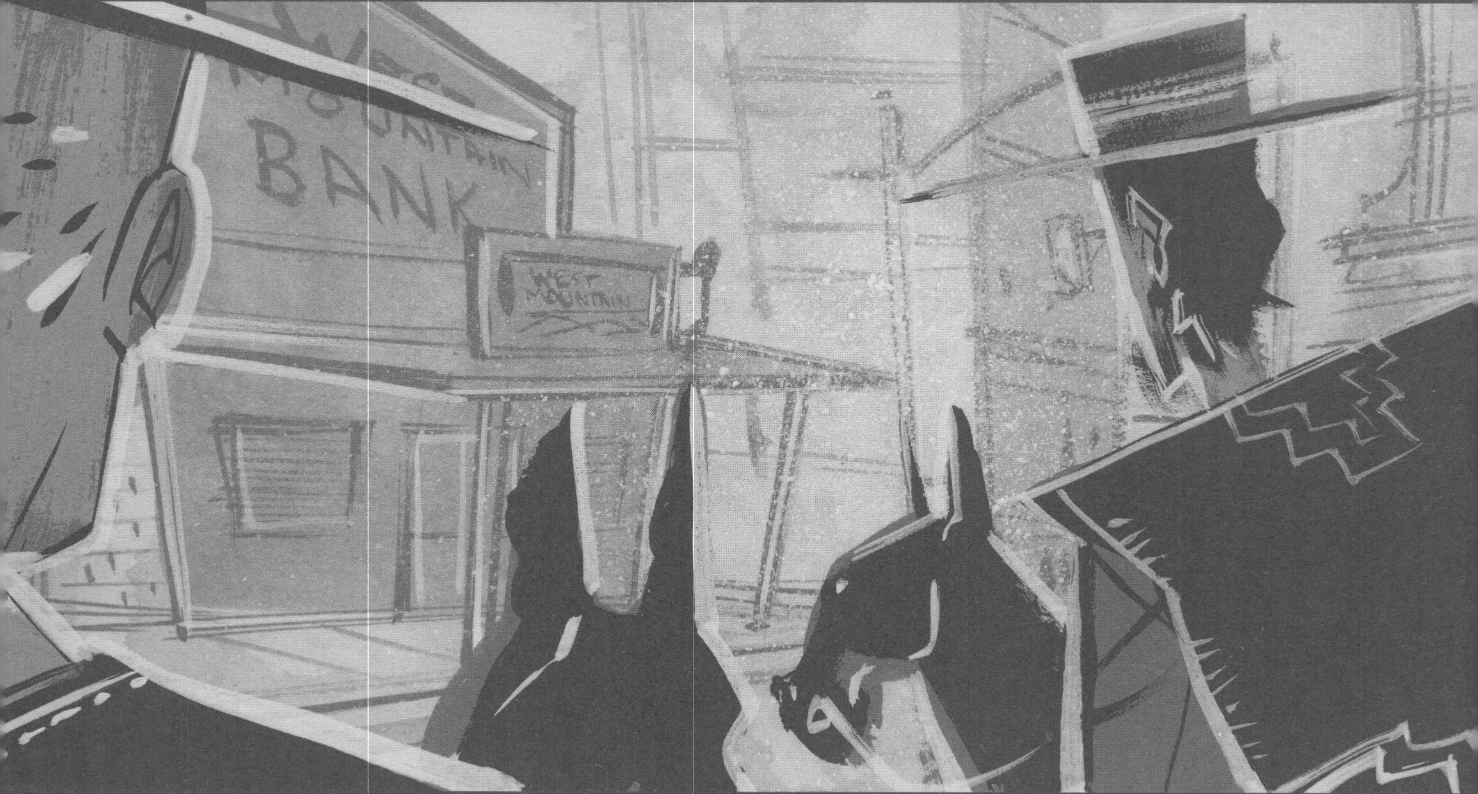
MOUNTAIN
BANK
WEST
MOUNTAIN

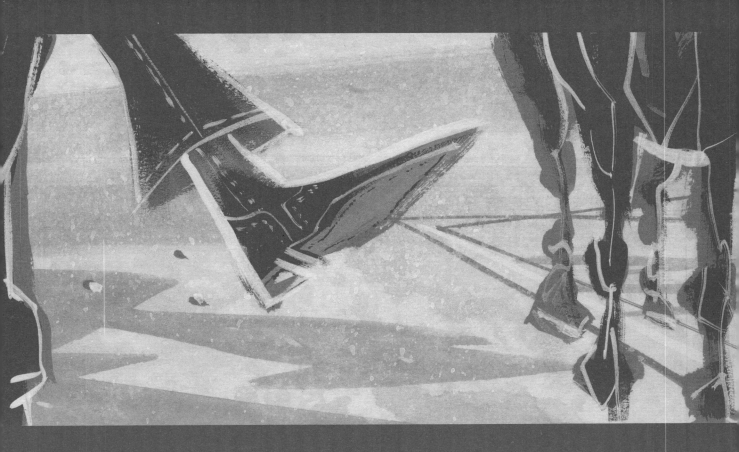

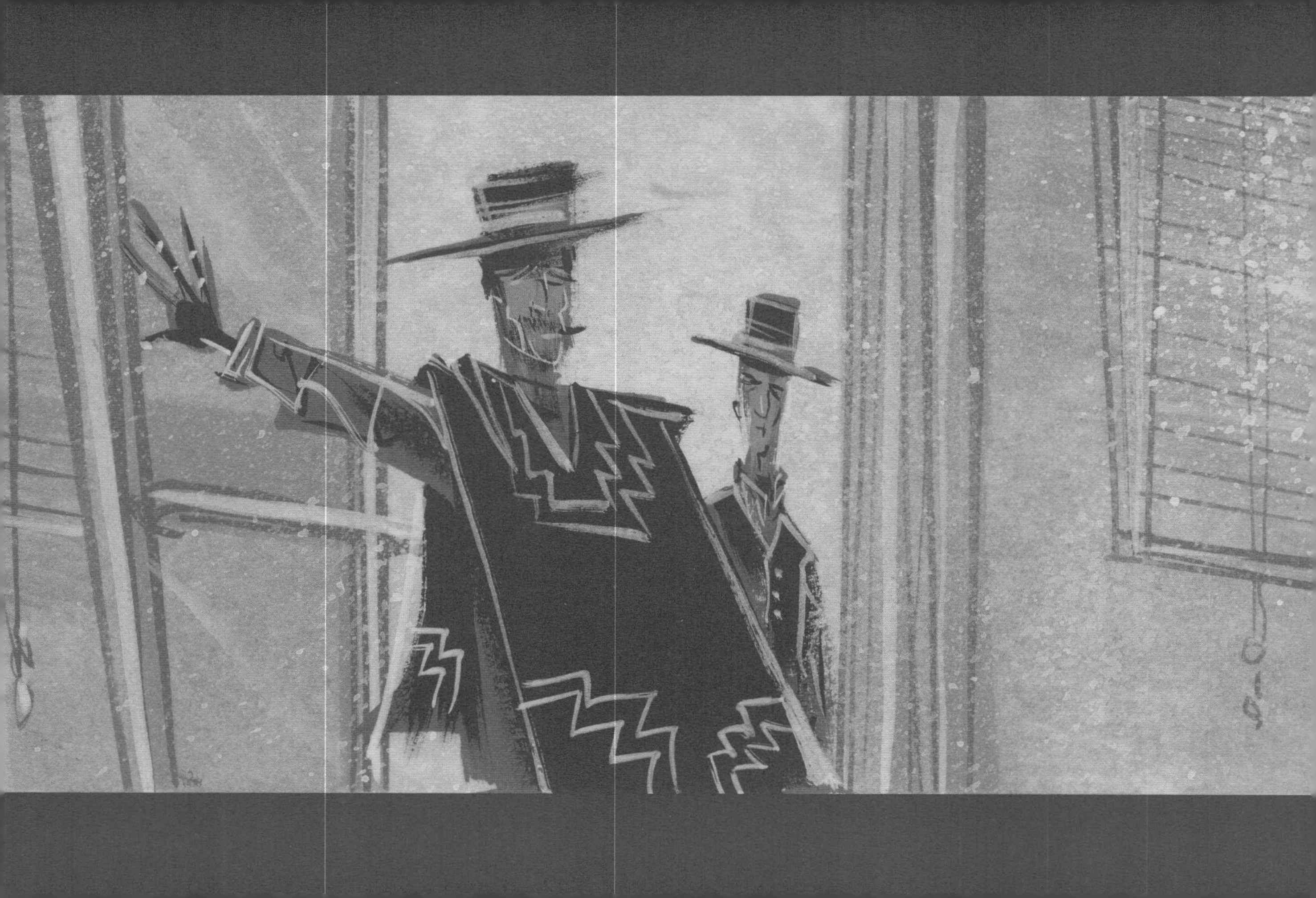

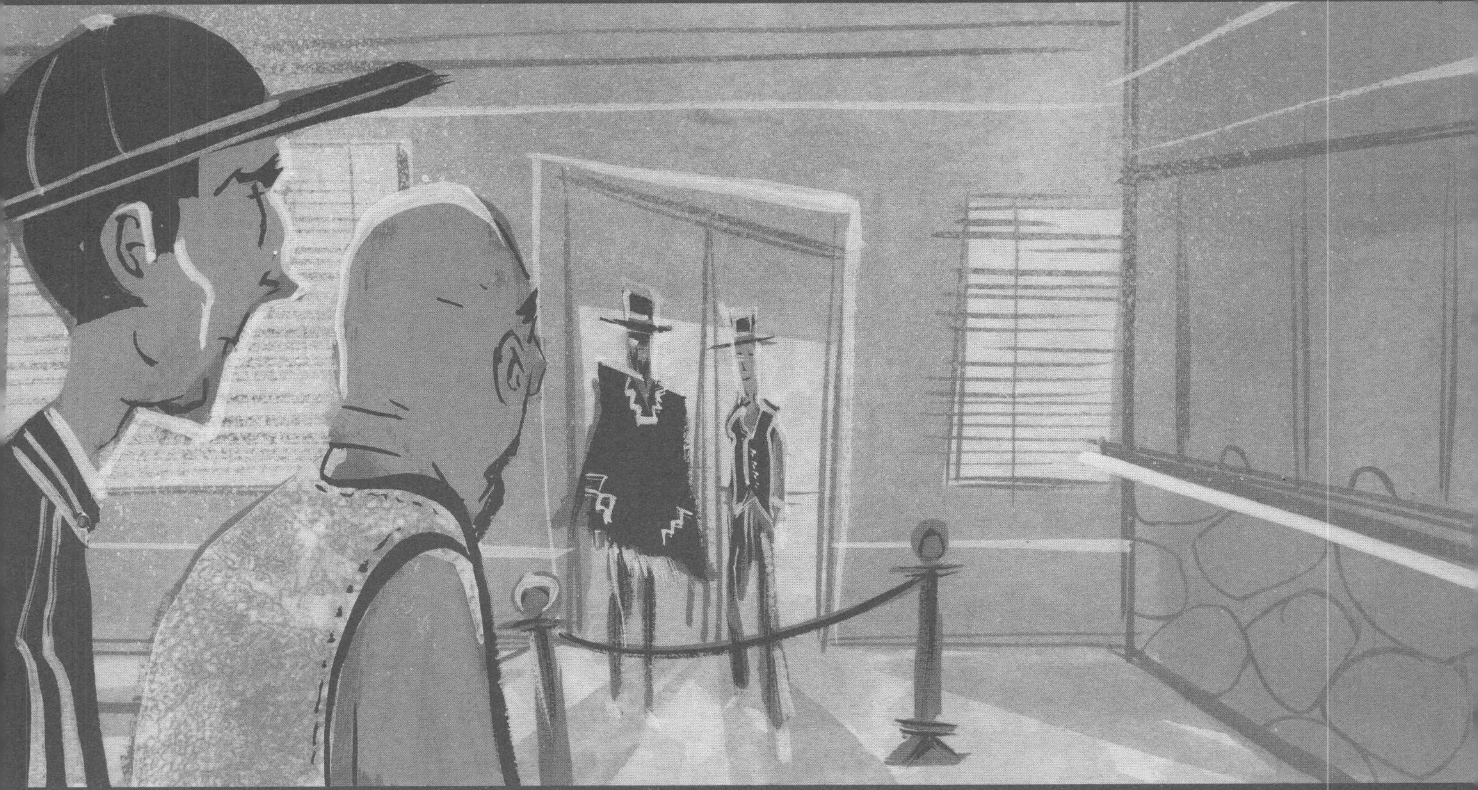

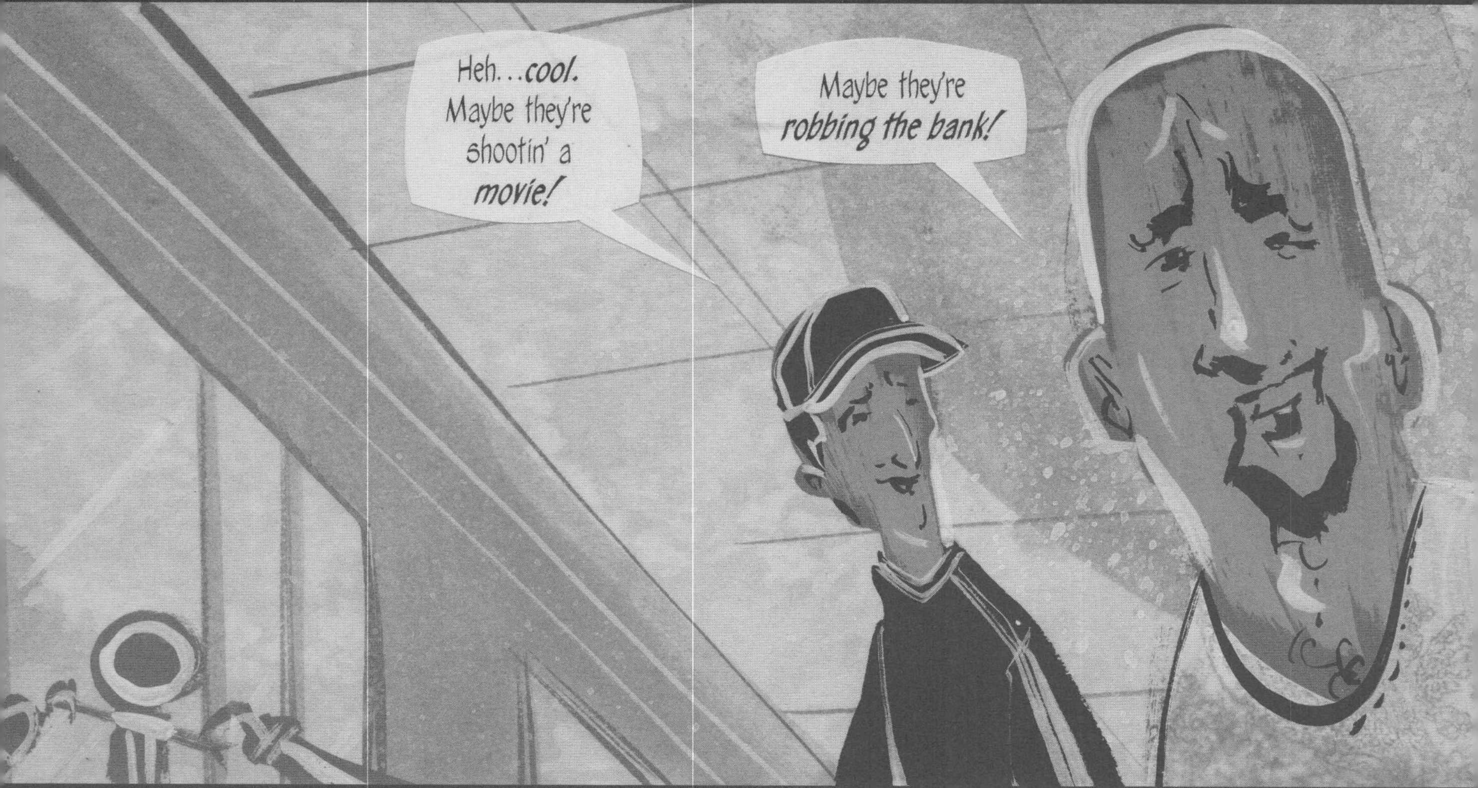
Heh...*cool.* Maybe they're shootin' a *movie!*
Maybe they're *robbing the bank!*

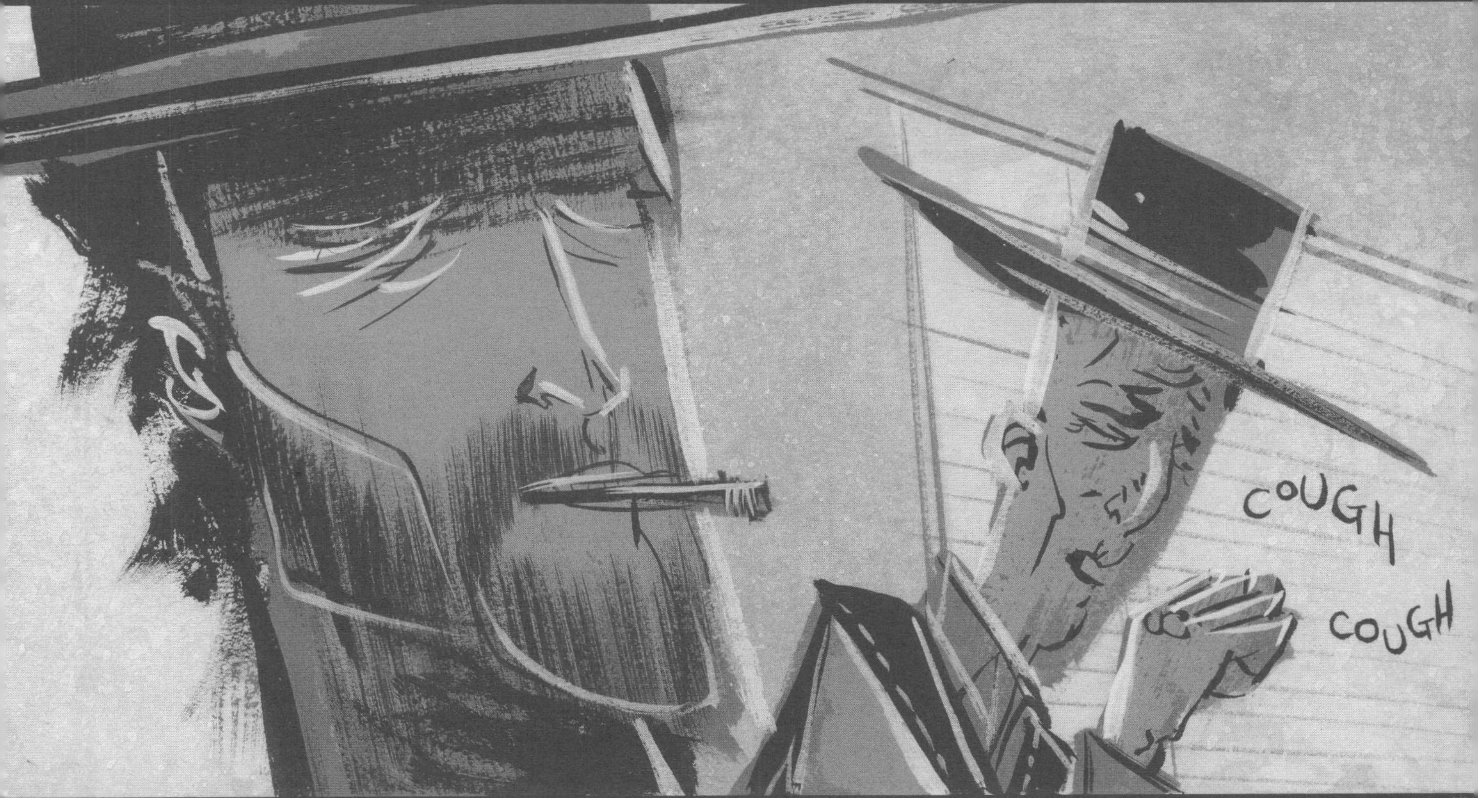
COUGH
COUGH

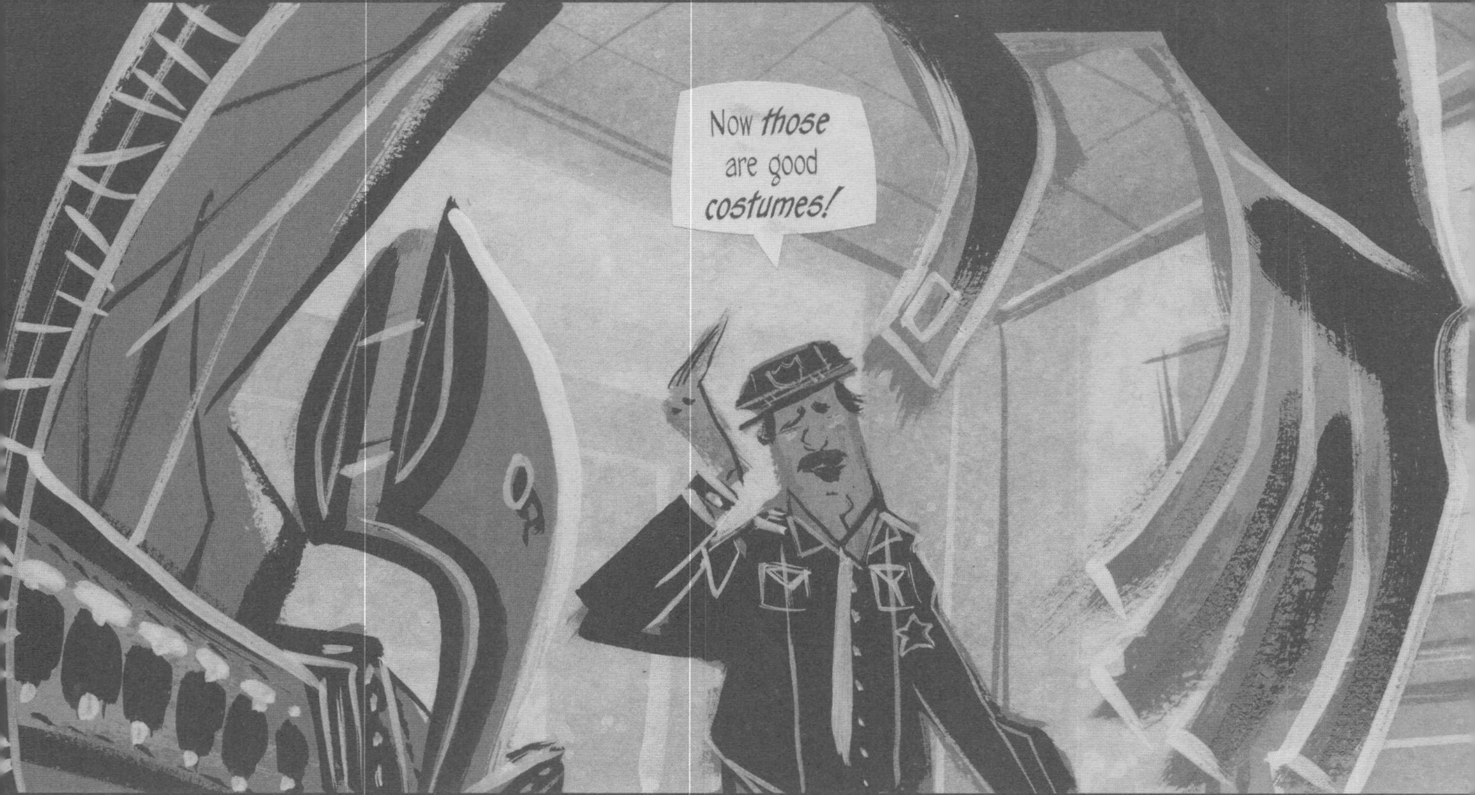
Now *those* are good *costumes!*

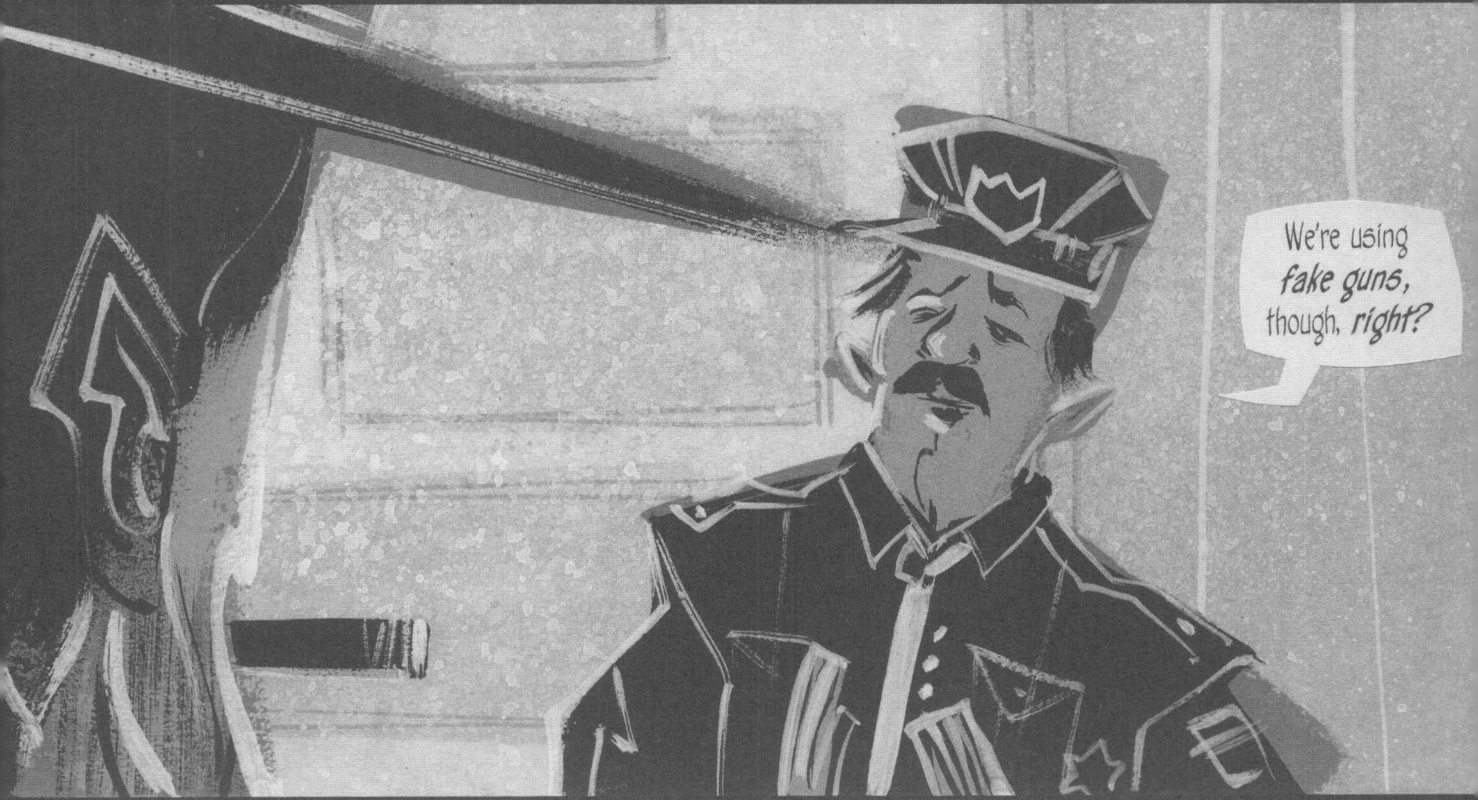
We're using *fake guns,* though, *right?*

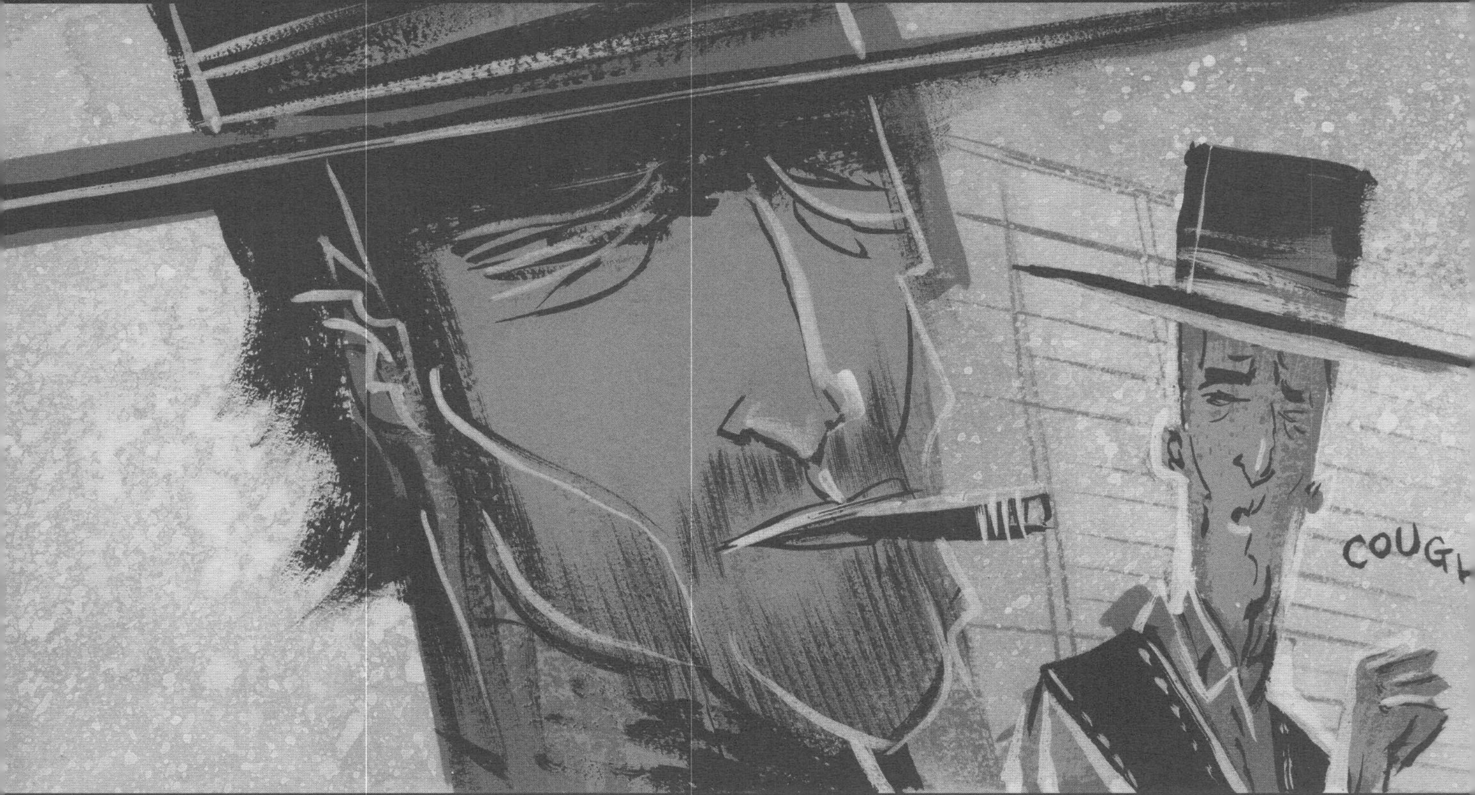
COUG

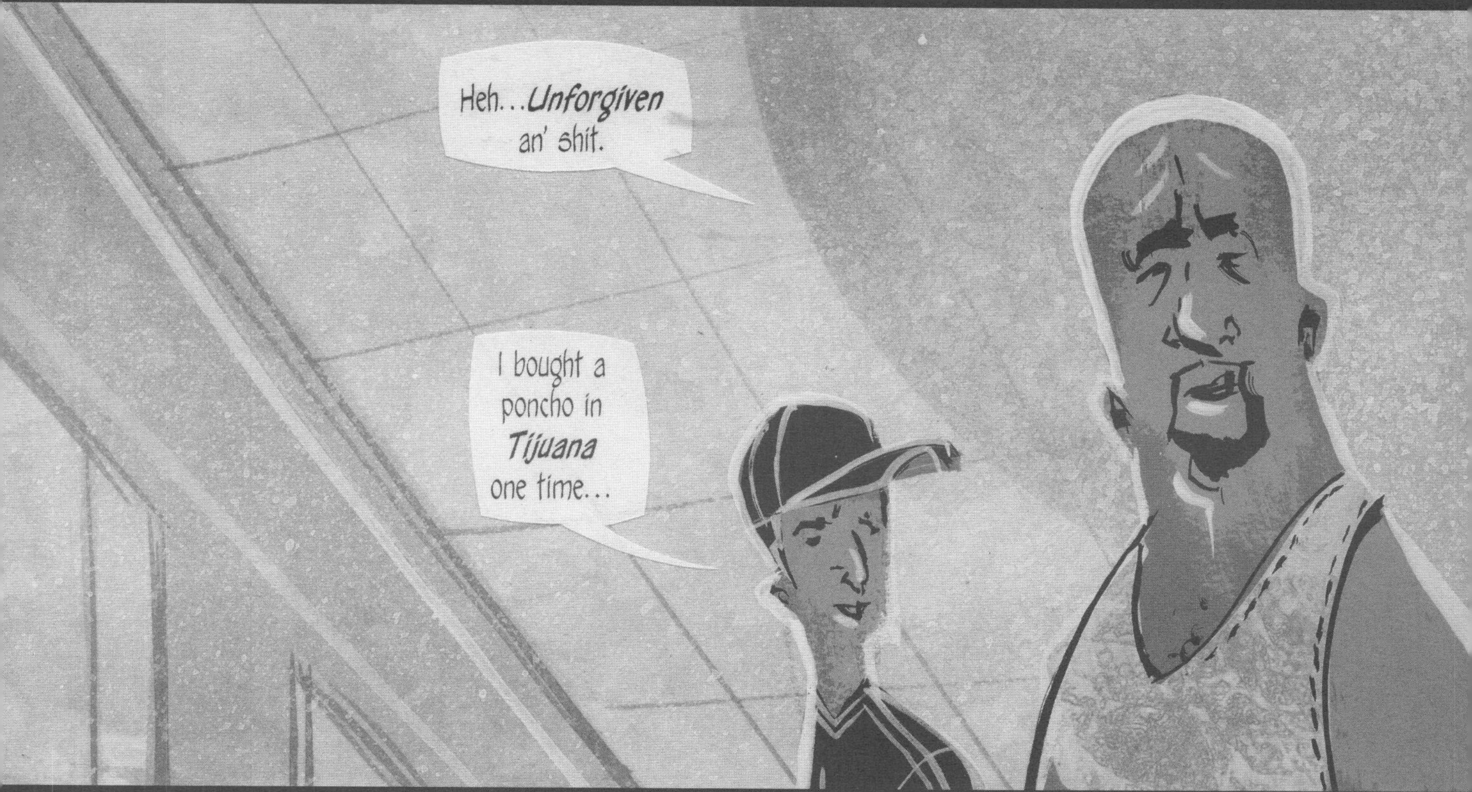
Heh...*Unforgiven* an' shit.
I bought a poncho in *Tijuana* one time...

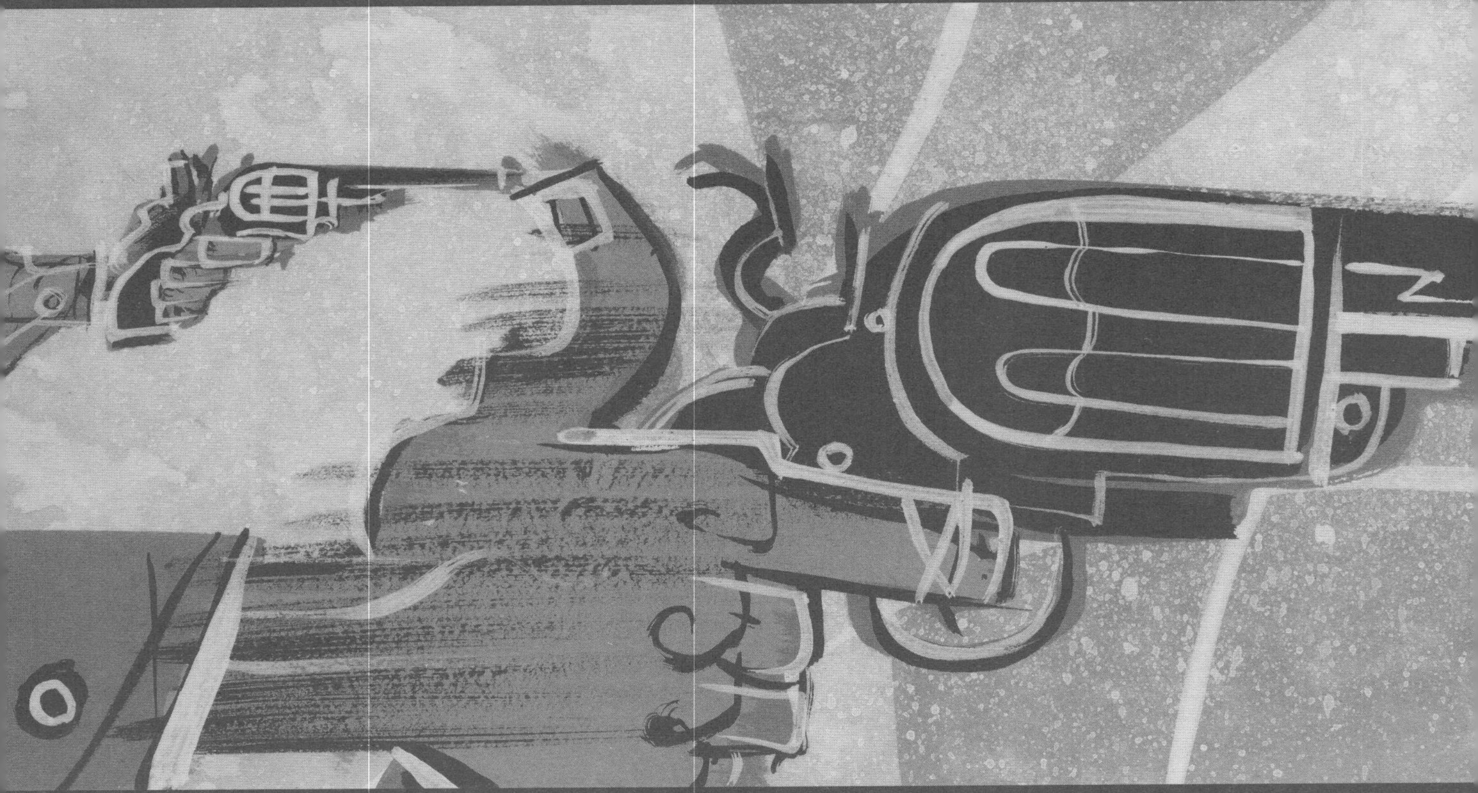

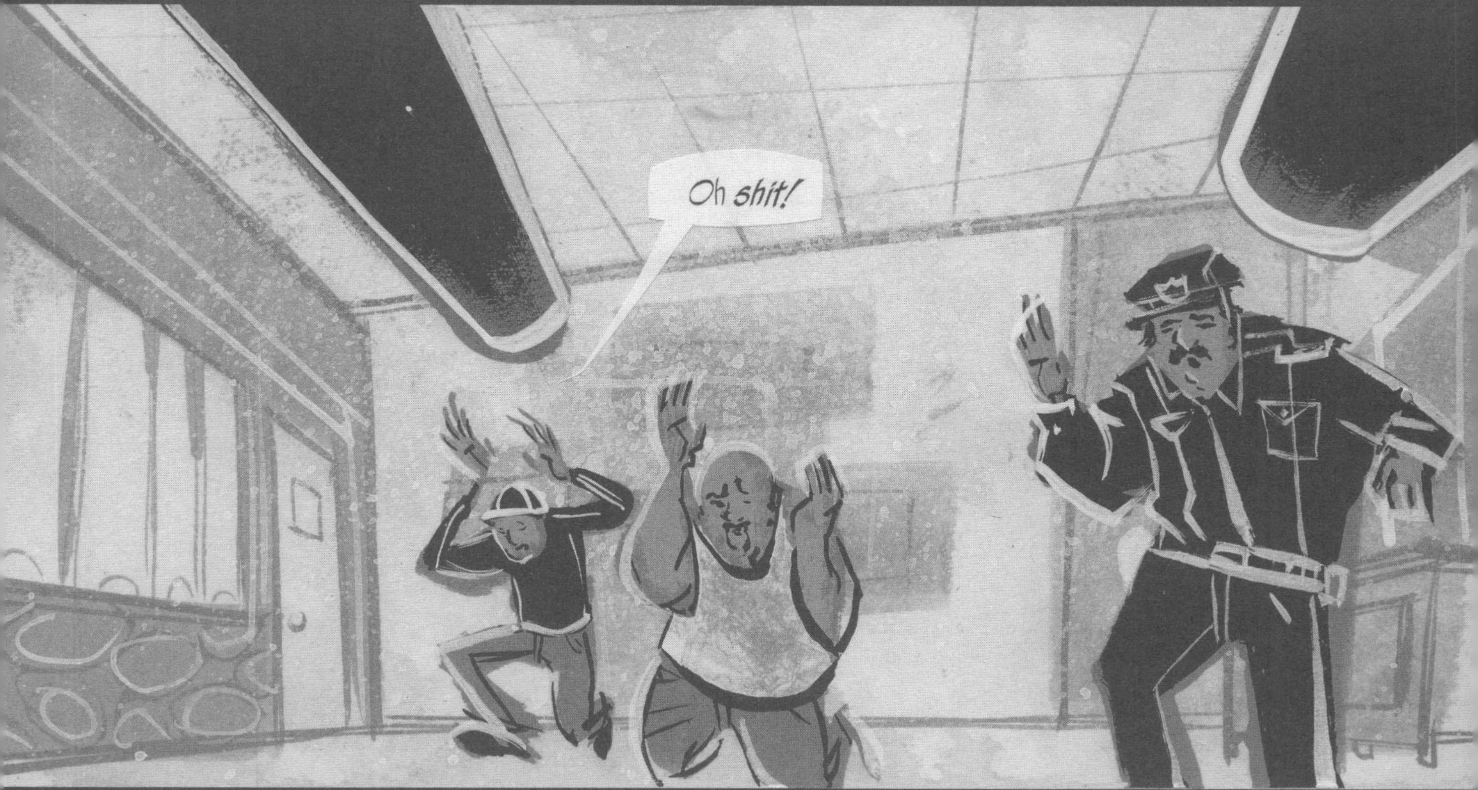
Oh shit!

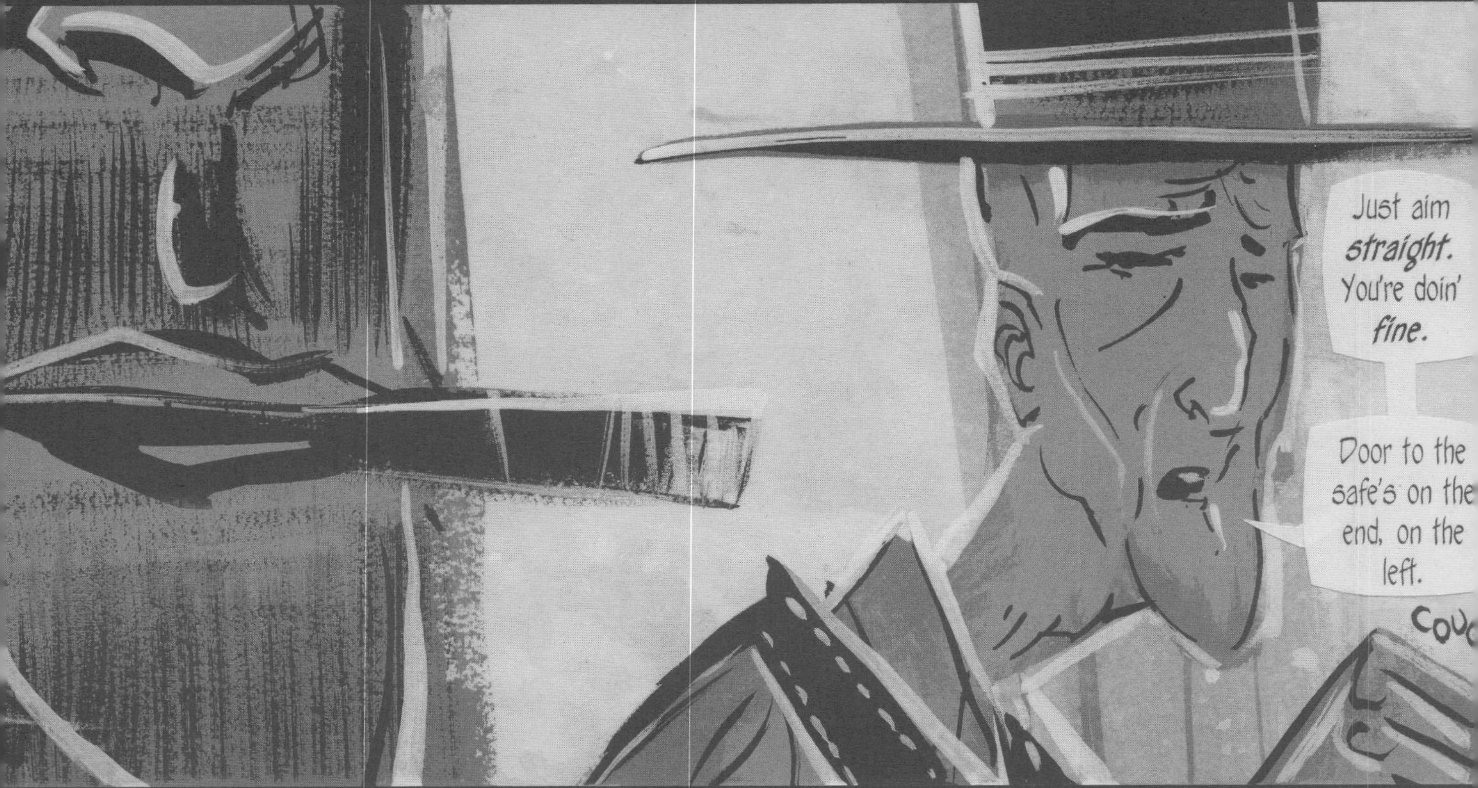
Just aim *straight*. You're doin' *fine*.
Door to the safe's on the end, on the left.
COUC

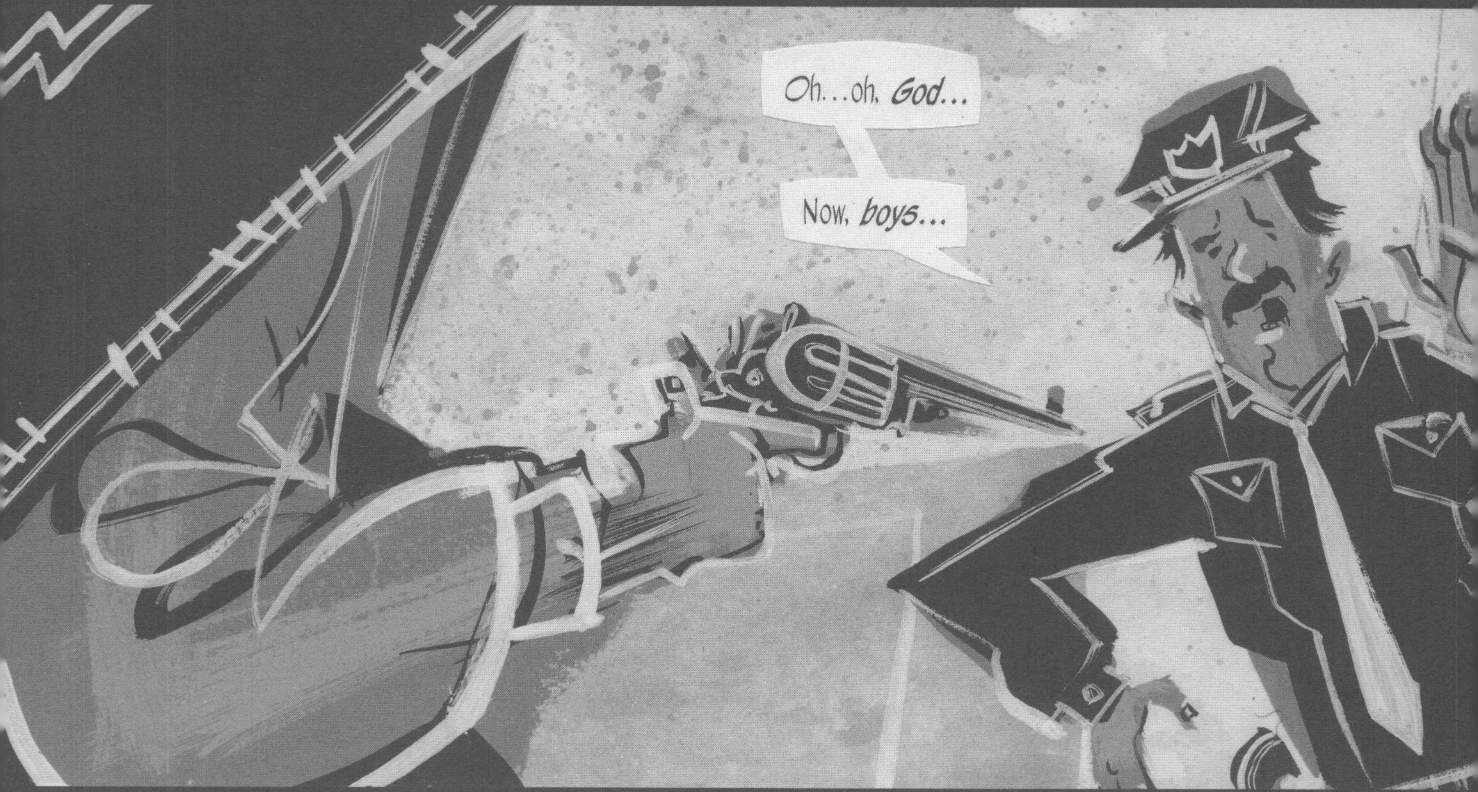
Oh...oh, God...
Now, boys...

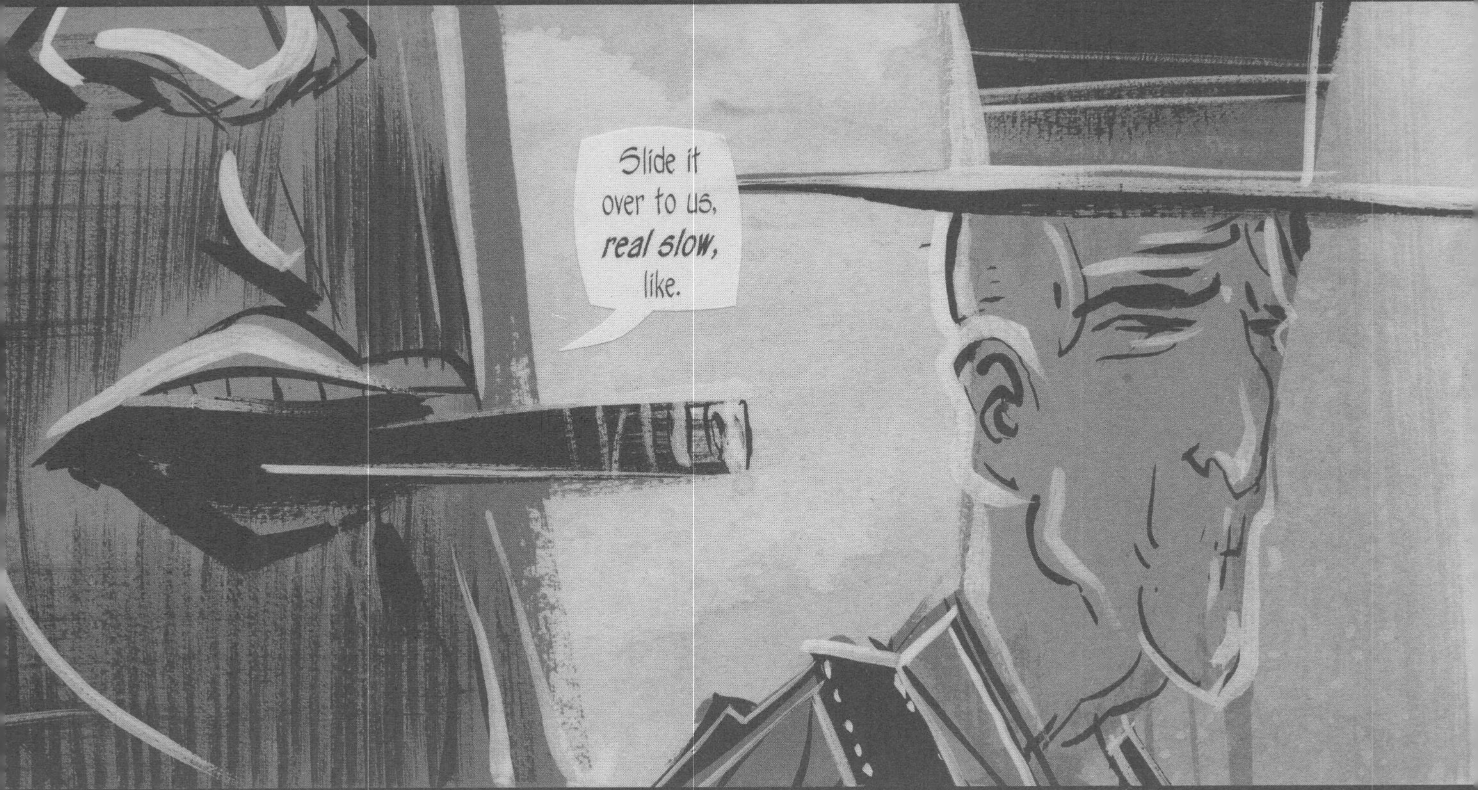
Slide it over to us, *real slow,* like.

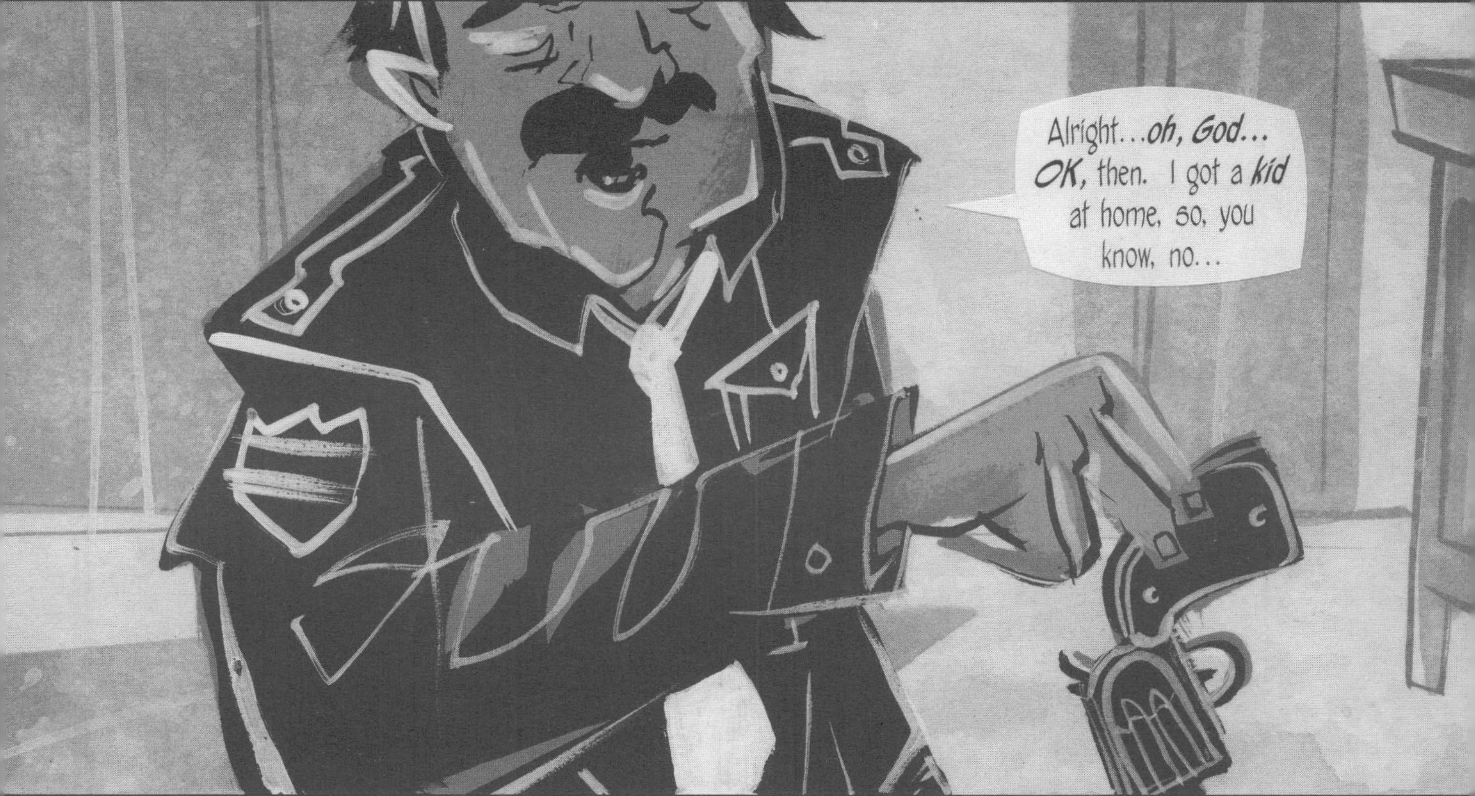
Alright...oh, God... OK, then. I got a kid at home, so, you know, no...

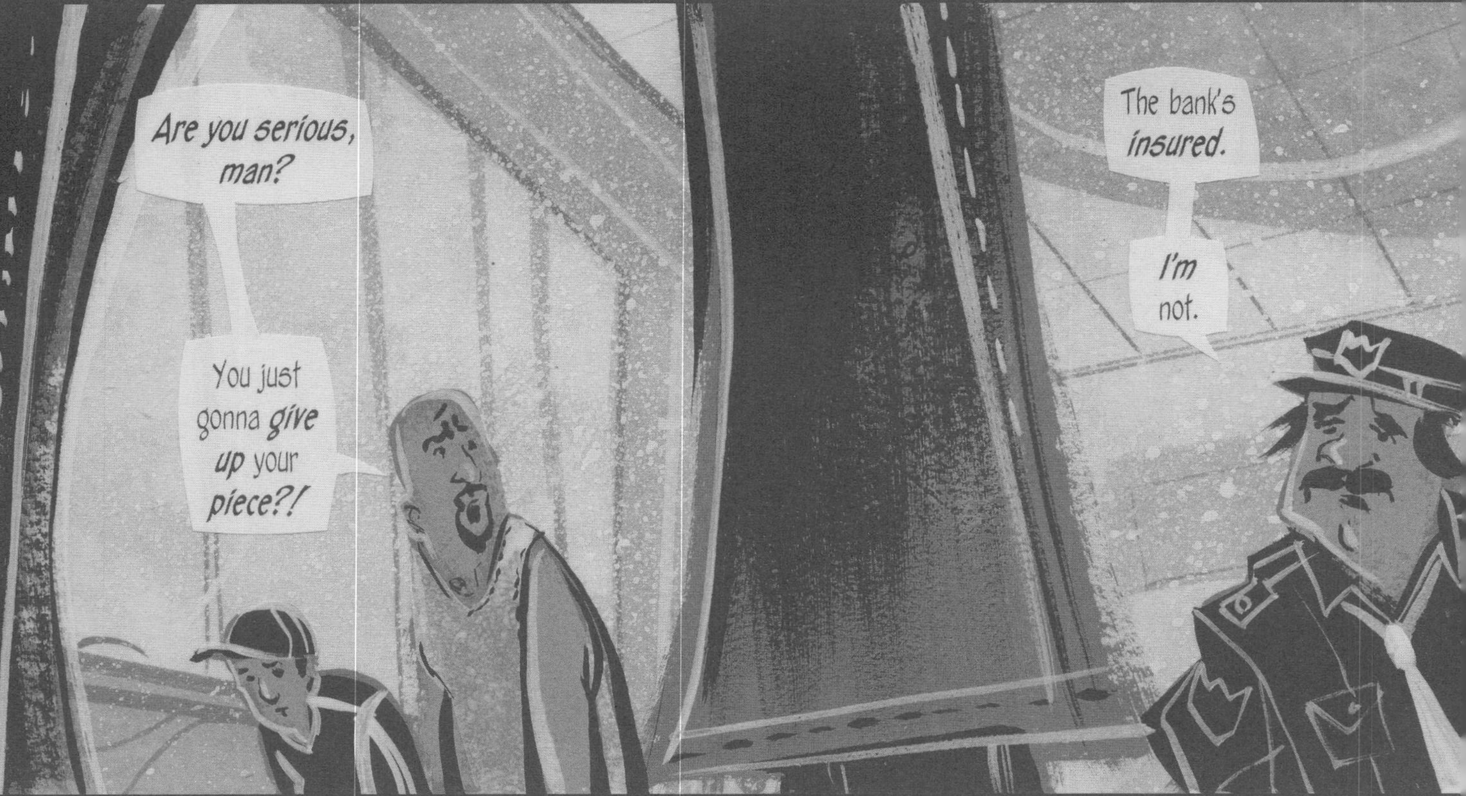
Are you serious, man?
You just gonna give up your piece?!
The bank's insured.
I'm not.

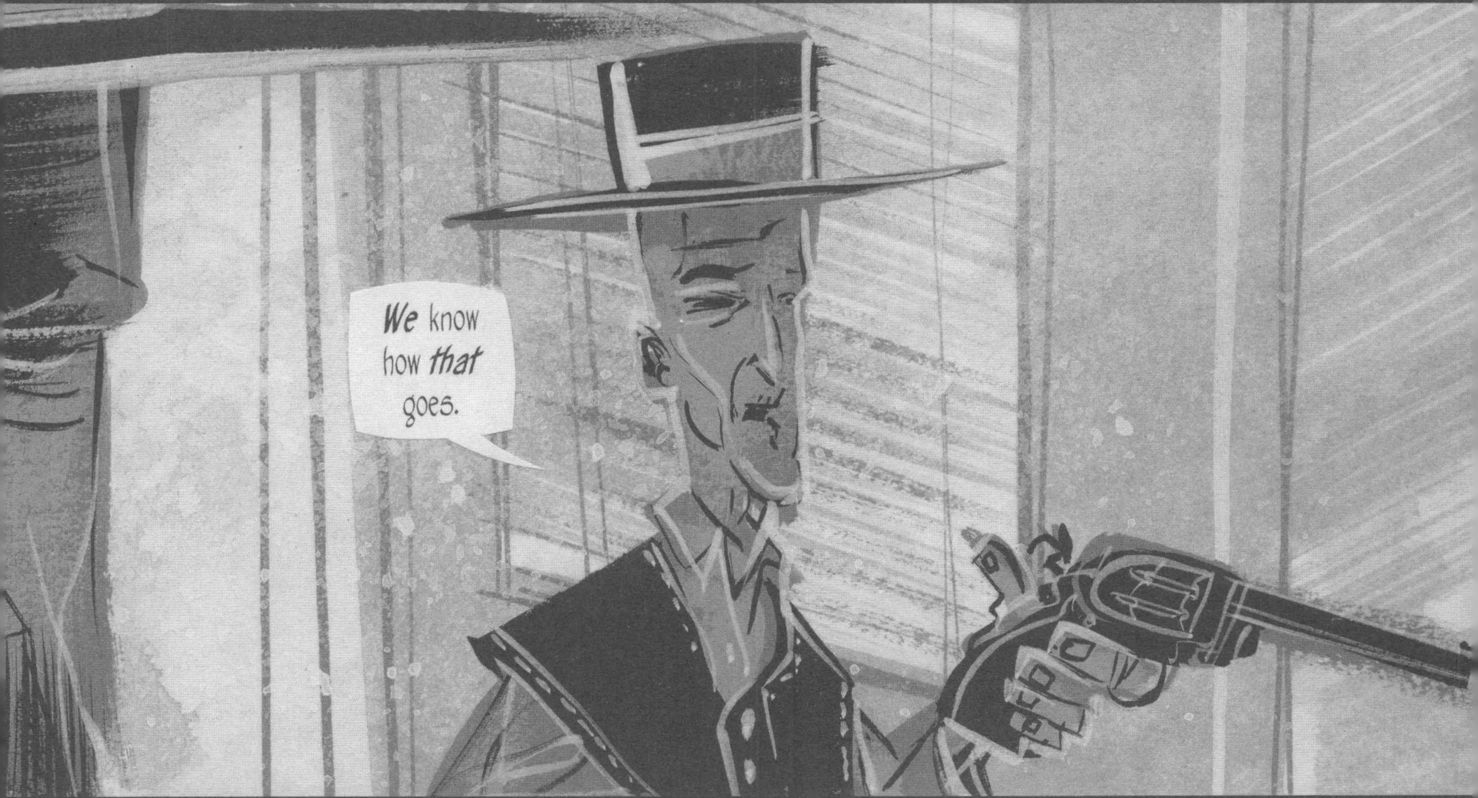

We know how that goes.

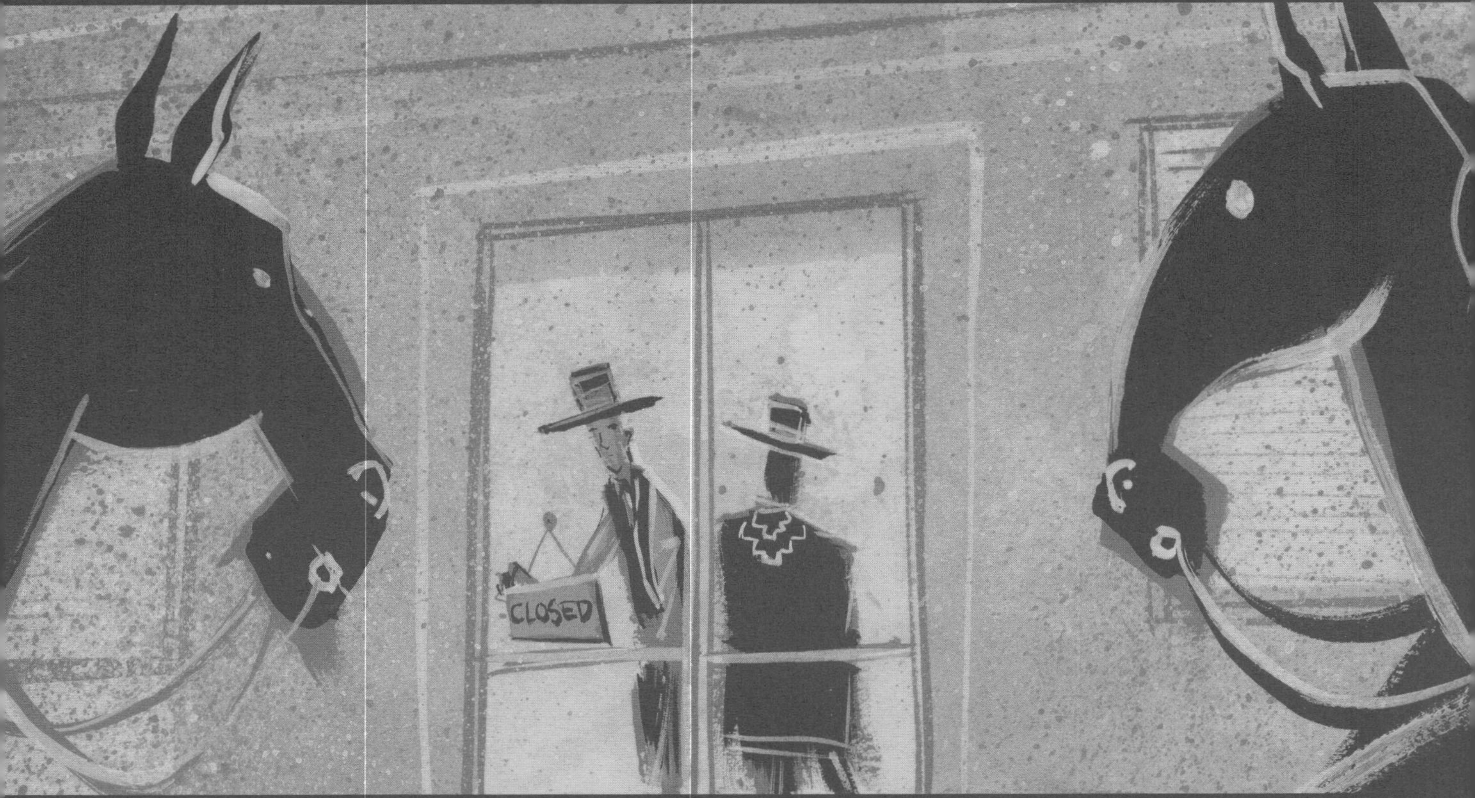
CLOSED

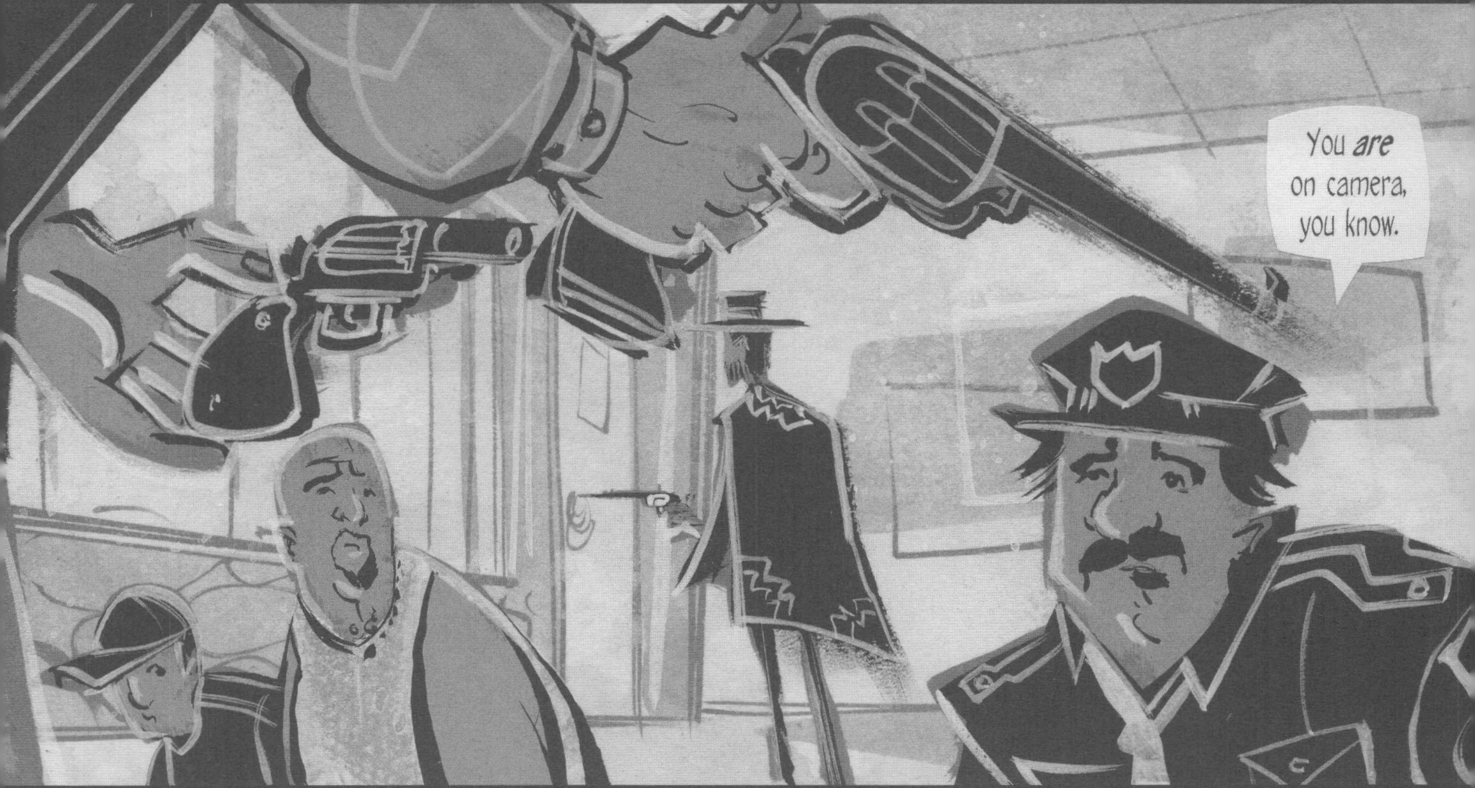
You *are* on camera, you know.

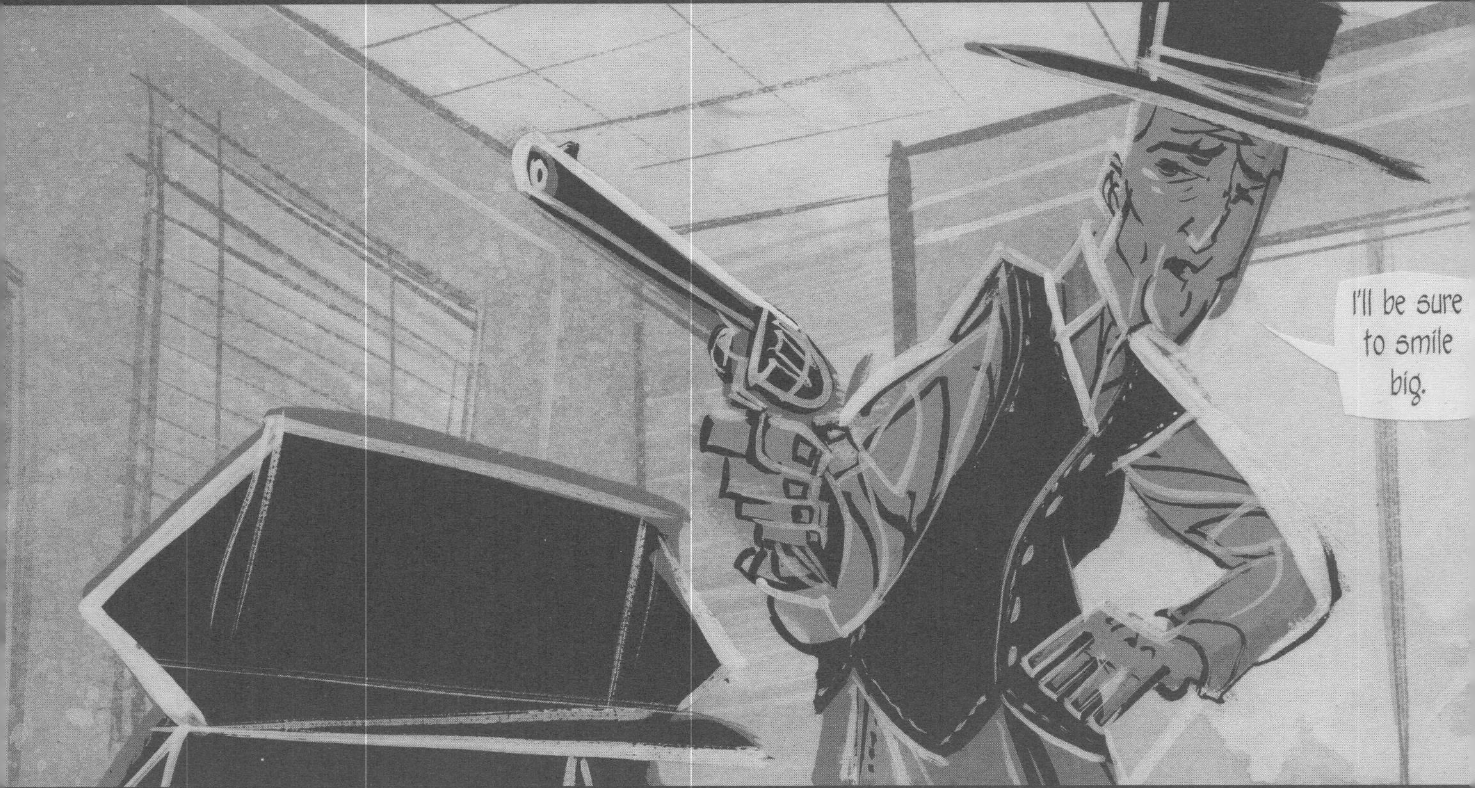
I'll be sure to smile big.

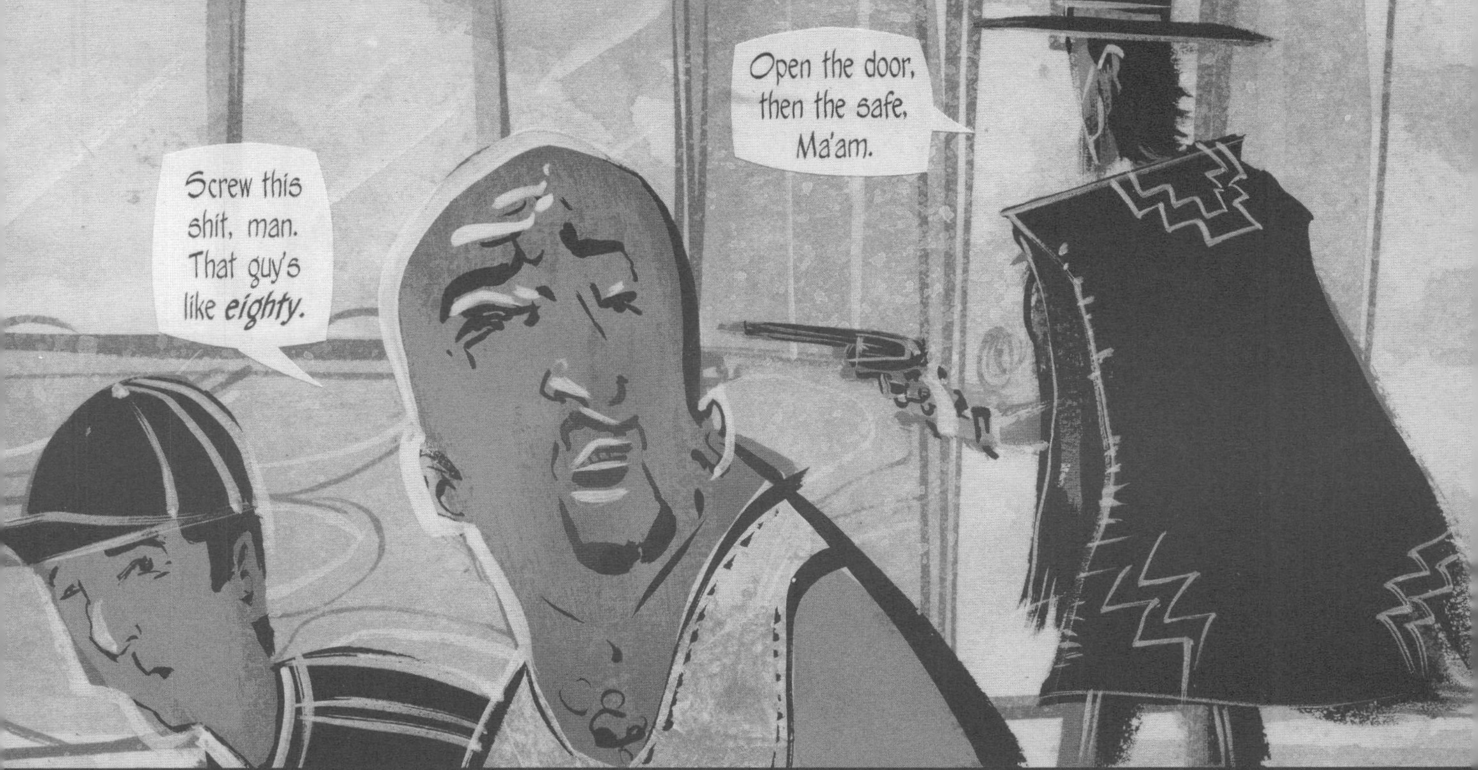
Screw this shit, man. That guy's like *eighty.*
Open the door, then the safe, Ma'am.

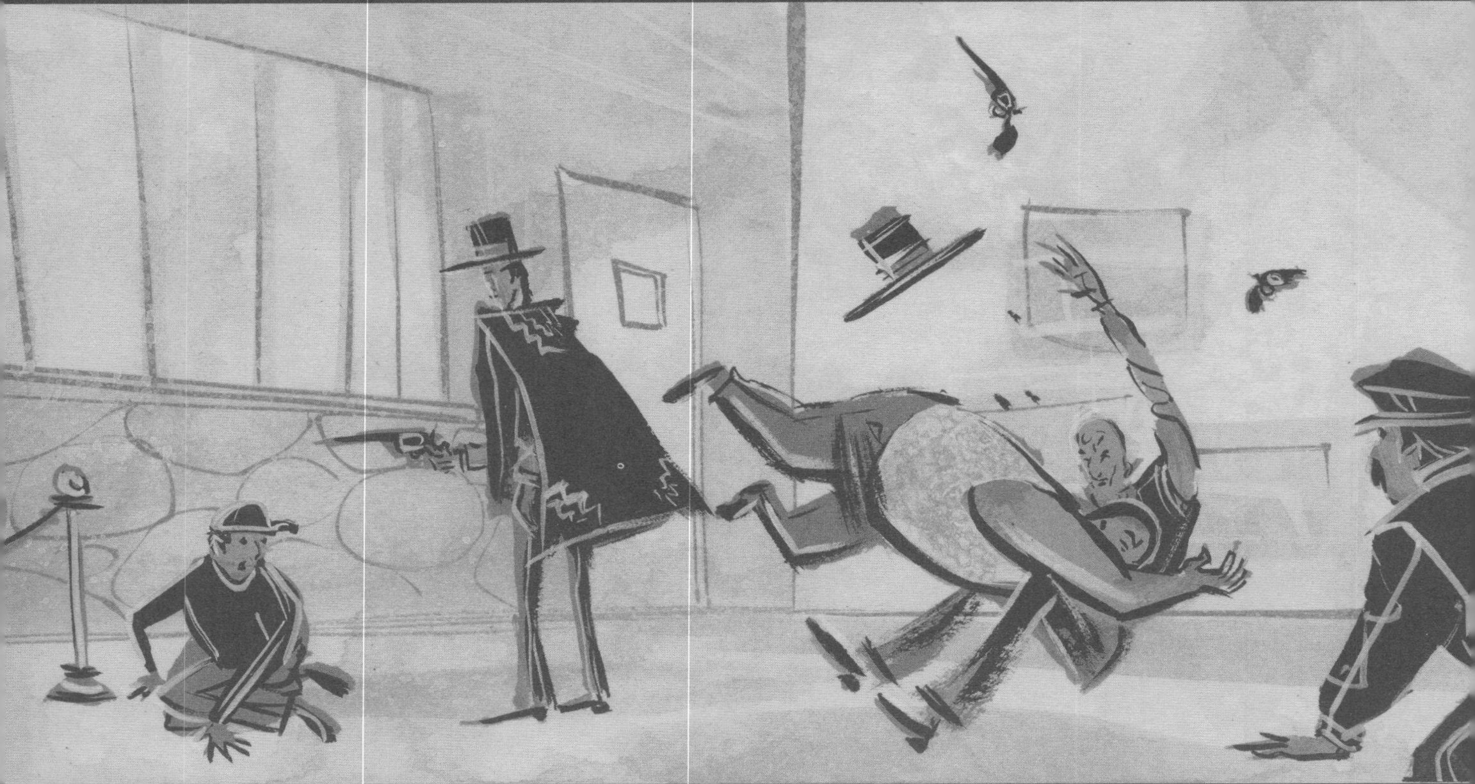

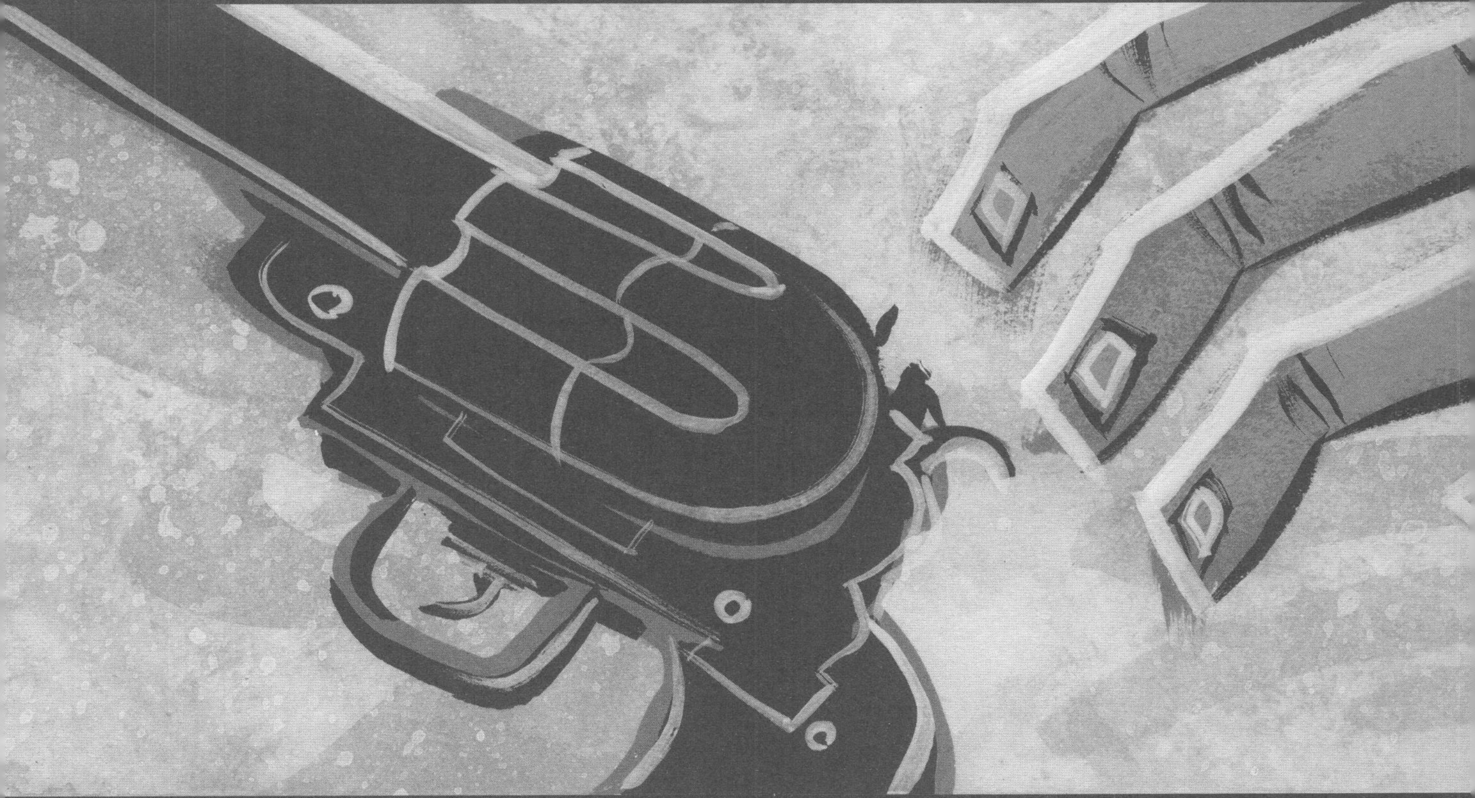

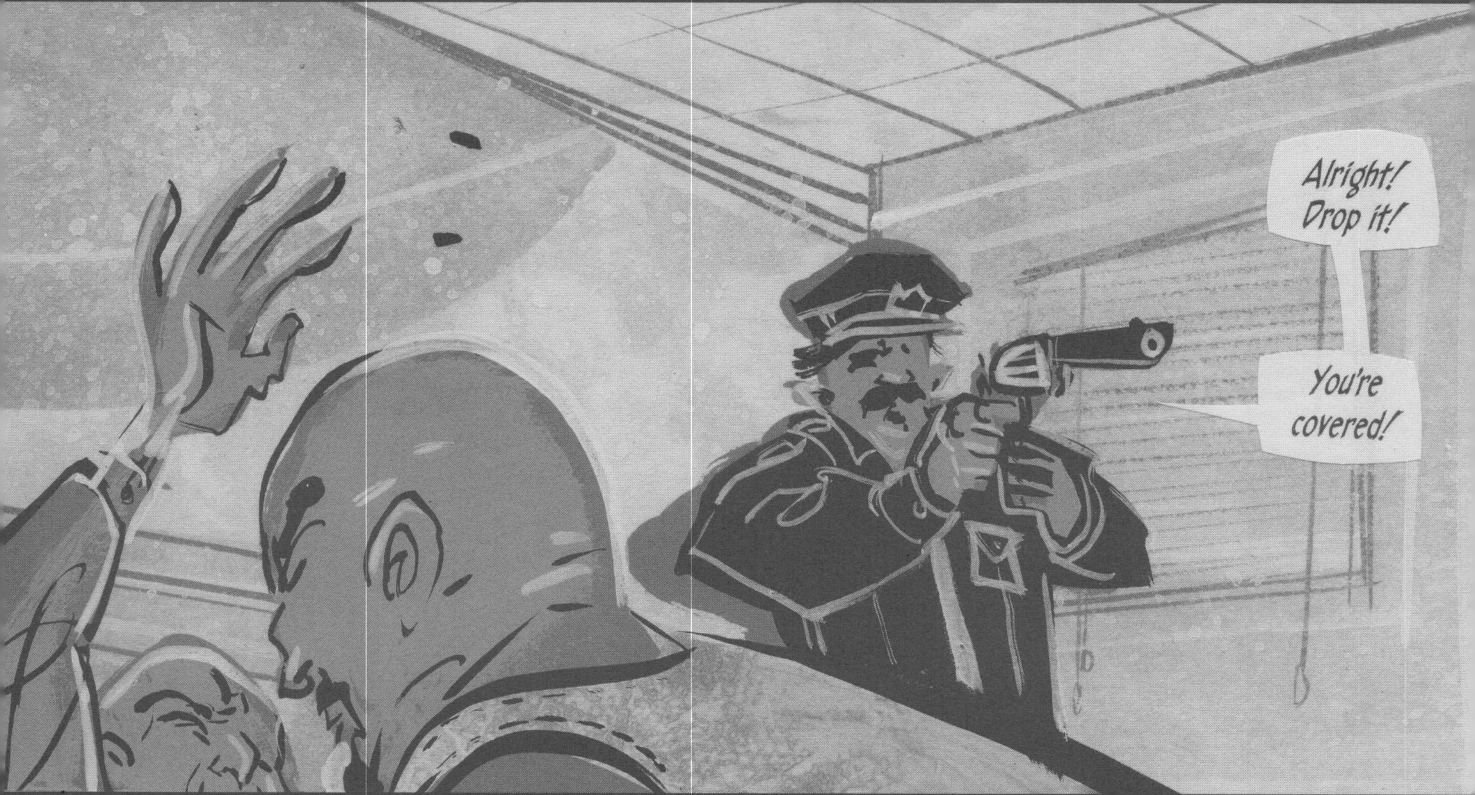
Alright! Drop it!
You're covered!

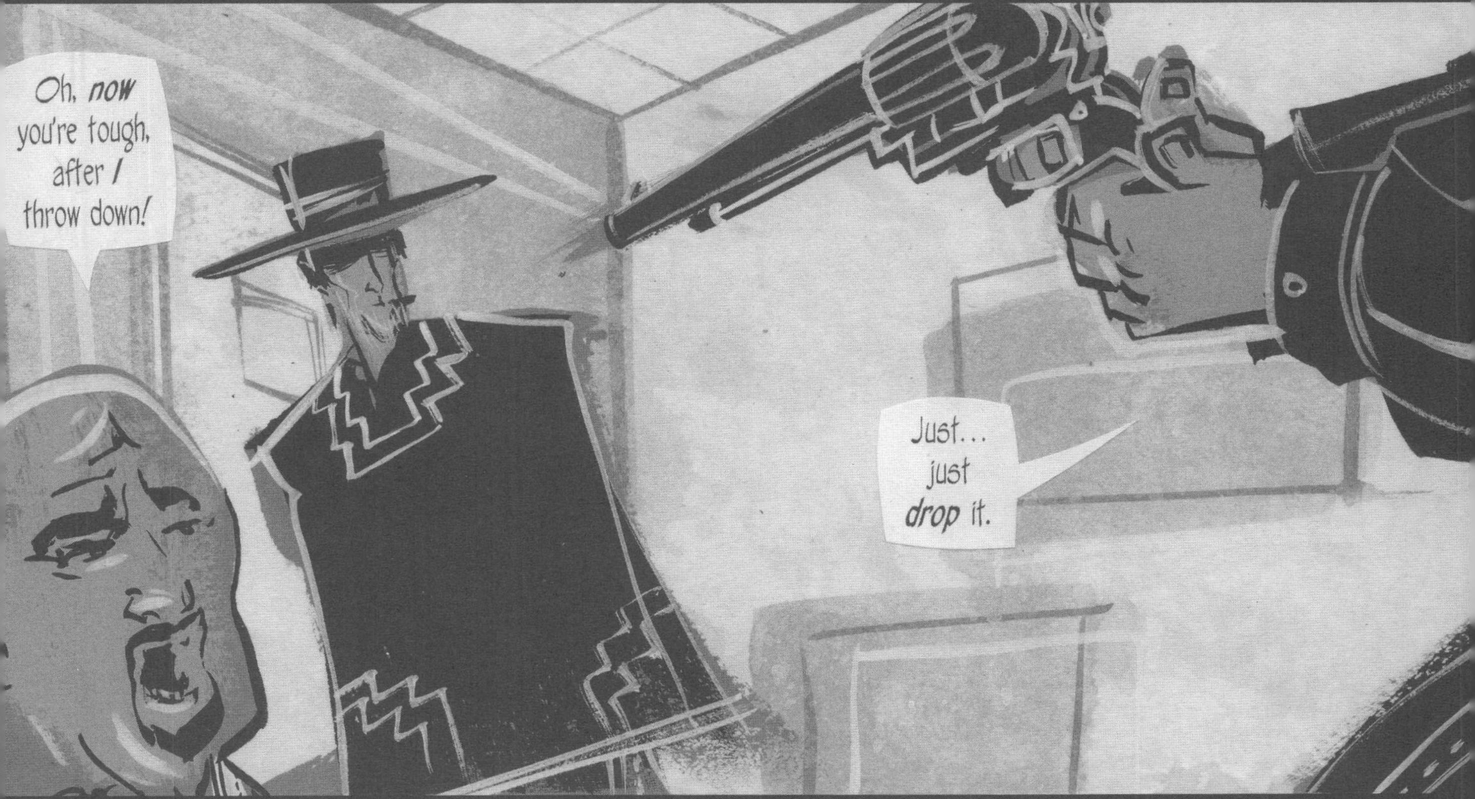
Oh, *now* you're tough, after *I* throw down!
Just... just *drop* it.

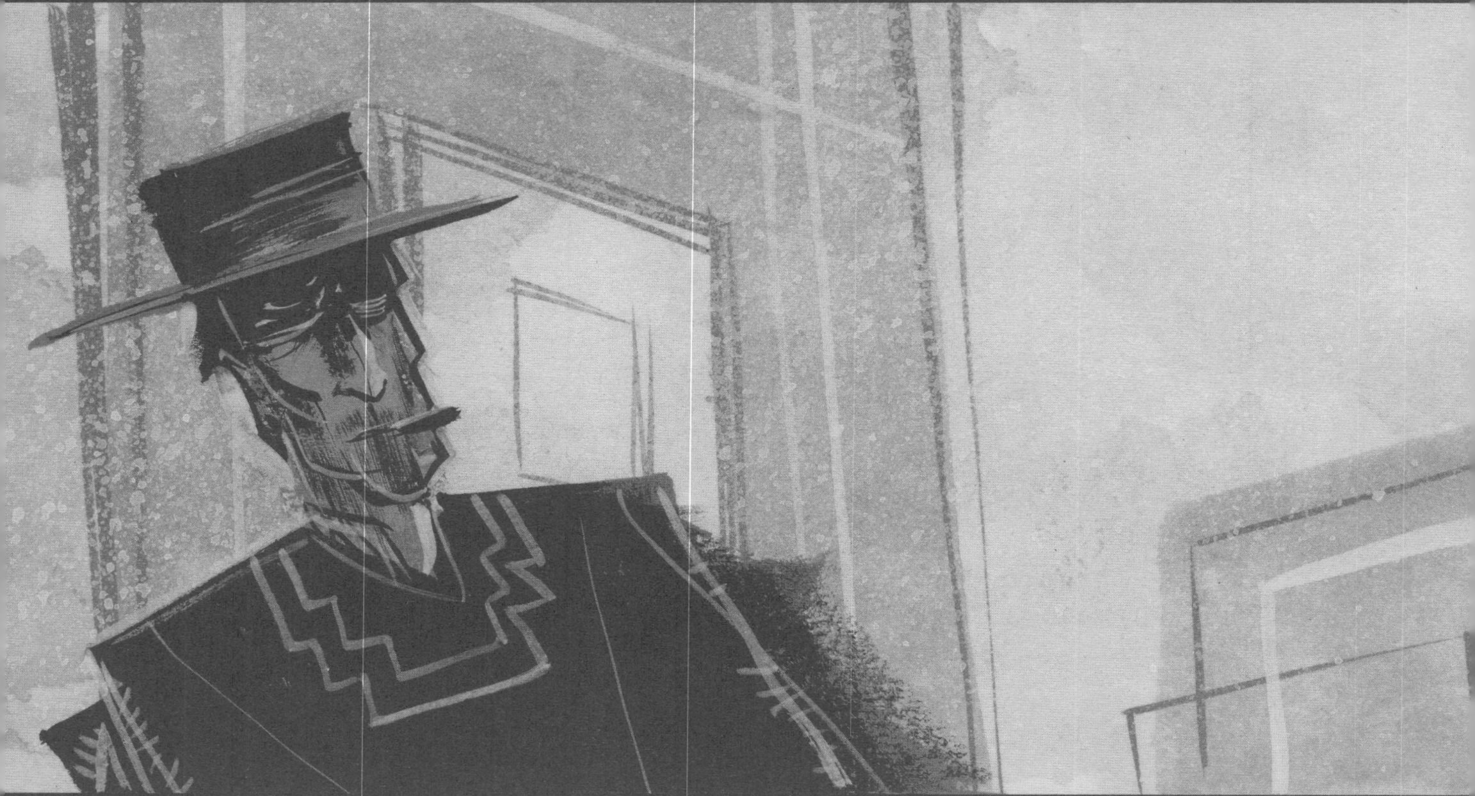

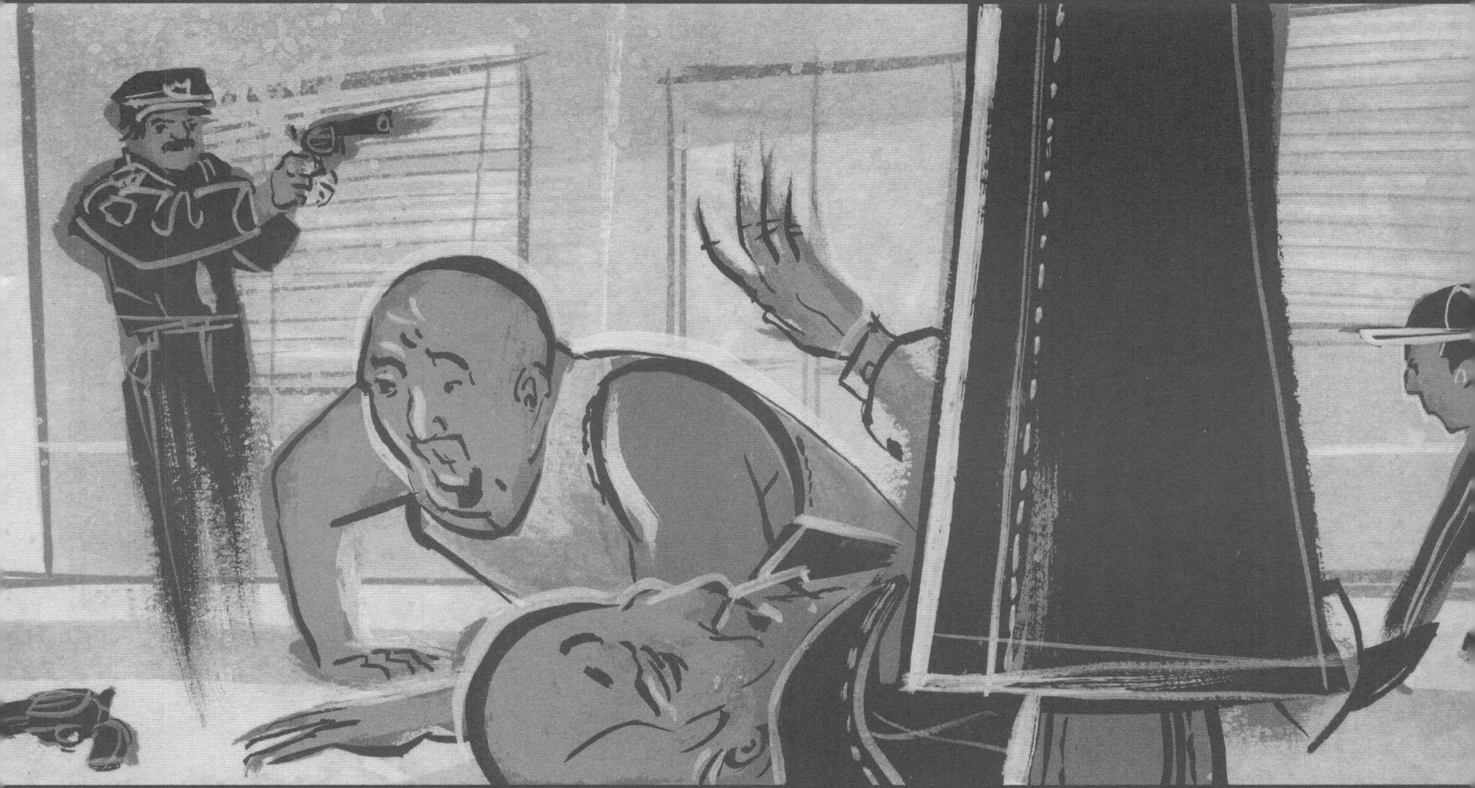

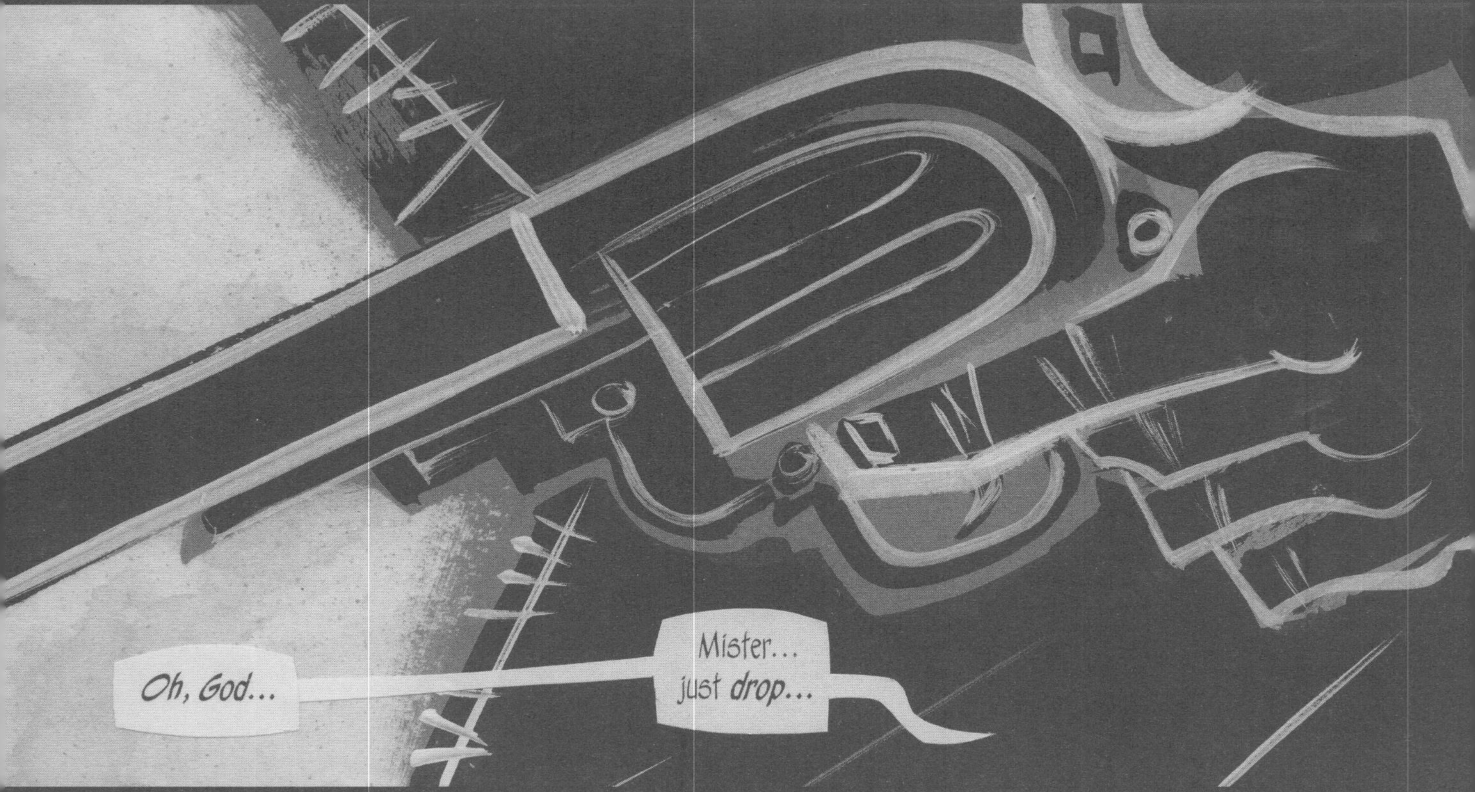
Oh, God...
Mister... just *drop*...

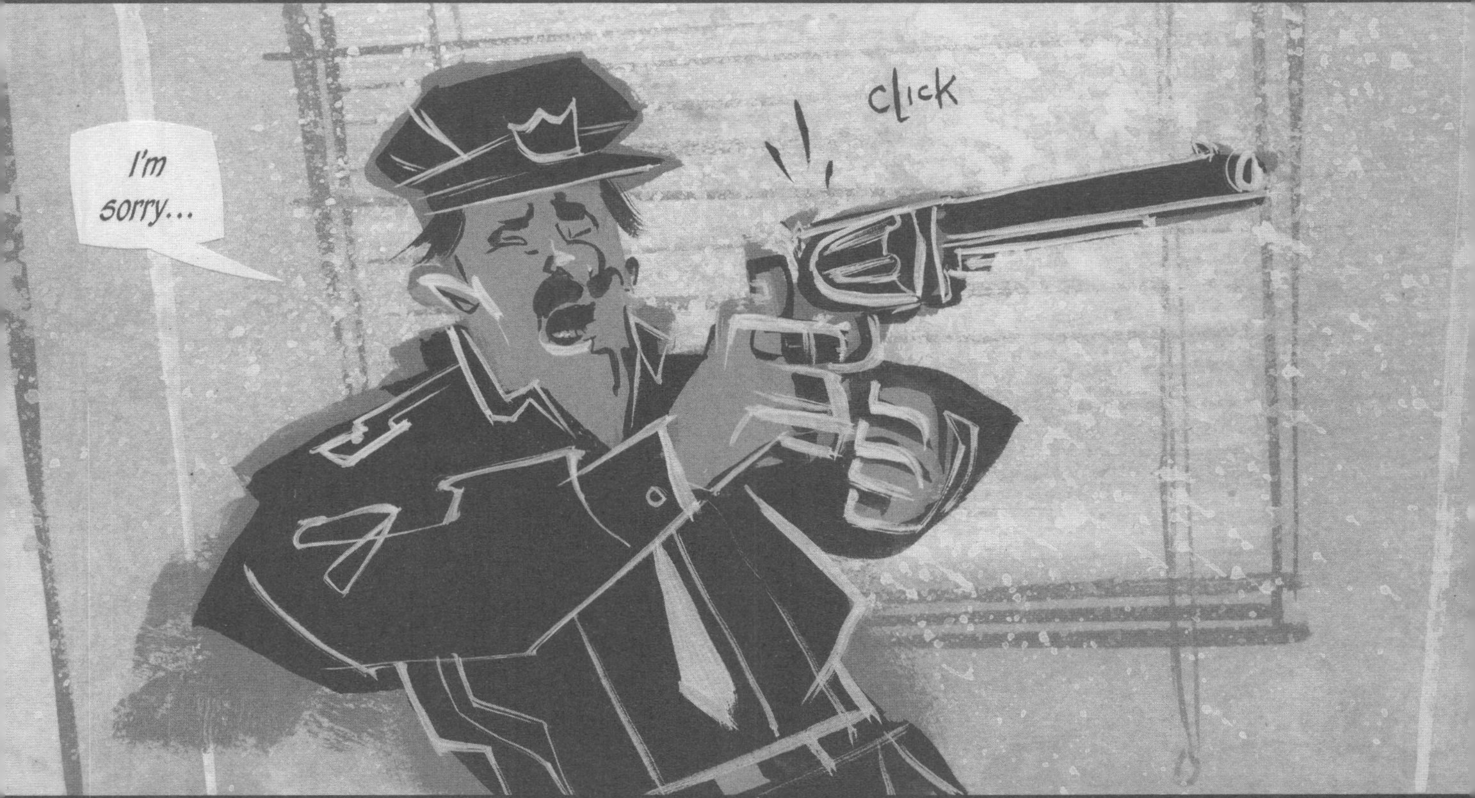
I'm sorry...
CLICK

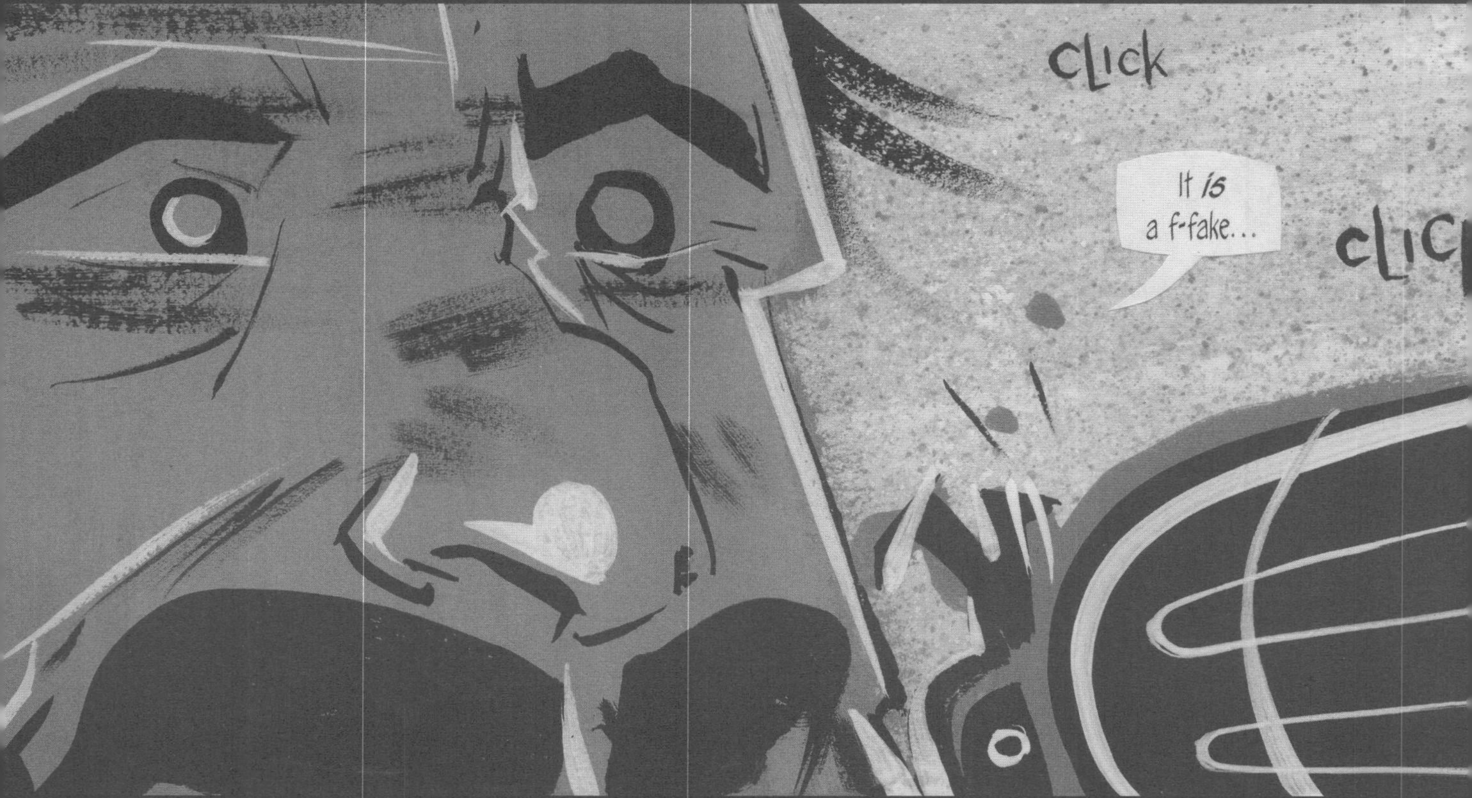
CLICK
It *is* a f-fake...
CLIC

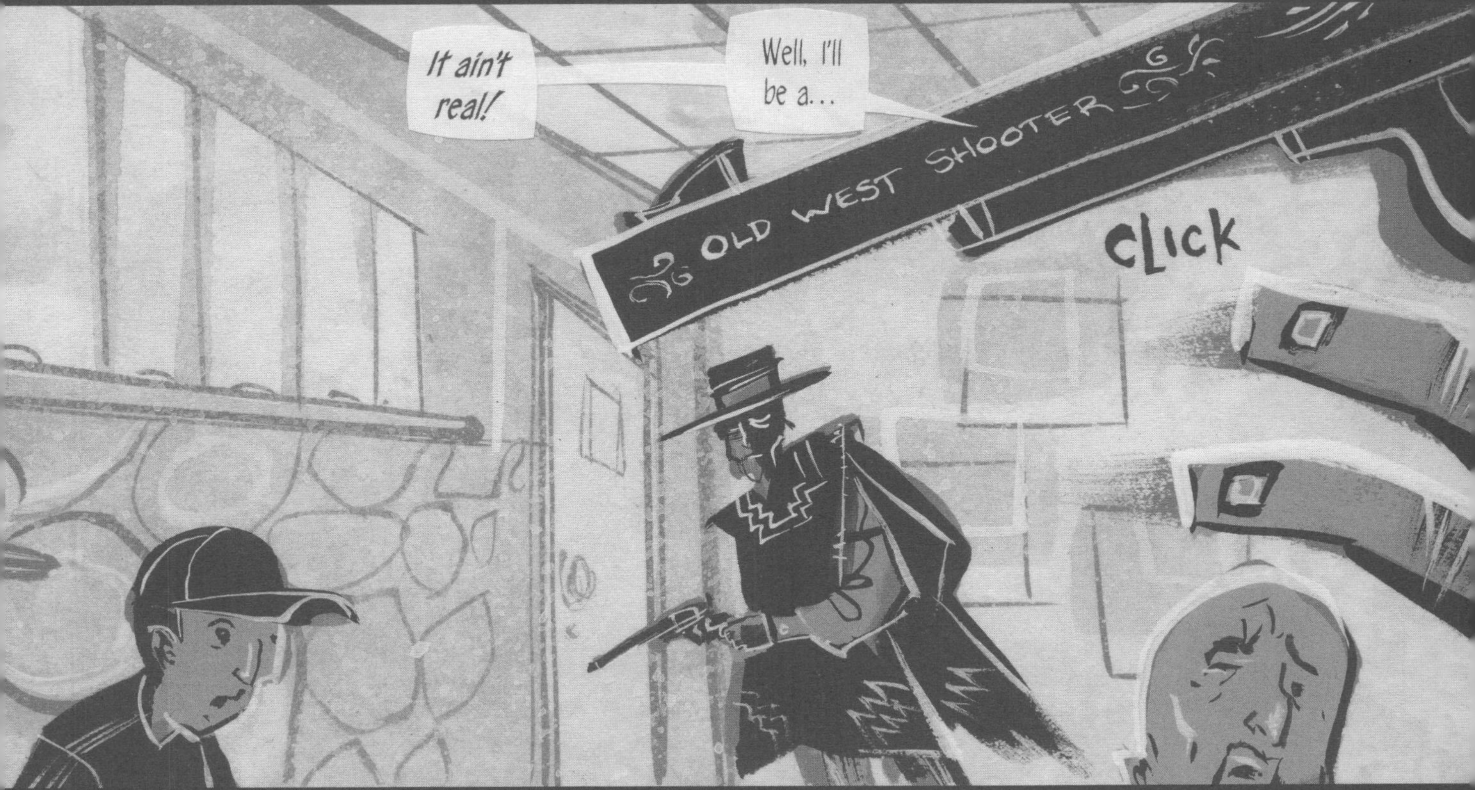

It ain't real!
Well, I'll be a...
OLD WEST SHOOTER
CLICK

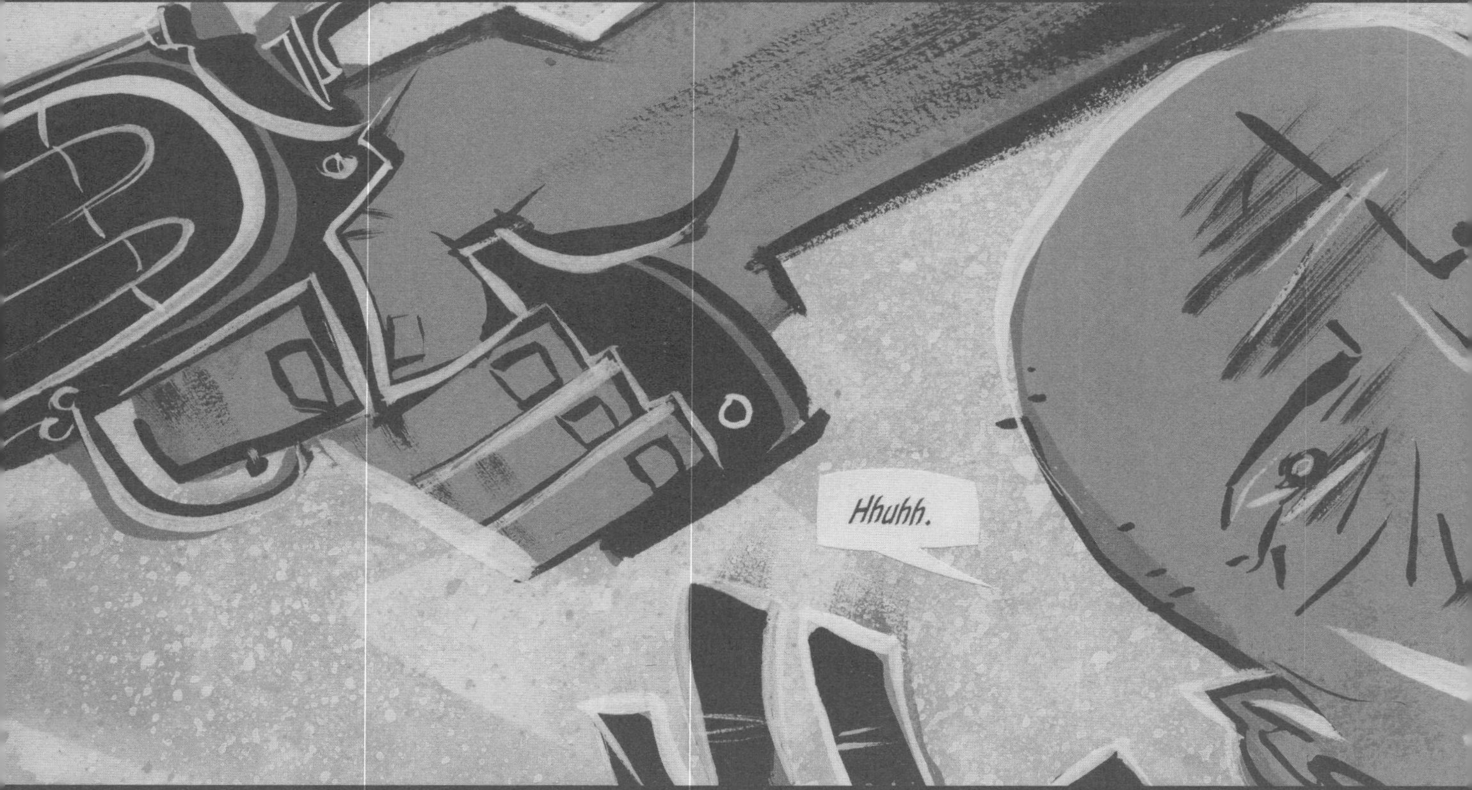
Hhuhh.

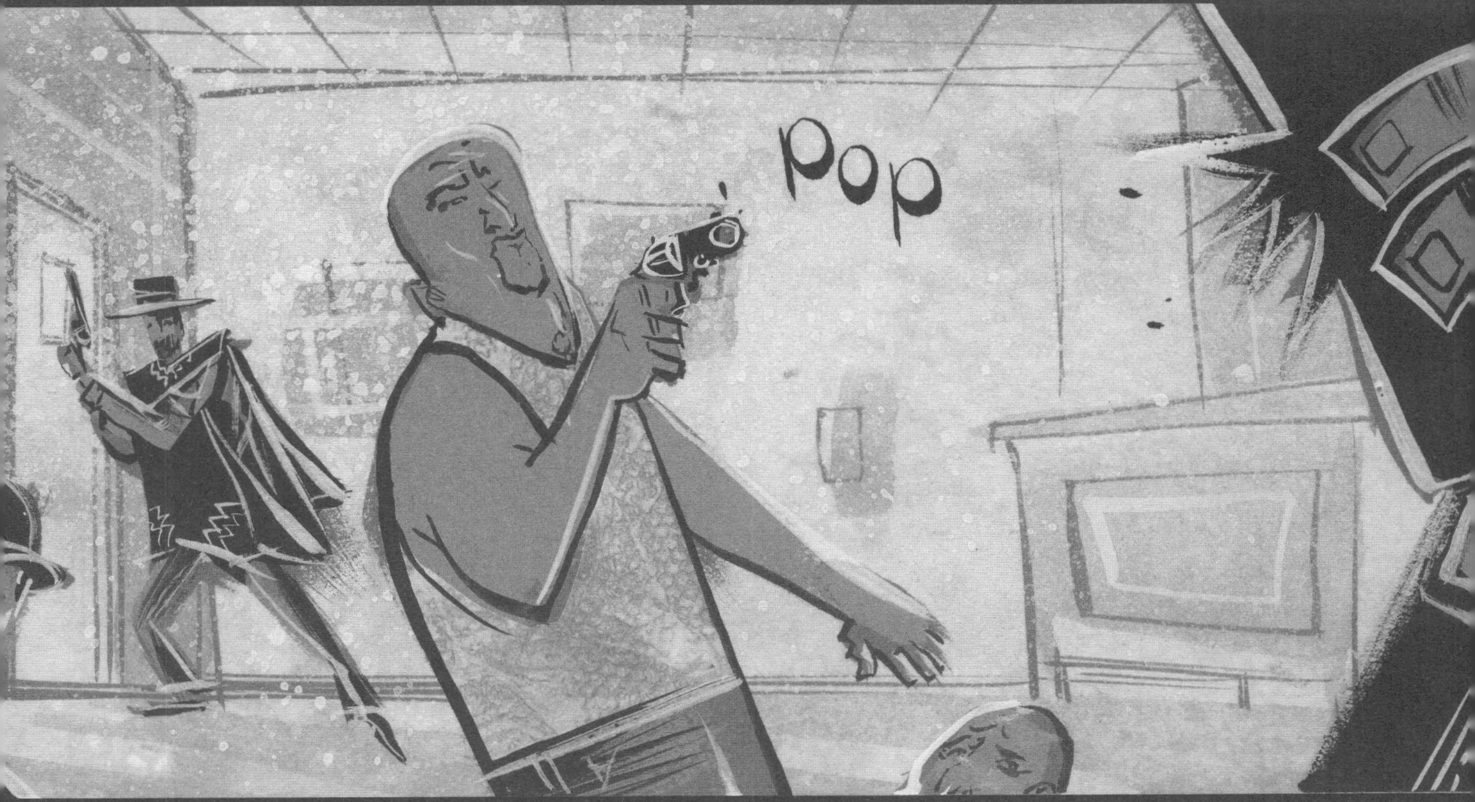
POP

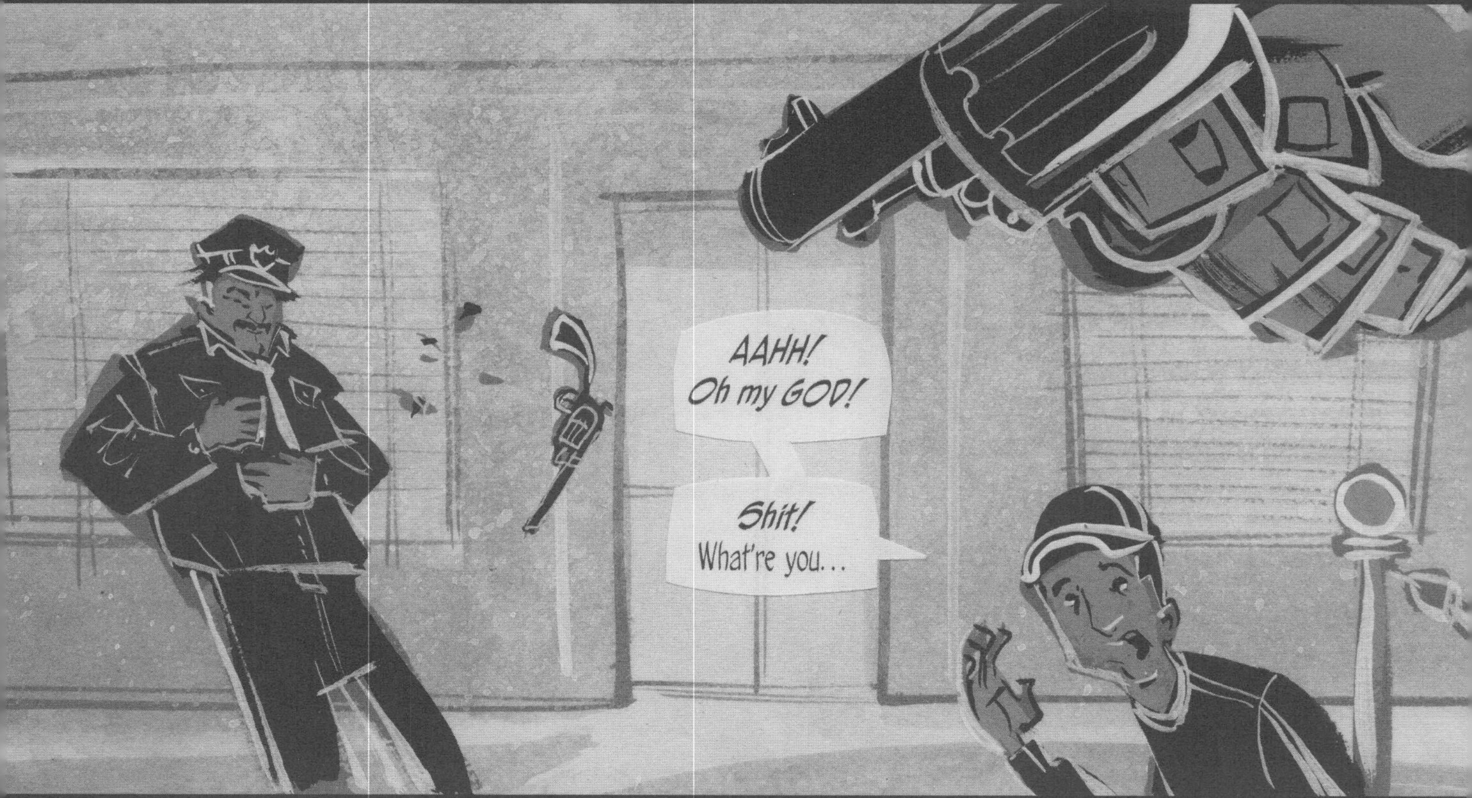
AAHH! Oh my GOD!
Shit! What're you...

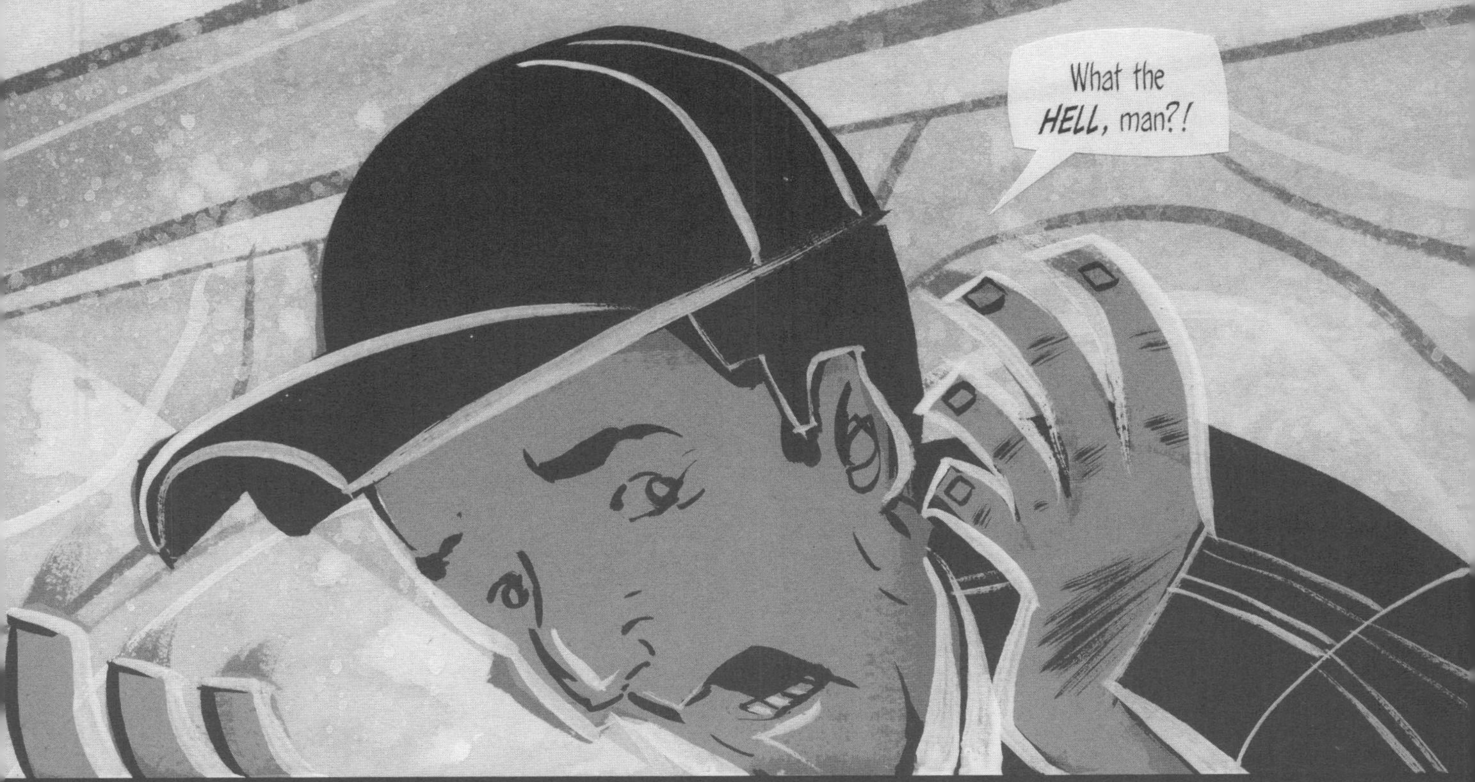
What the HELL, man?!

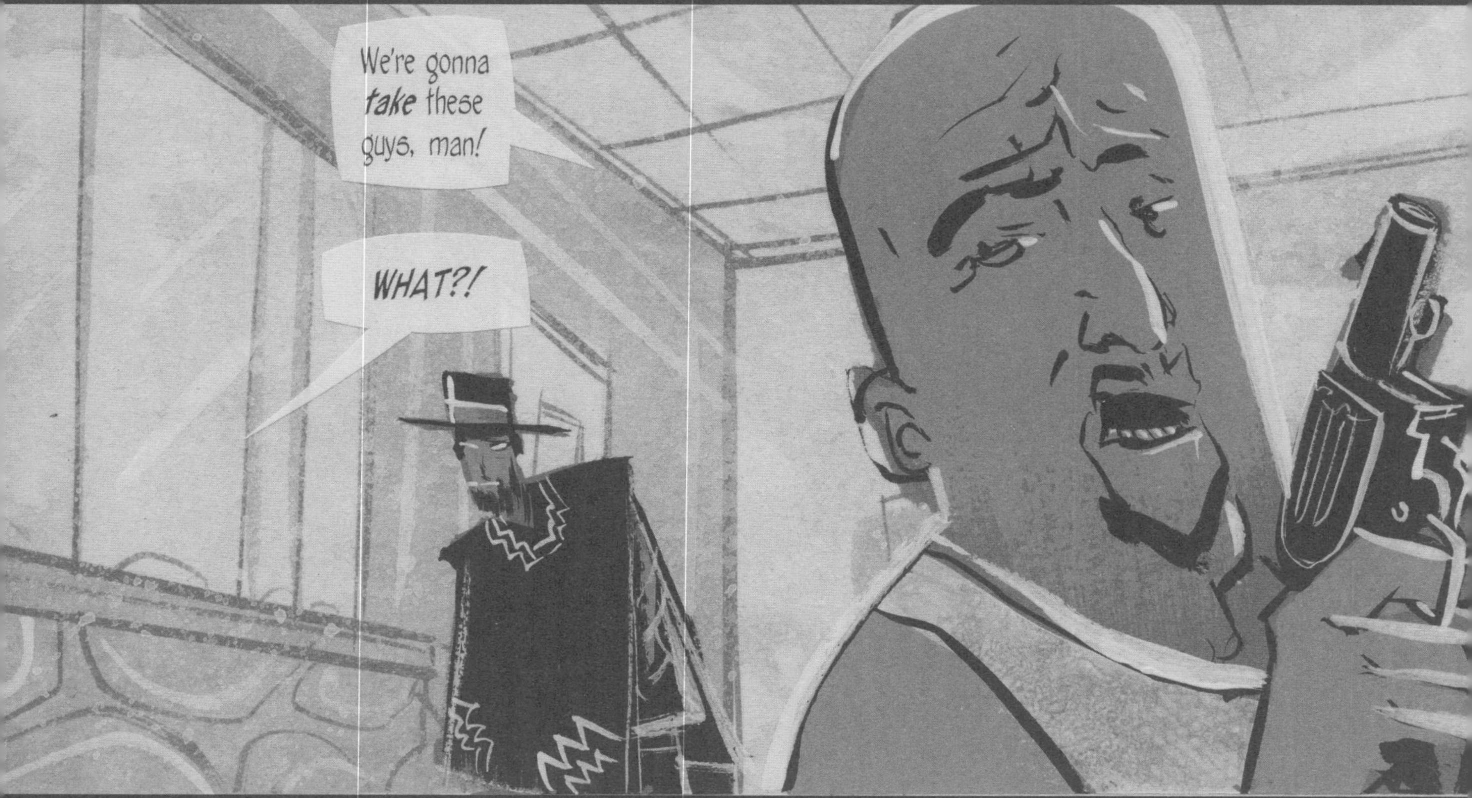
We're gonna *take* these guys, man!
WHAT?!

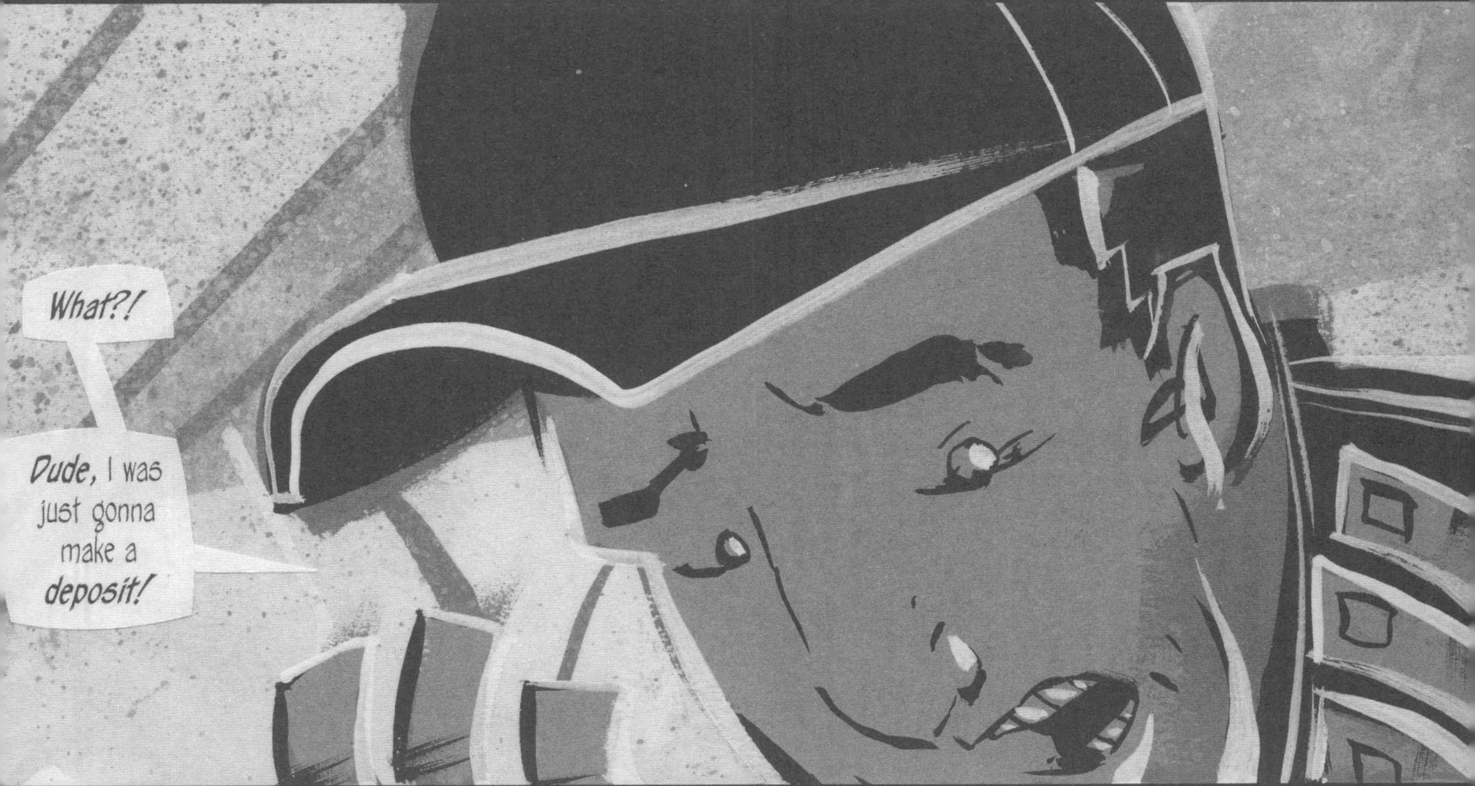
What?!
Dude, I was just gonna make a deposit!

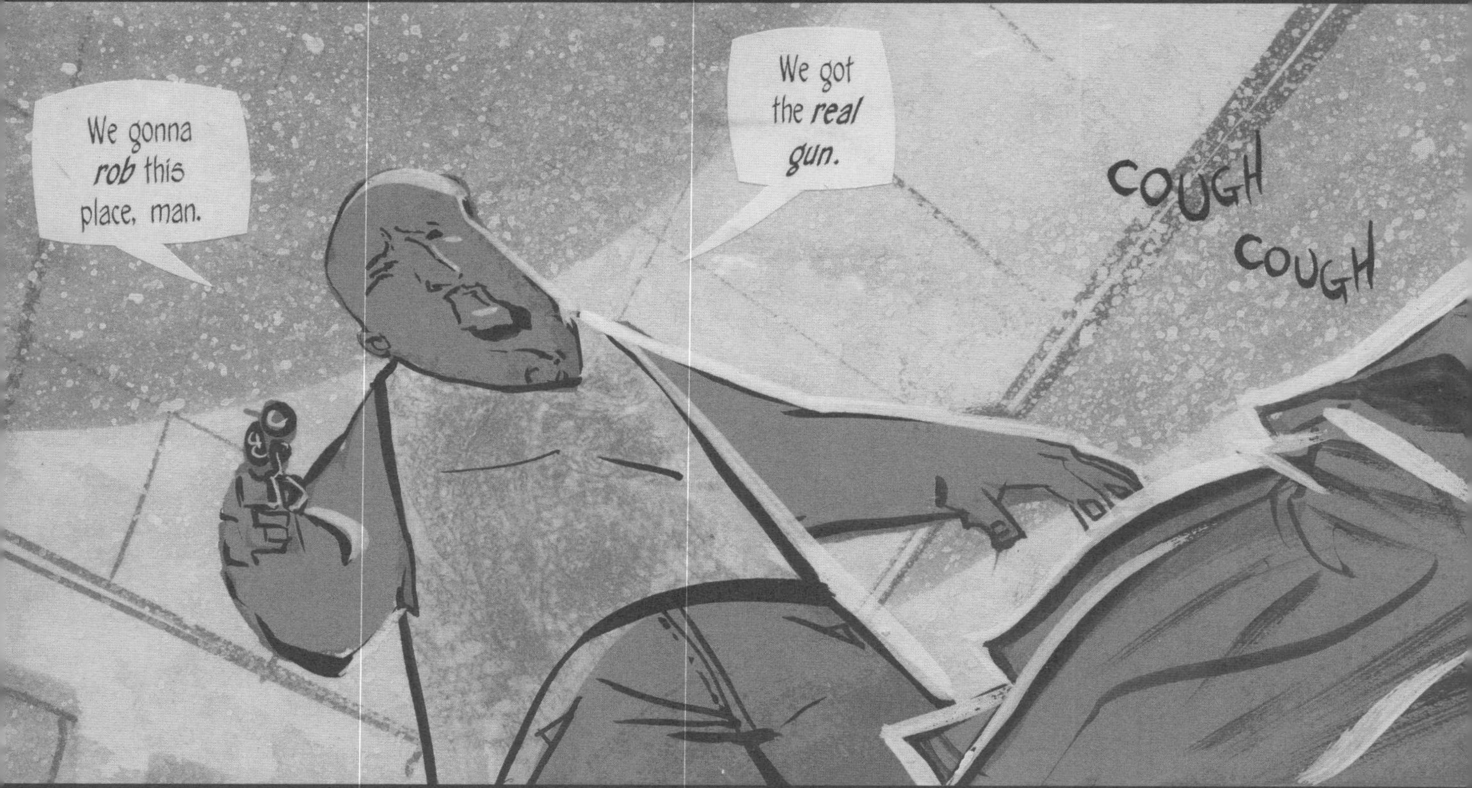
We gonna *rob* this place, man.
We got the *real* gun.
COUGH
COUGH

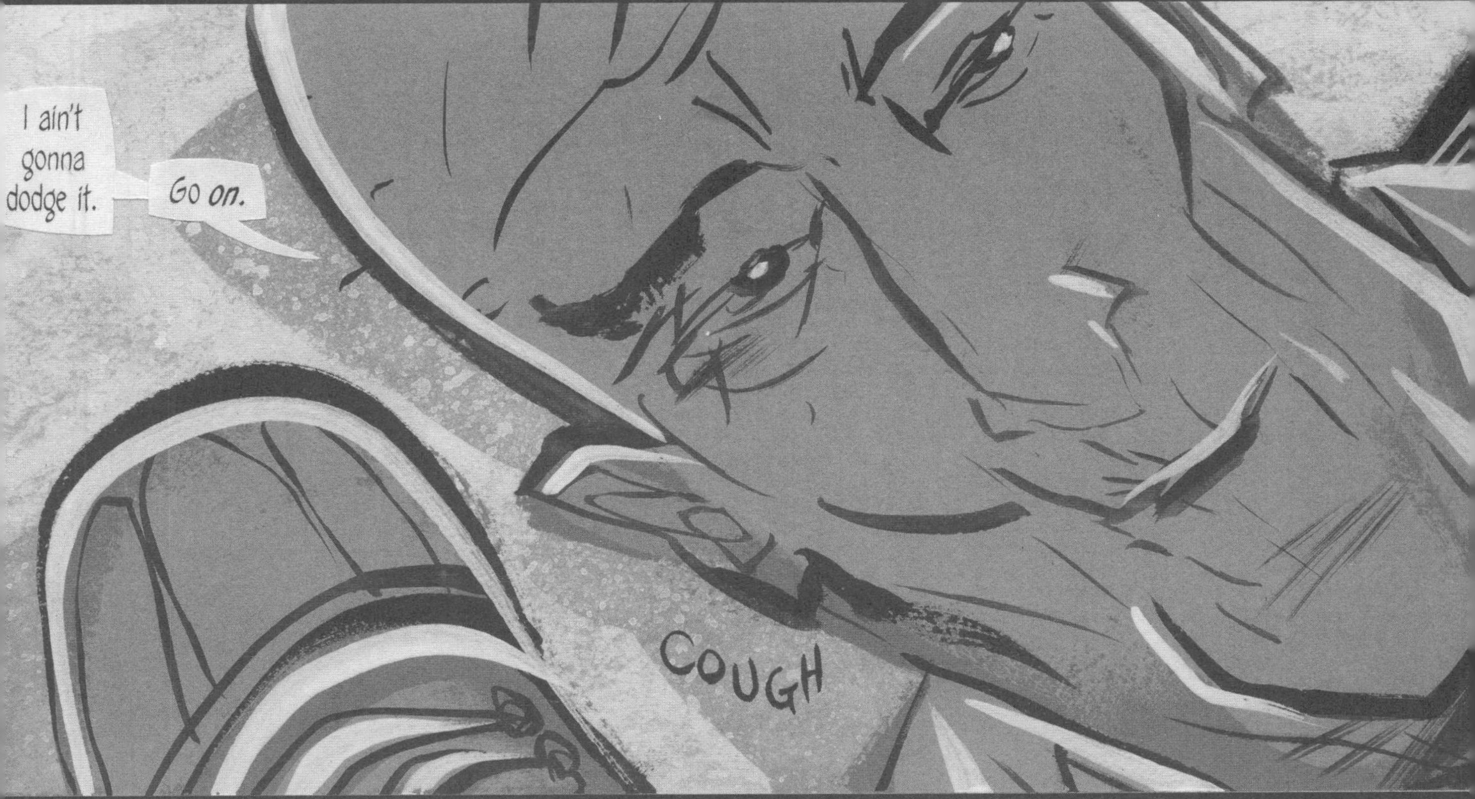
I ain't gonna dodge it.
Go on.
COUGH

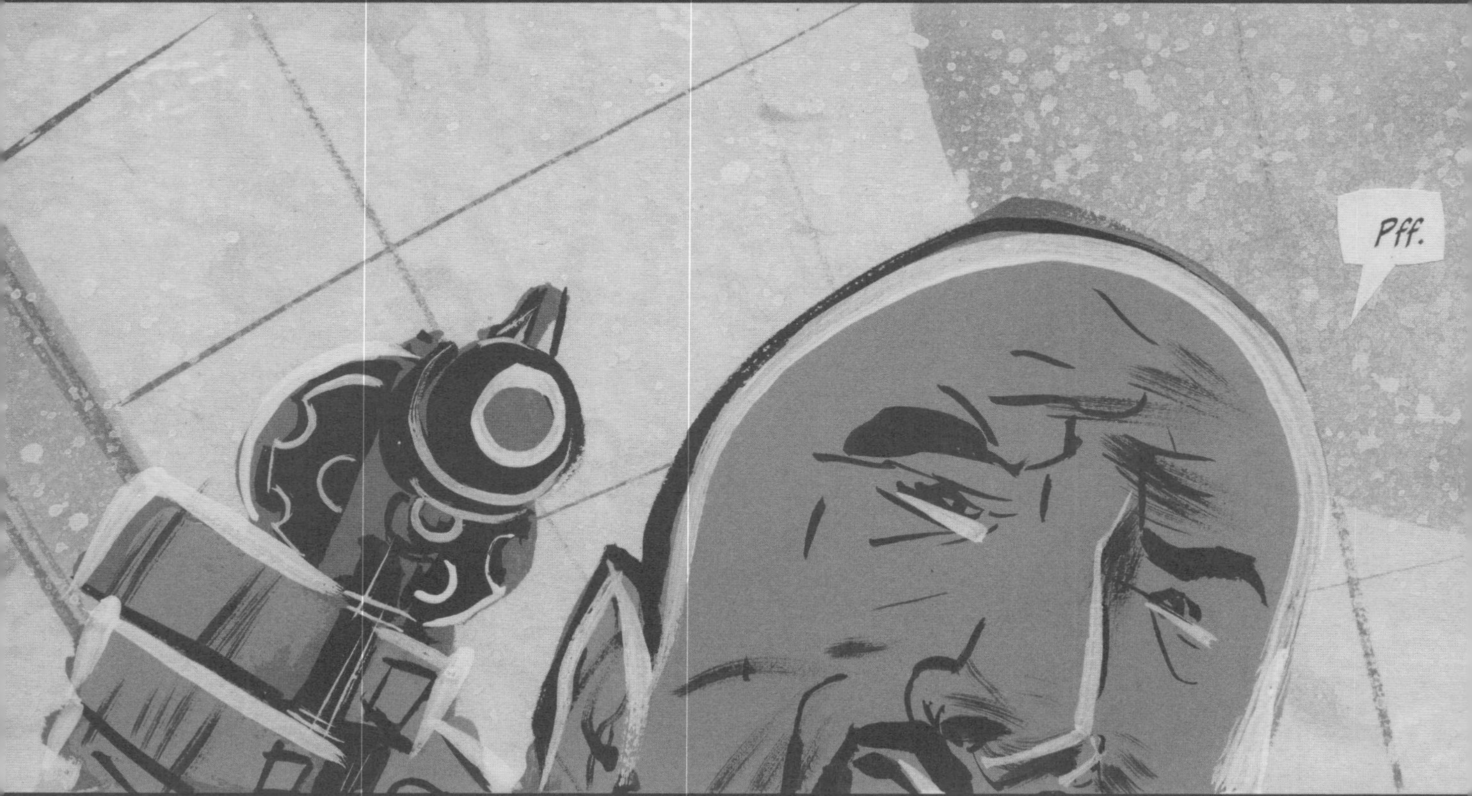
Pff.

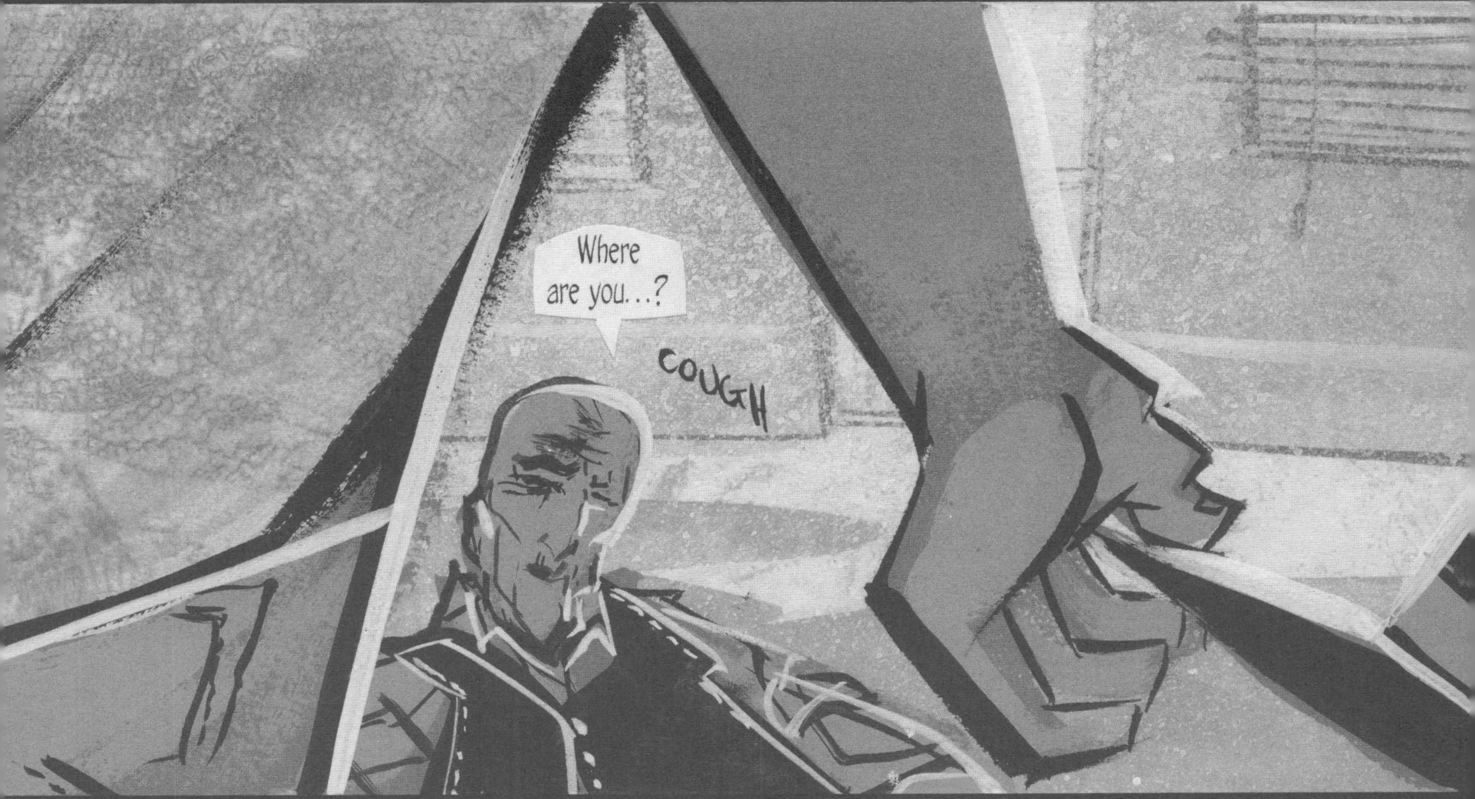
Where are you...?
COUGH

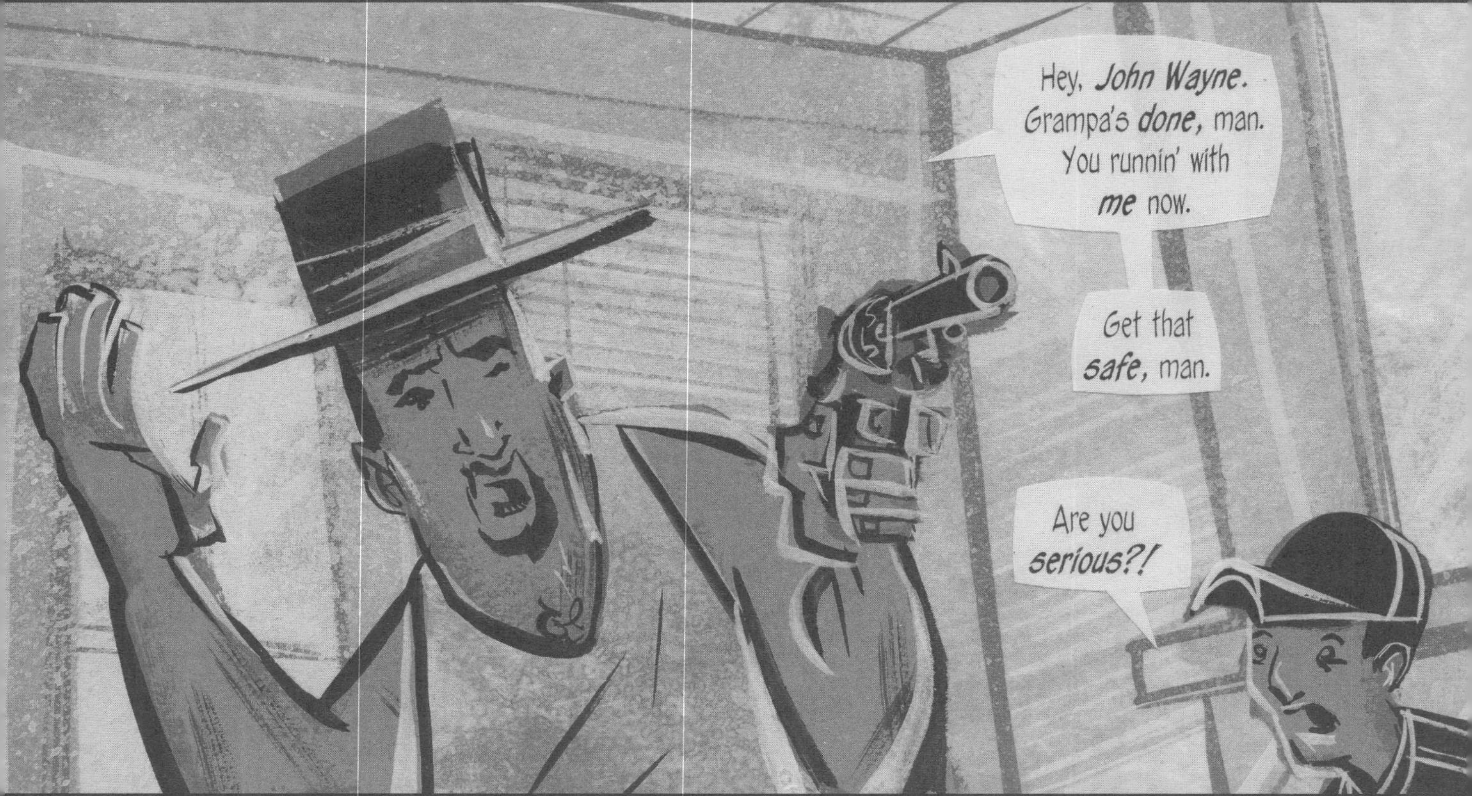
Hey, John Wayne. Grampa's done, man. You runnin' with me now.
Get that safe, man.
Are you serious?!

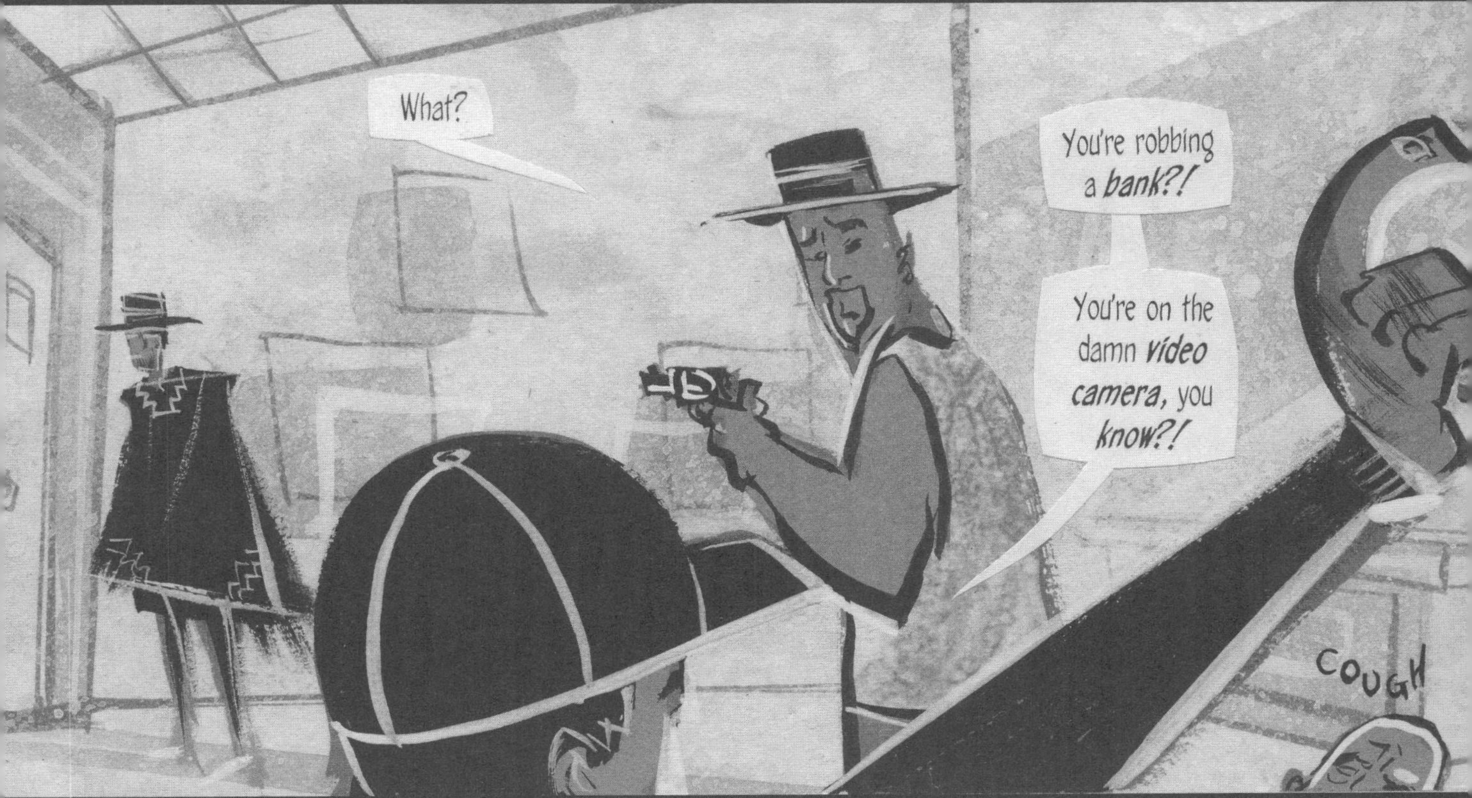
What?
You're robbing a bank?!
You're on the damn video camera, you know?!
COUGH

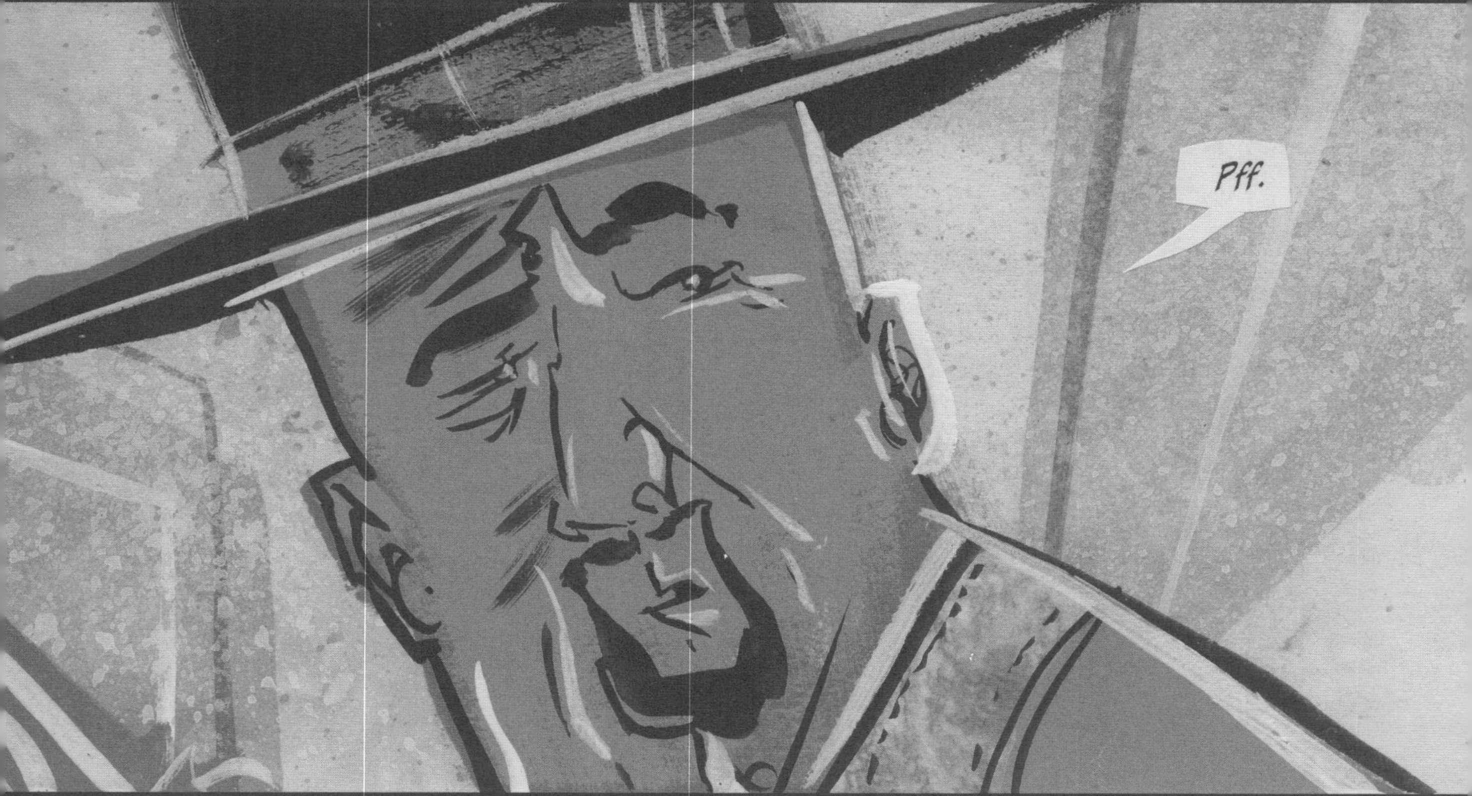
Pff.

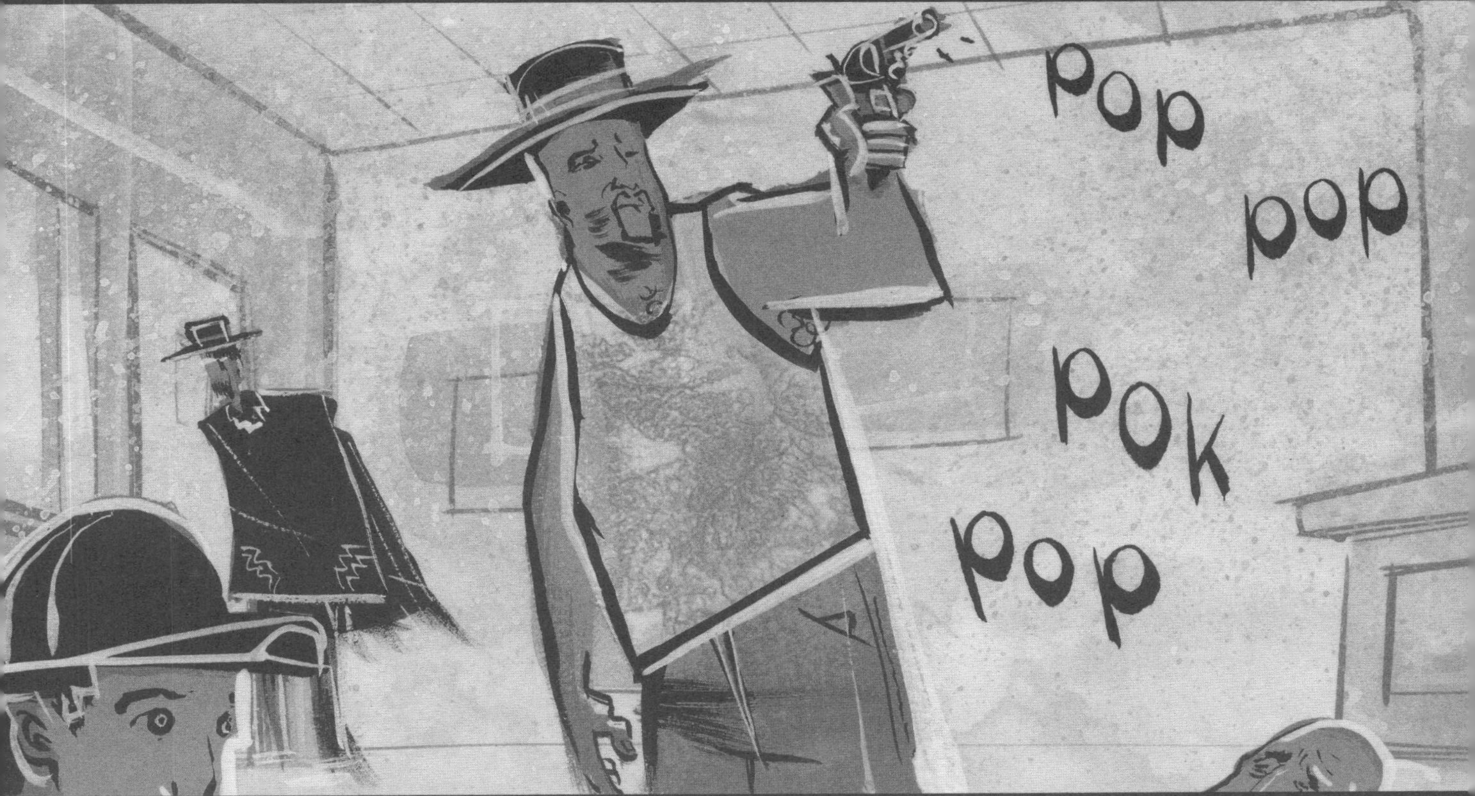
pop
pop
pok
pop

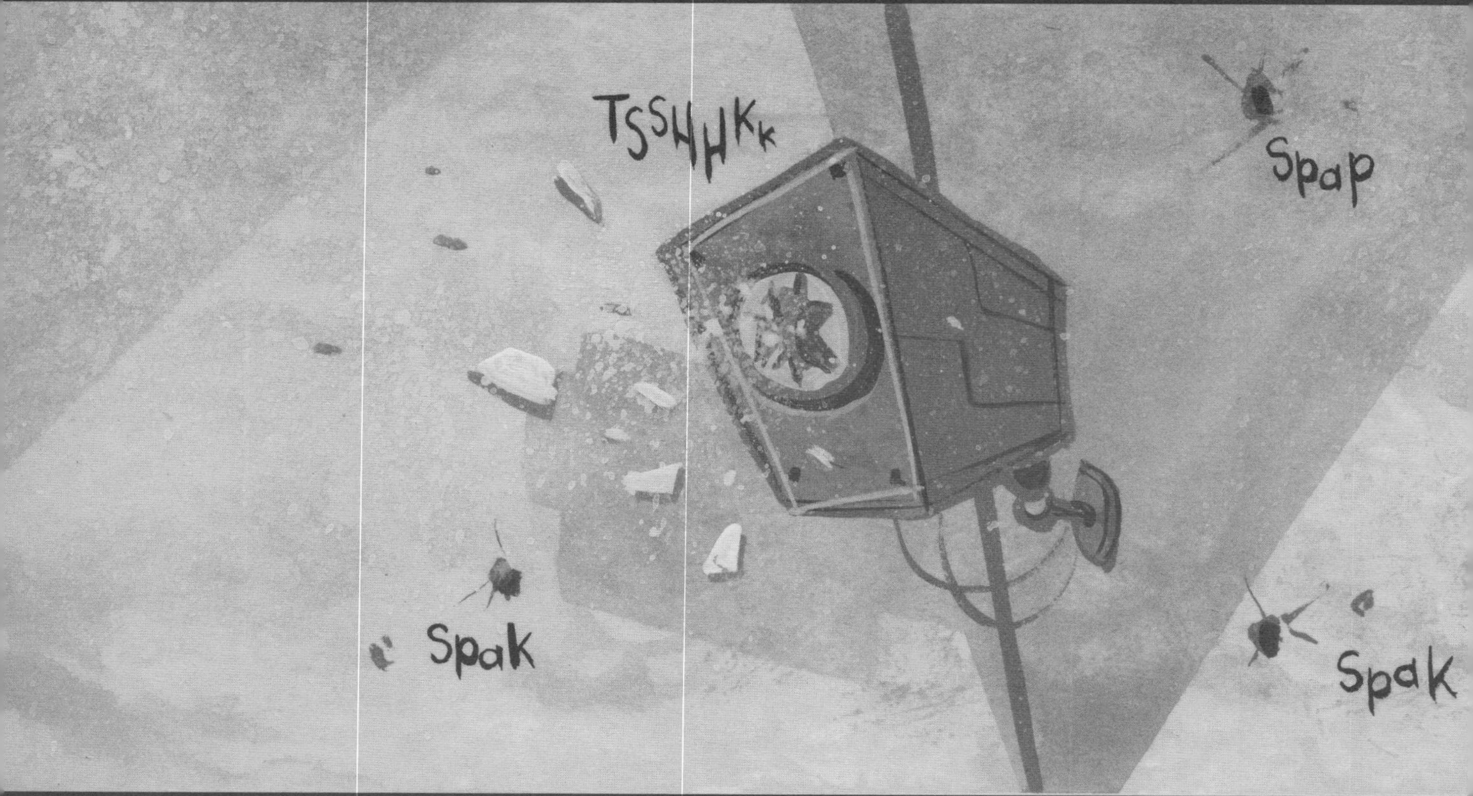
TSSHHKk
Spap
Spak
Spak

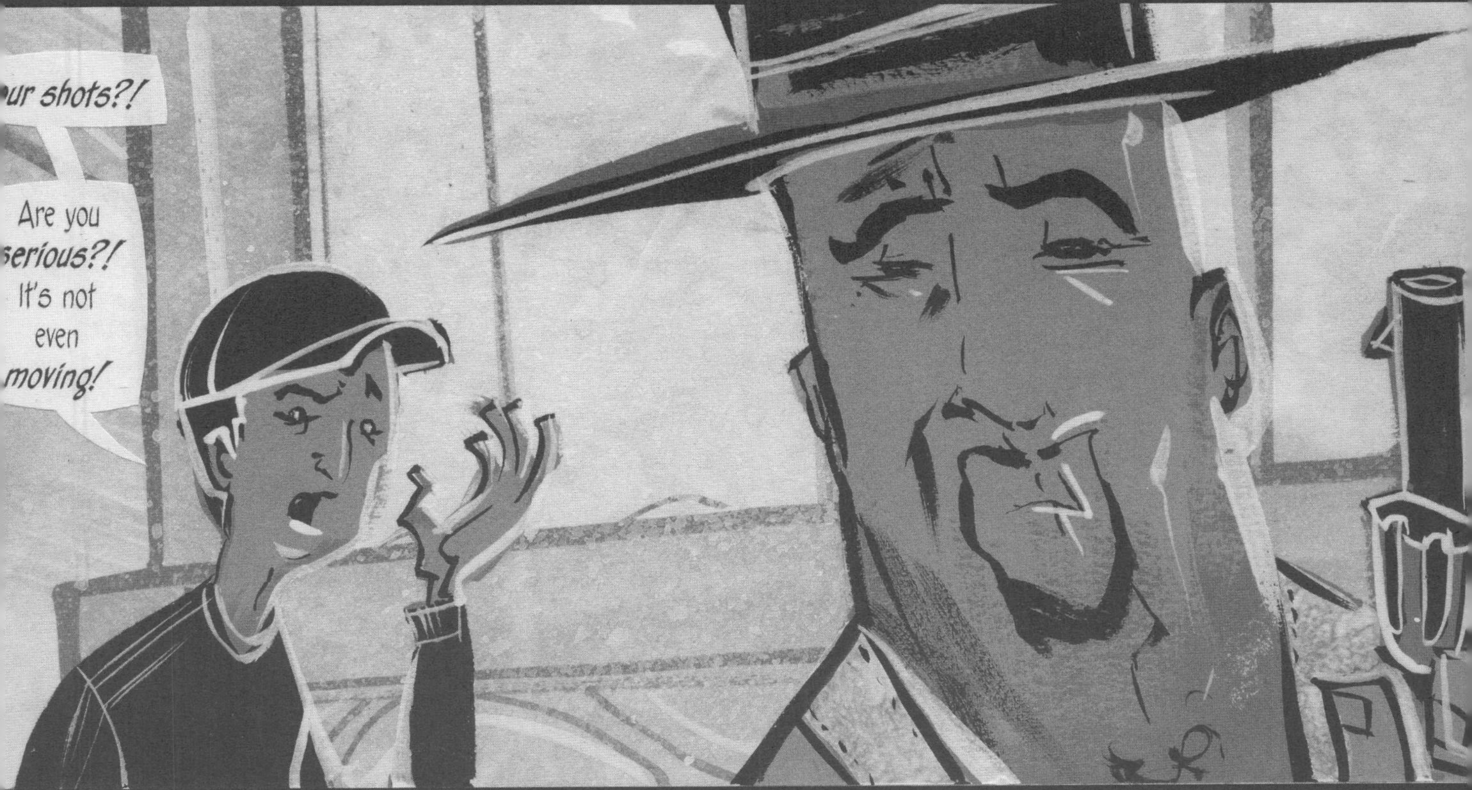
our shots?!
Are you serious?! It's not even moving!

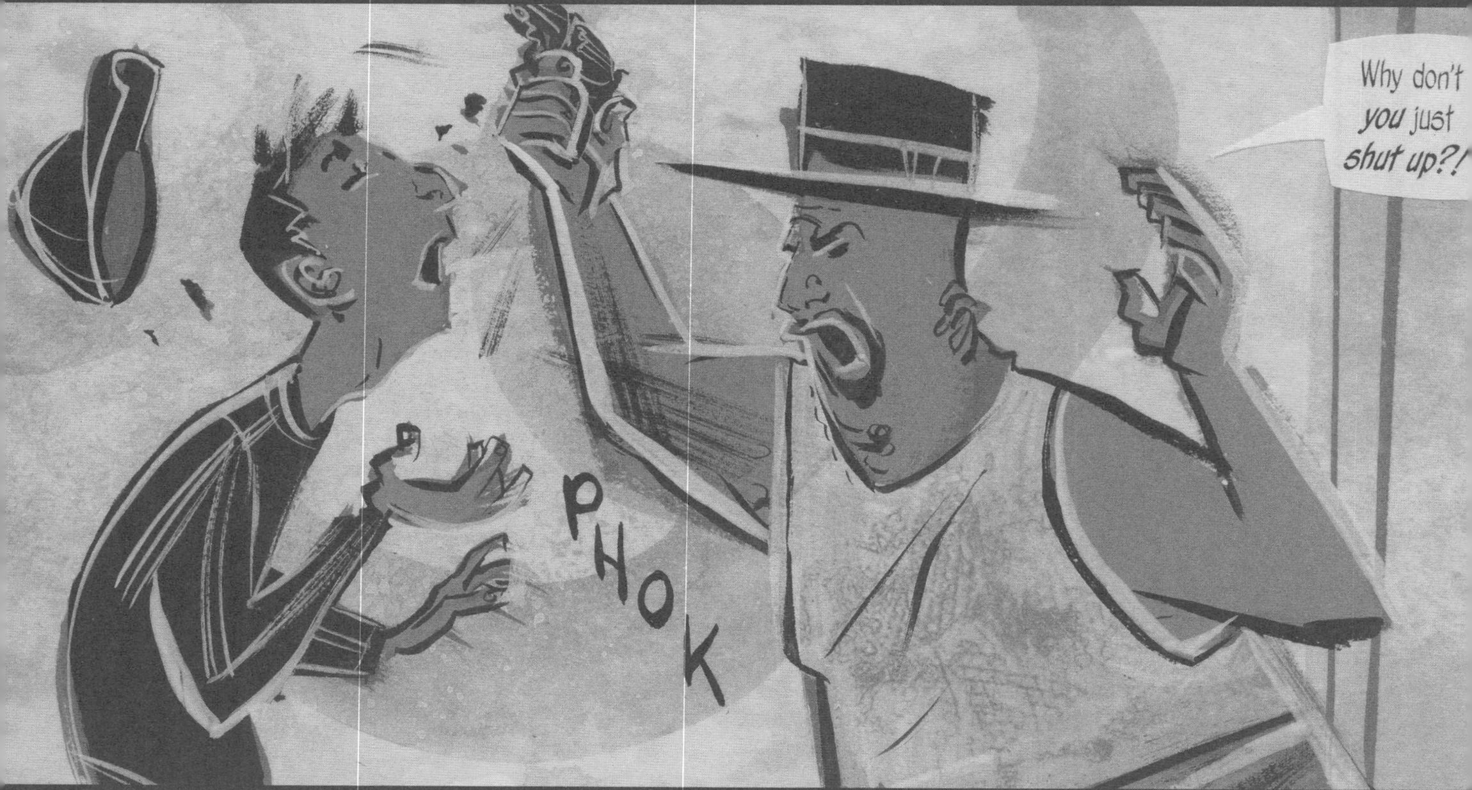
Why don't you just shut up?!
PHOK

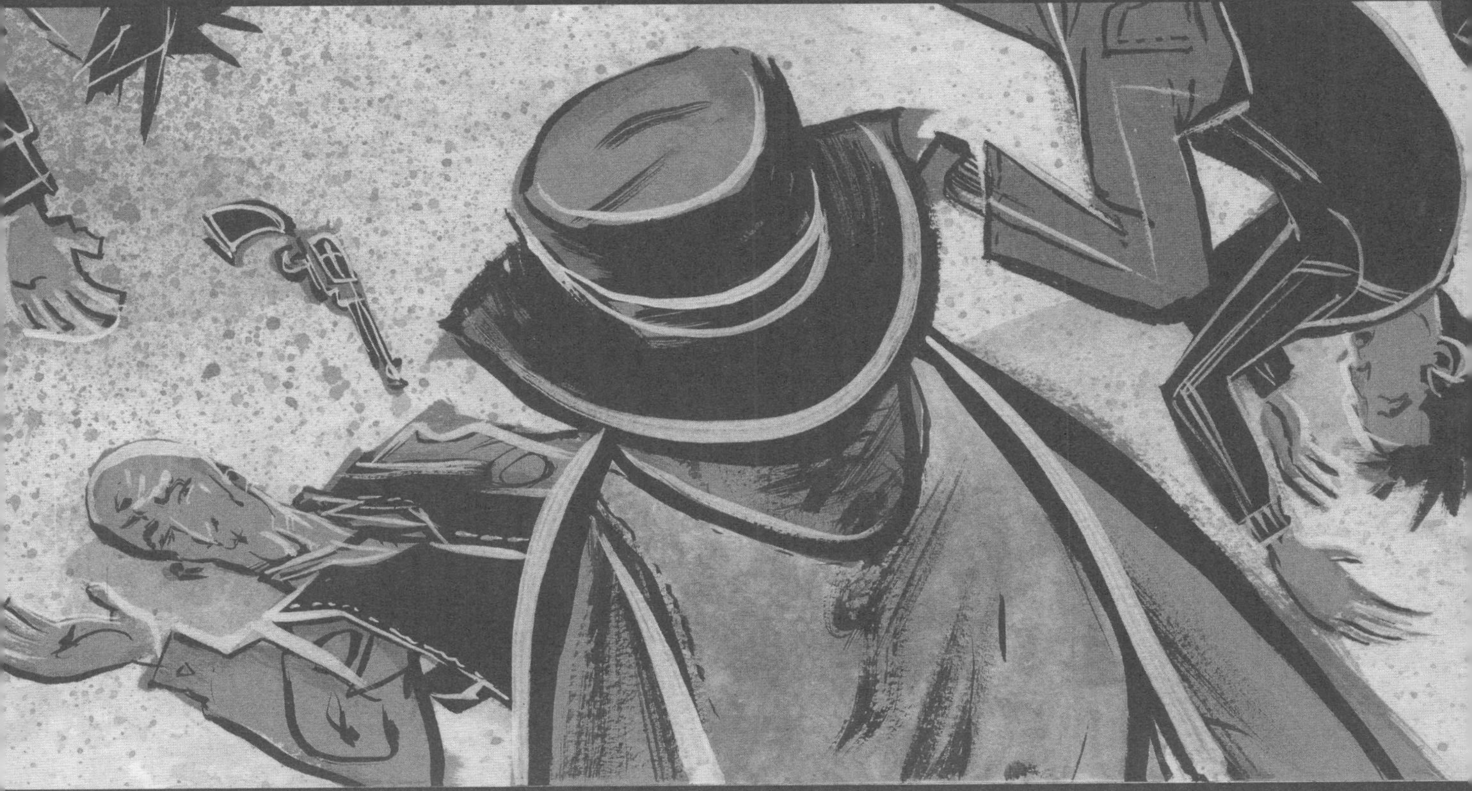

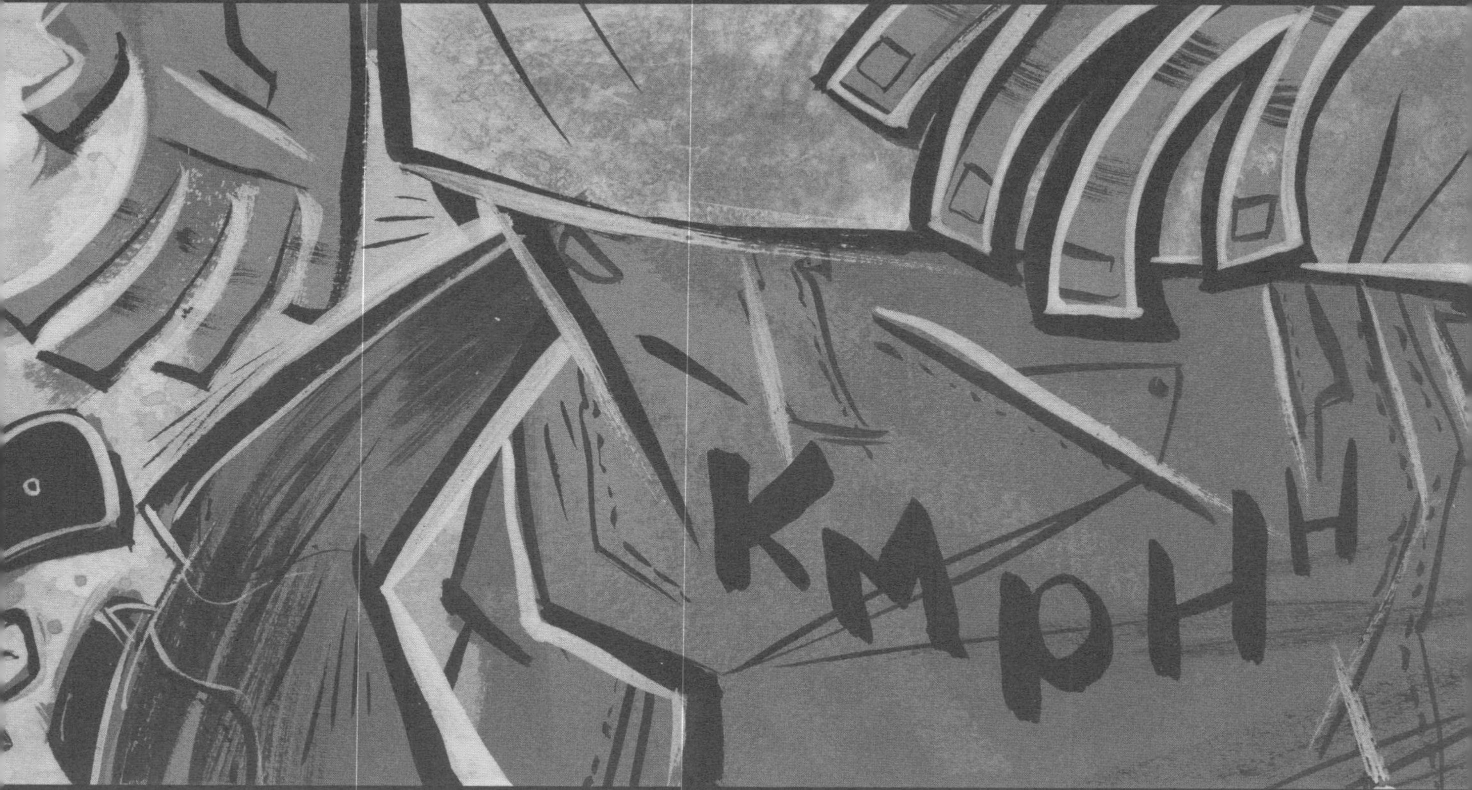
KMPHH

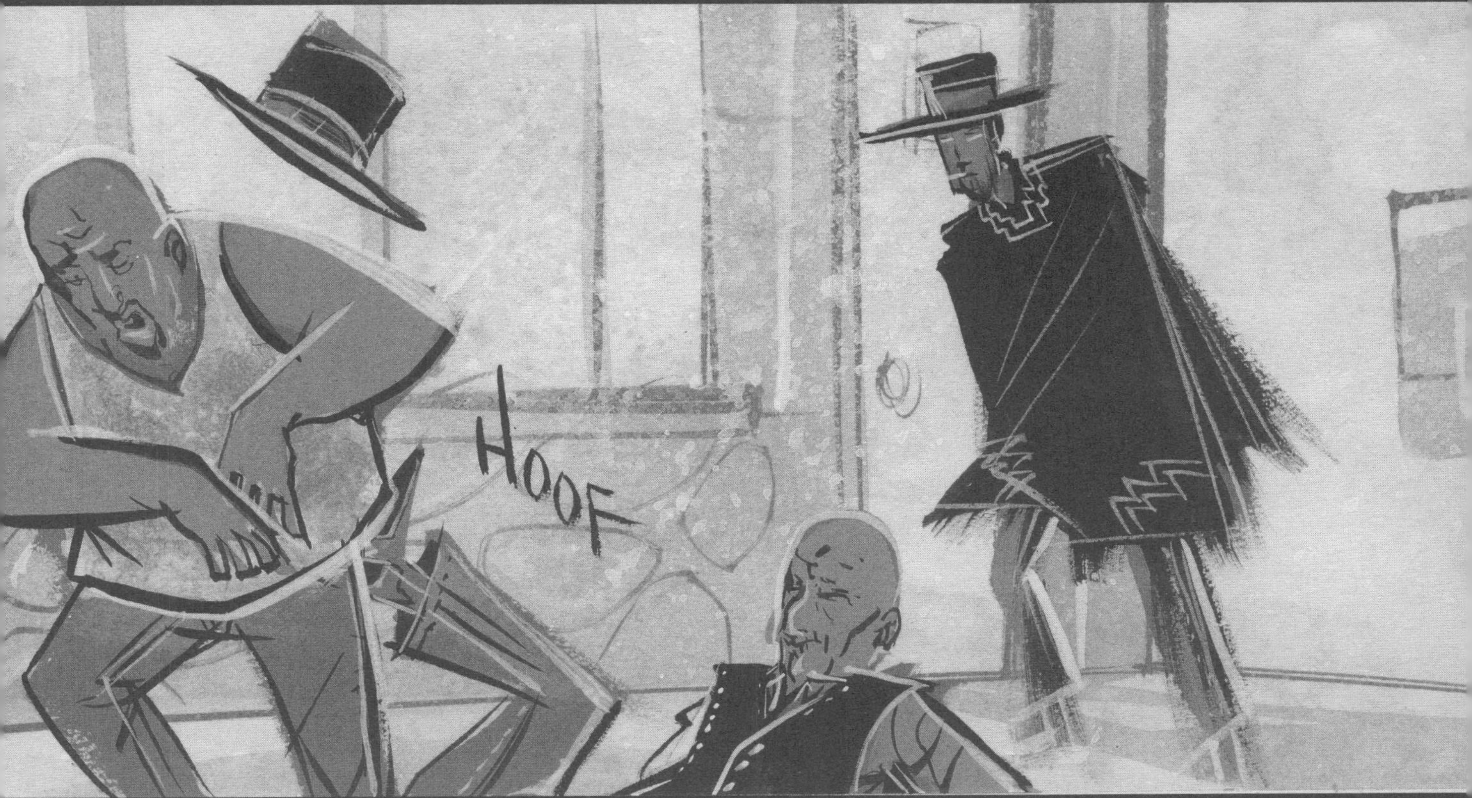
HOOF

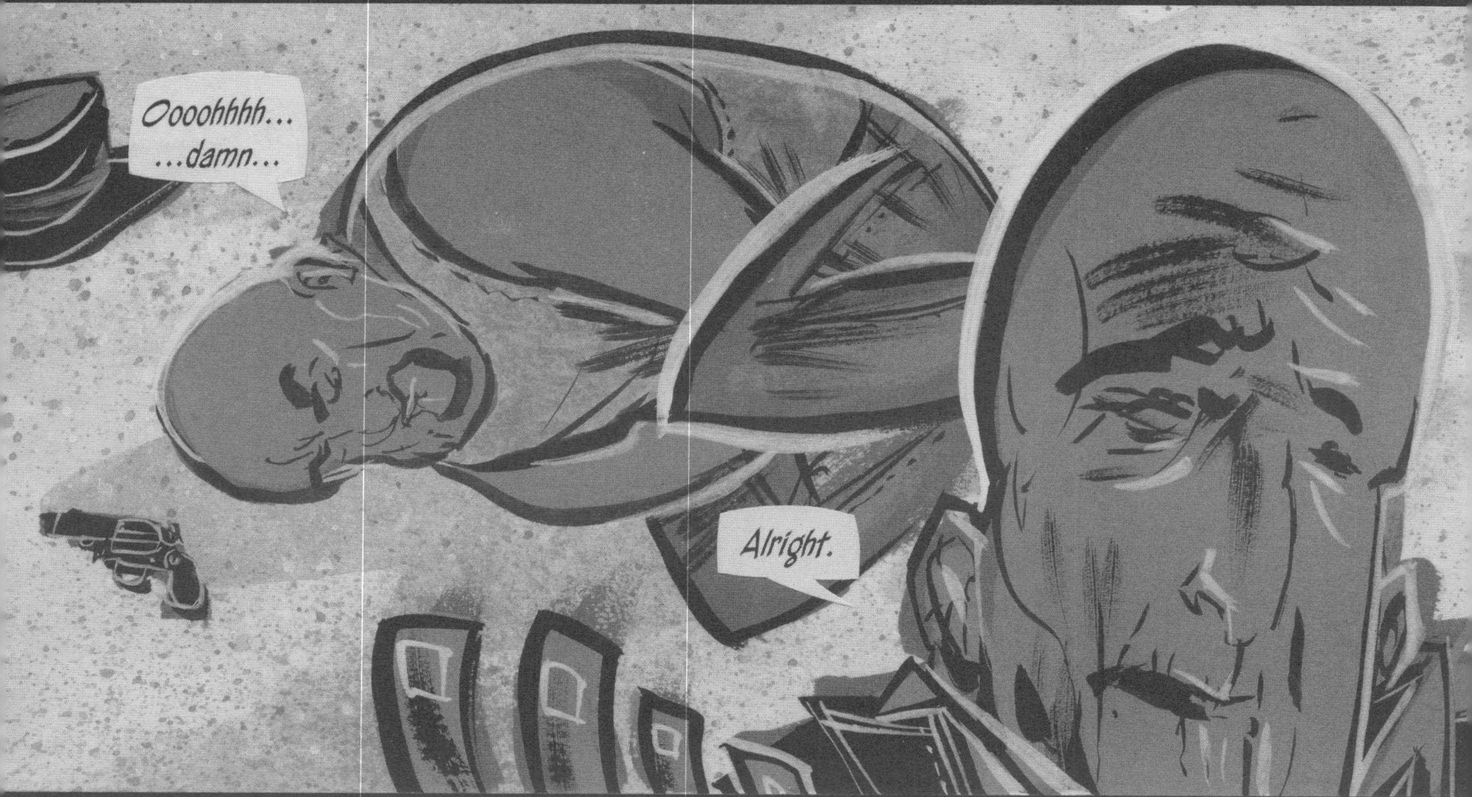
Oooohhhh...
...damn...
Alright.

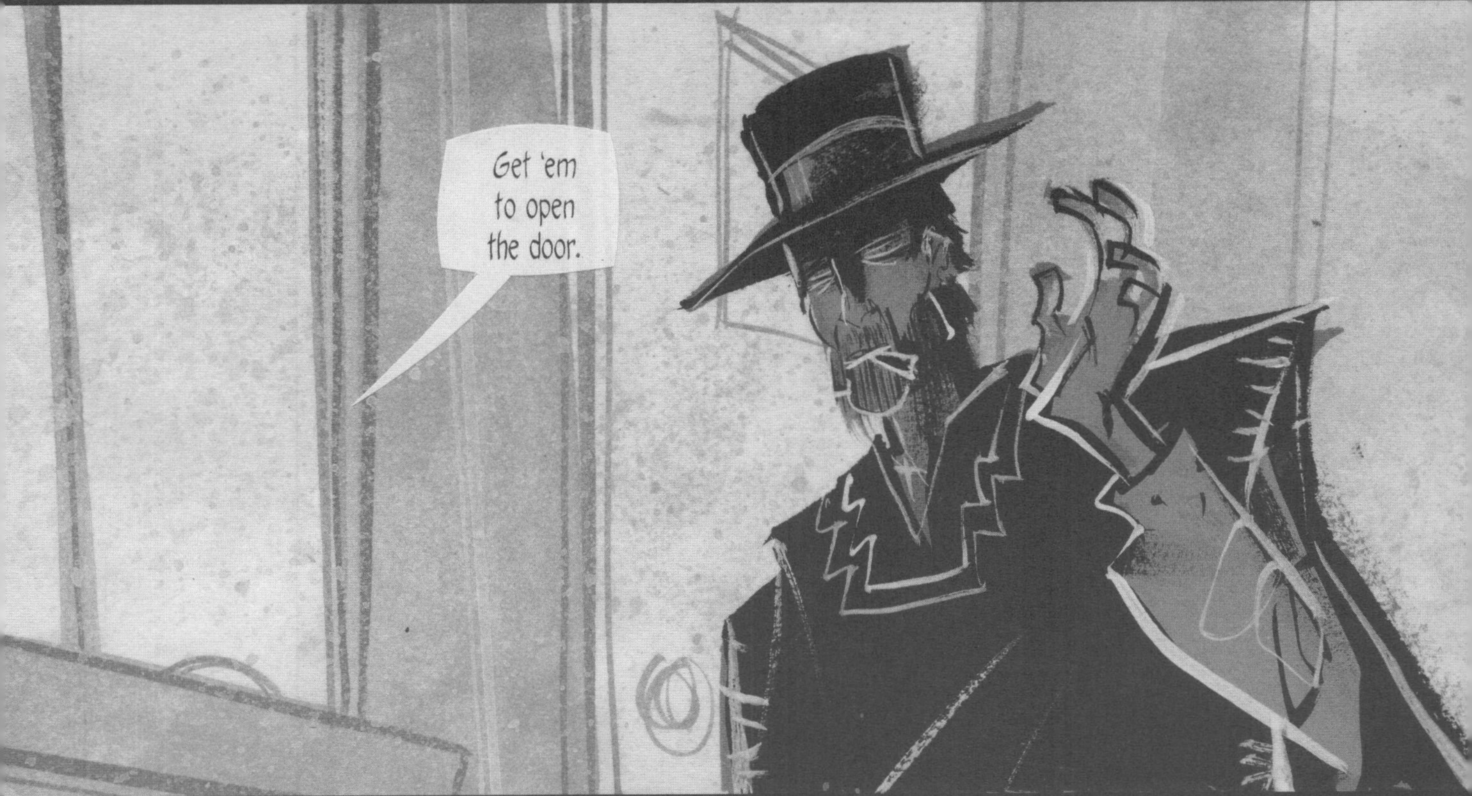
Get 'em to open the door.

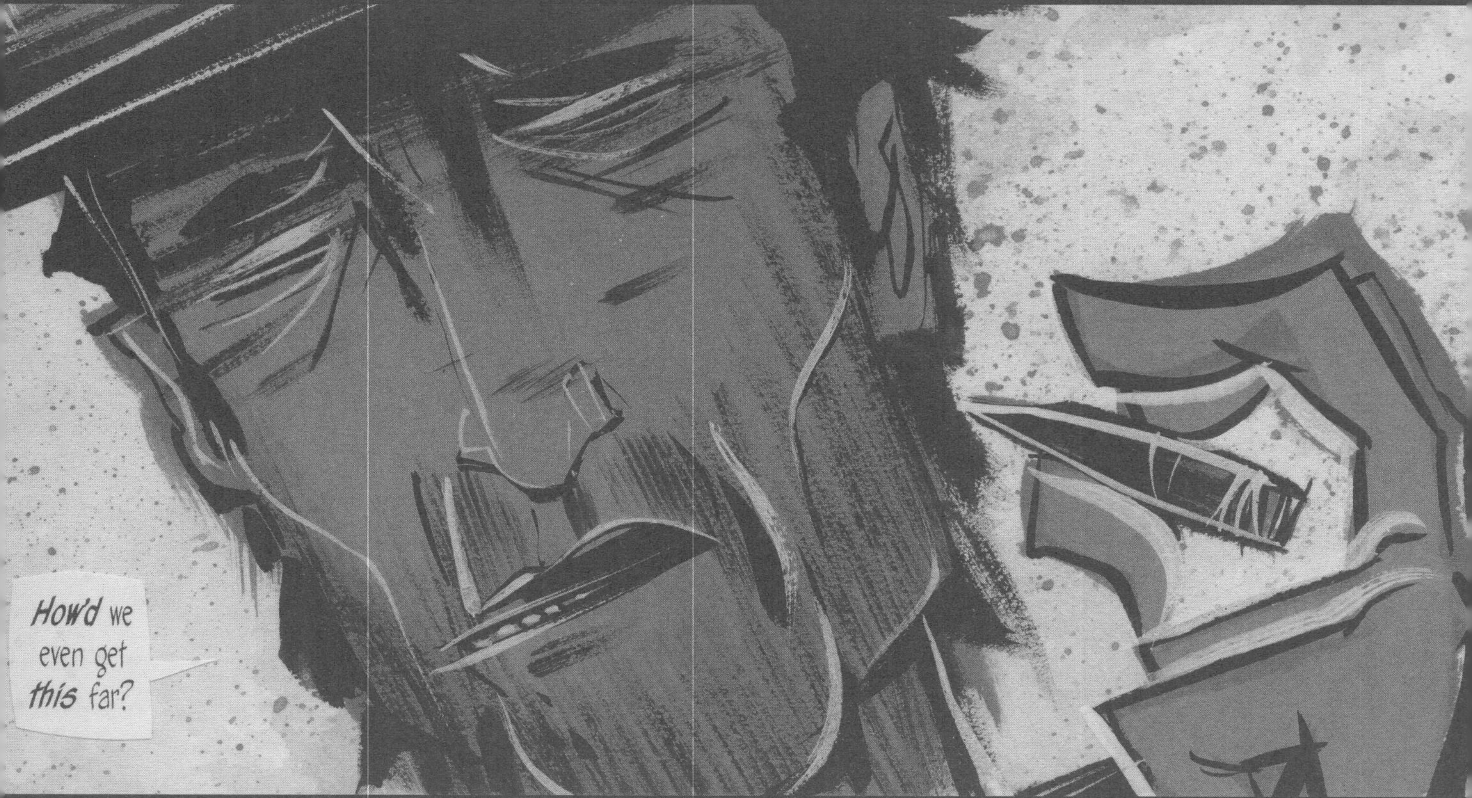
How'd we even get *this* far?

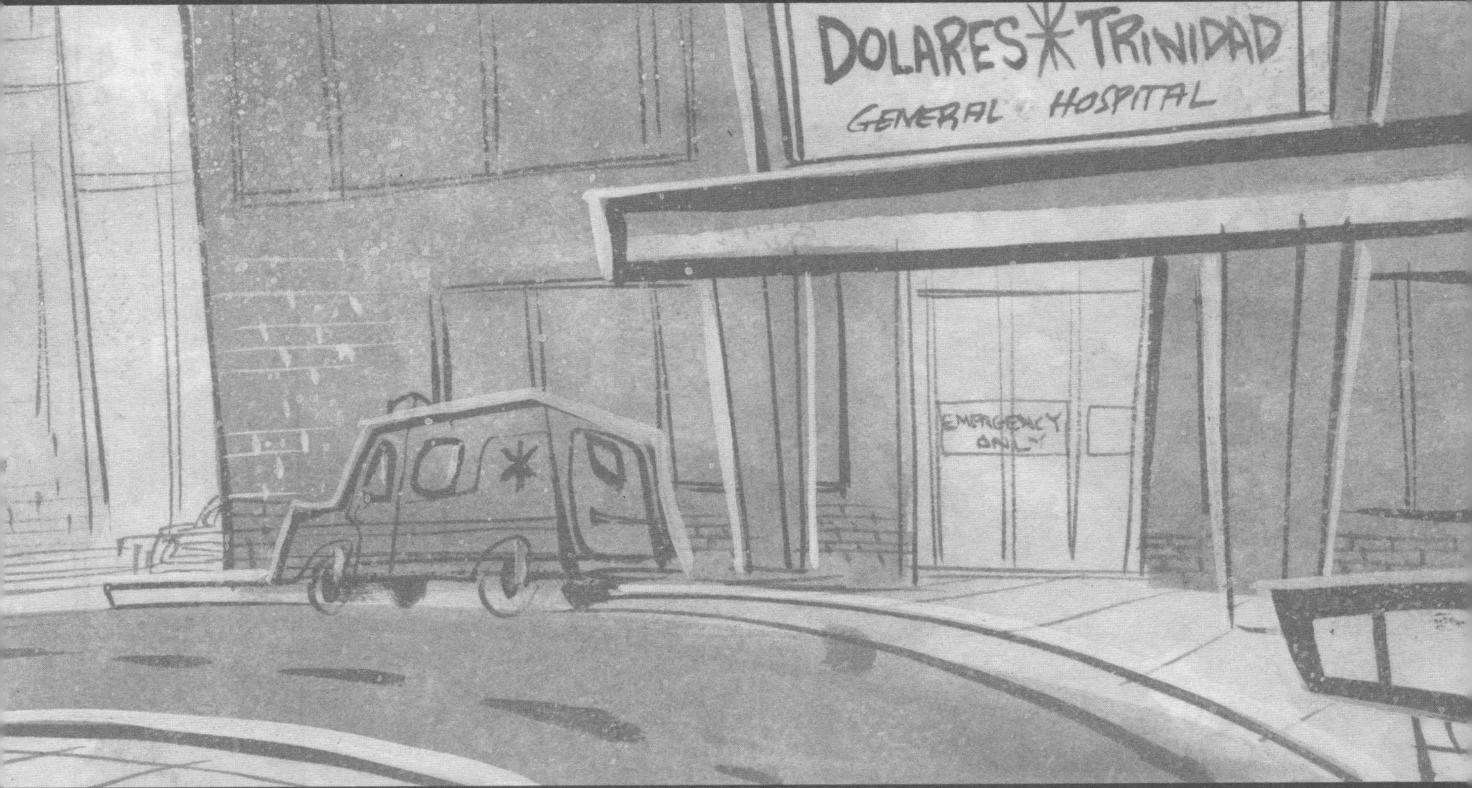
DOLARES TRINIDAD
GENERAL HOSPITAL
EMERGENCY ONLY

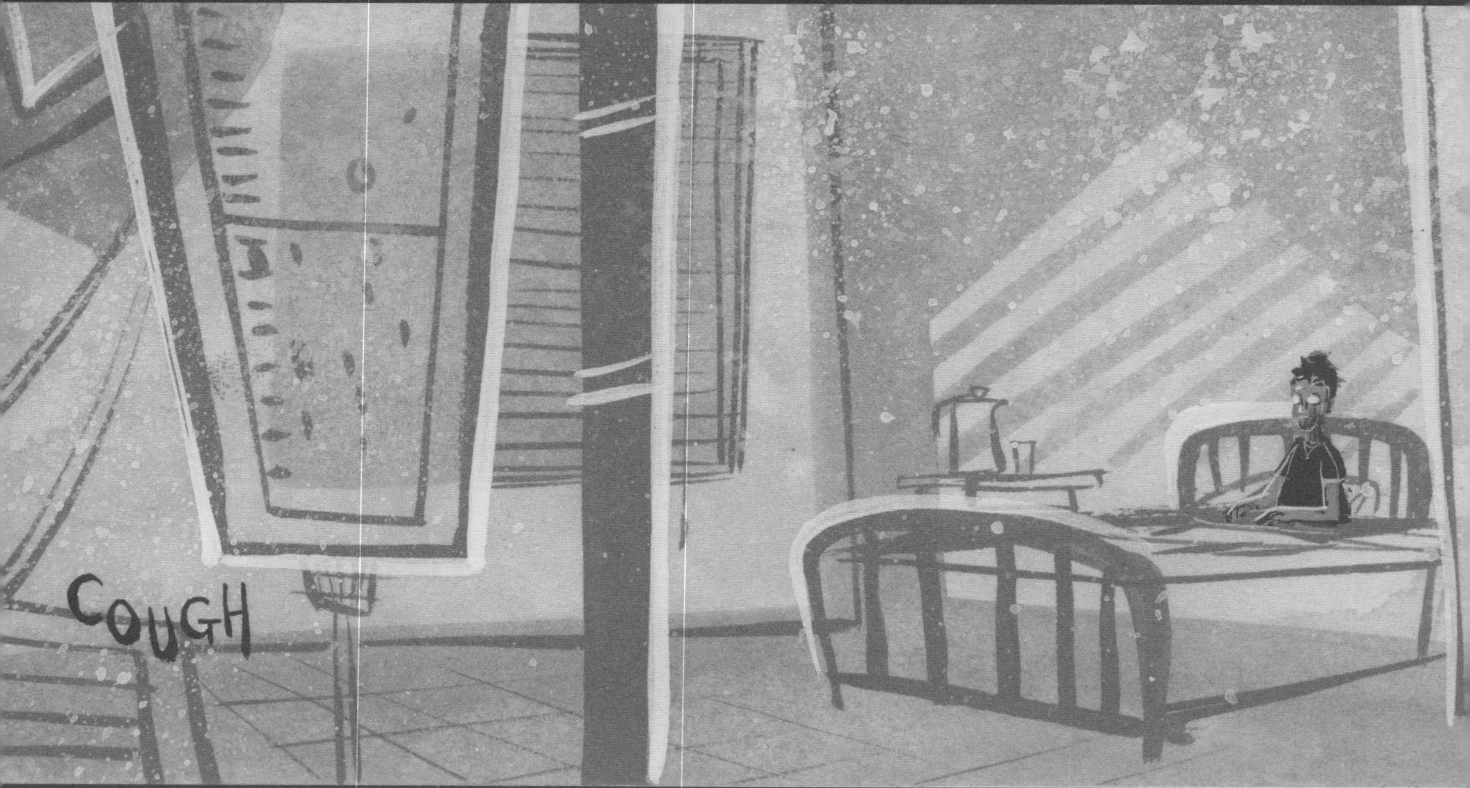
COUGH

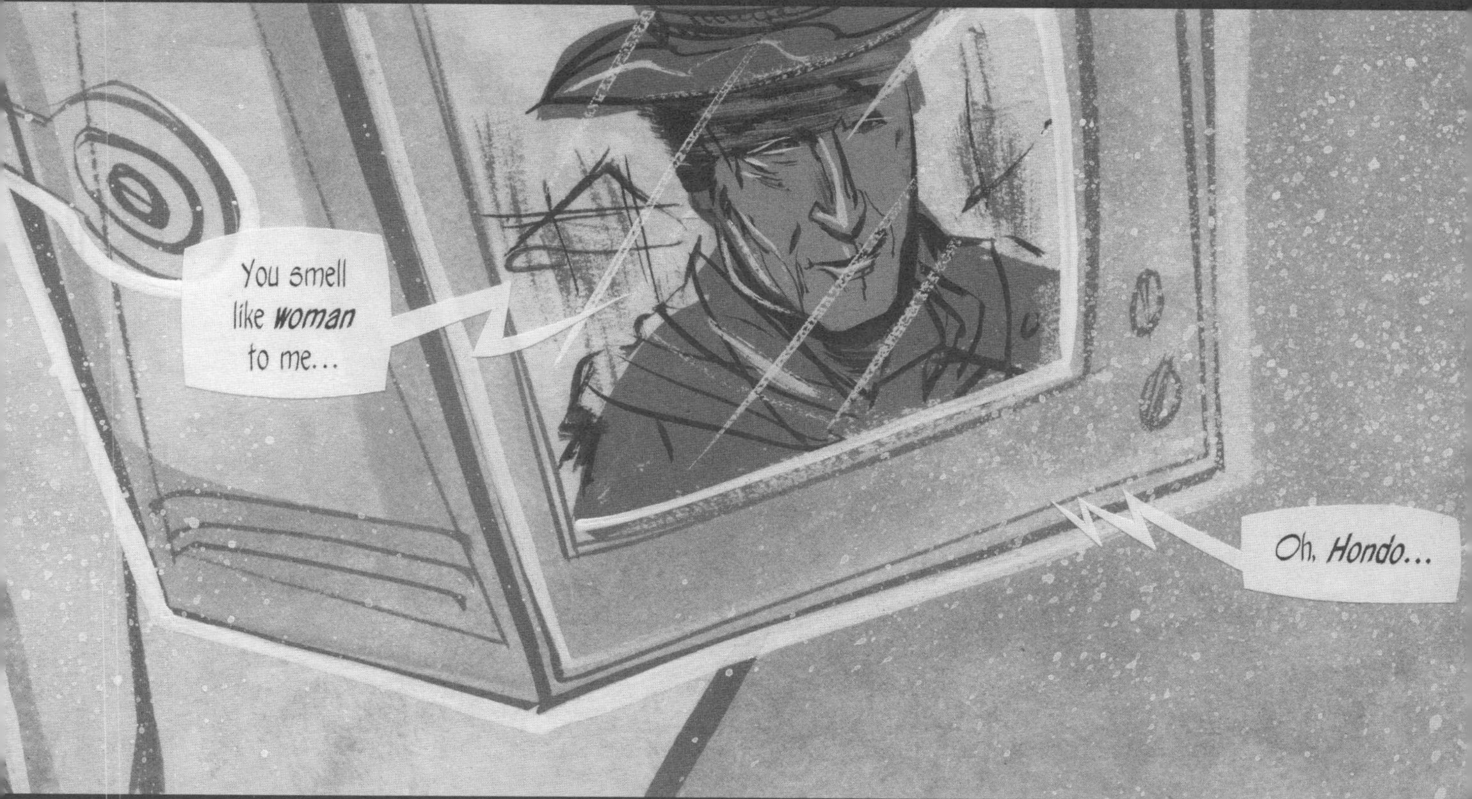
You smell like ***woman*** to me...
Oh, *Hondo*...

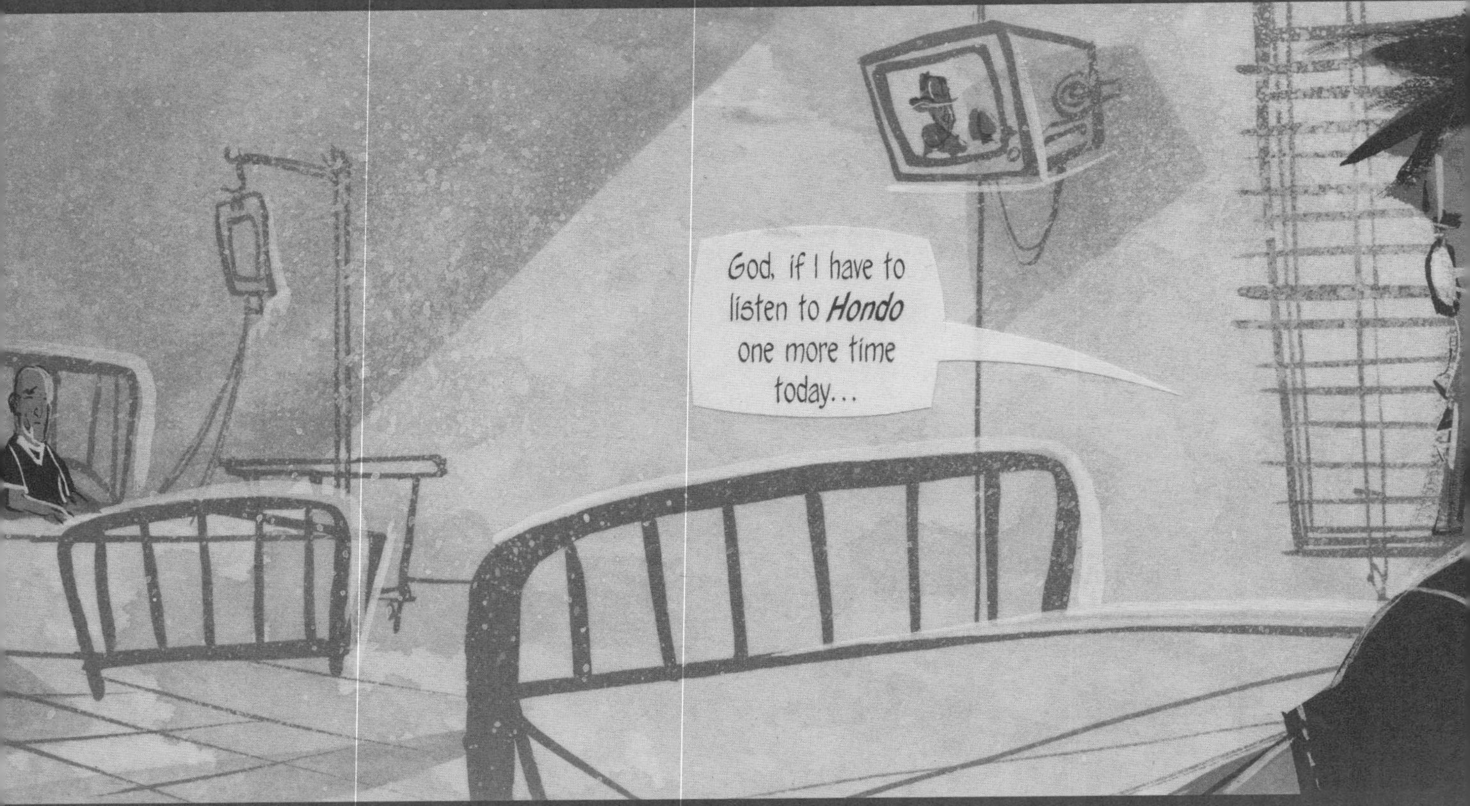
God, if I have to listen to *Hondo* one more time today...

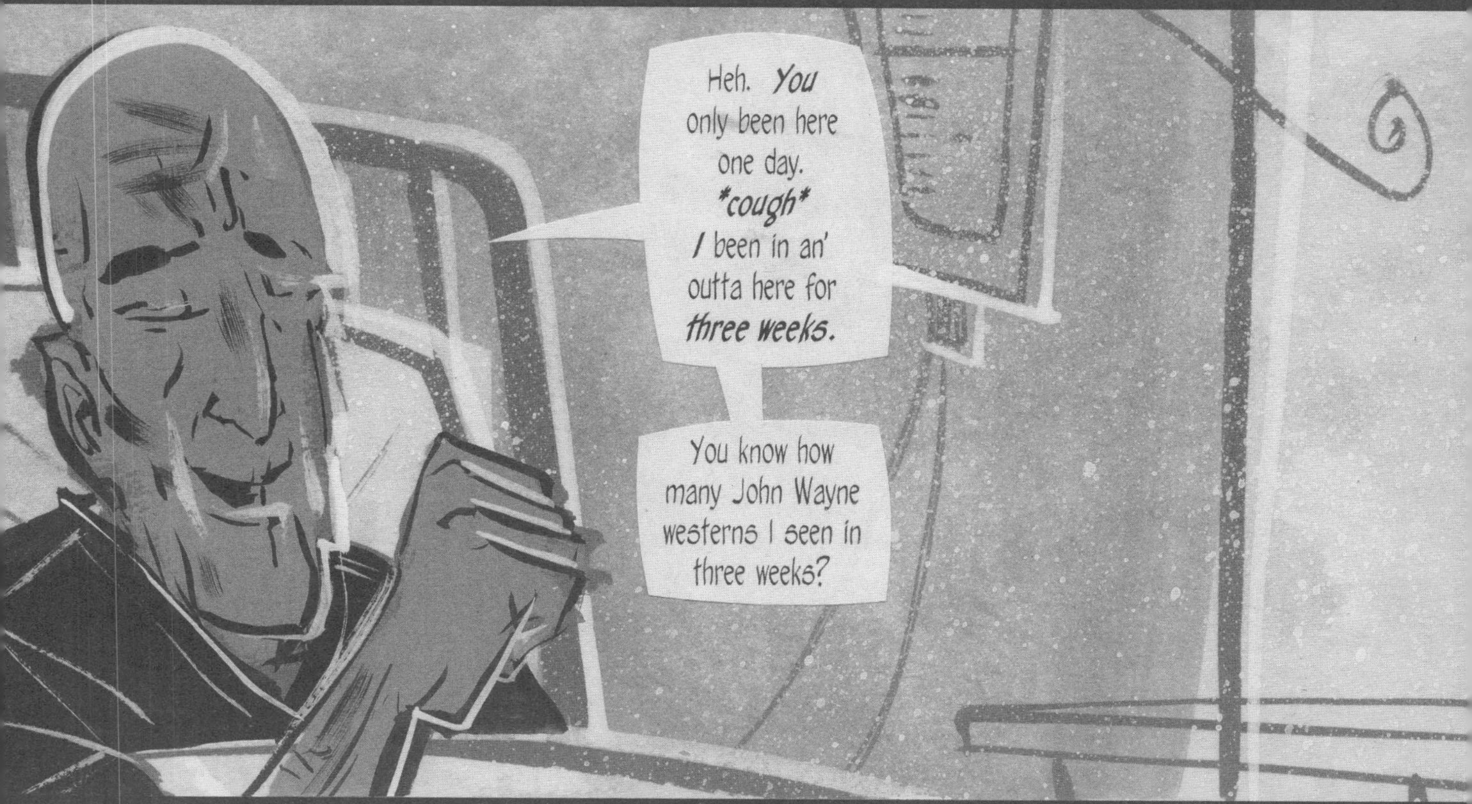
Heh. *You* only been here one day. ***cough*** *I* been in an' outta here for ***three weeks.***
You know how many John Wayne westerns I seen in three weeks?

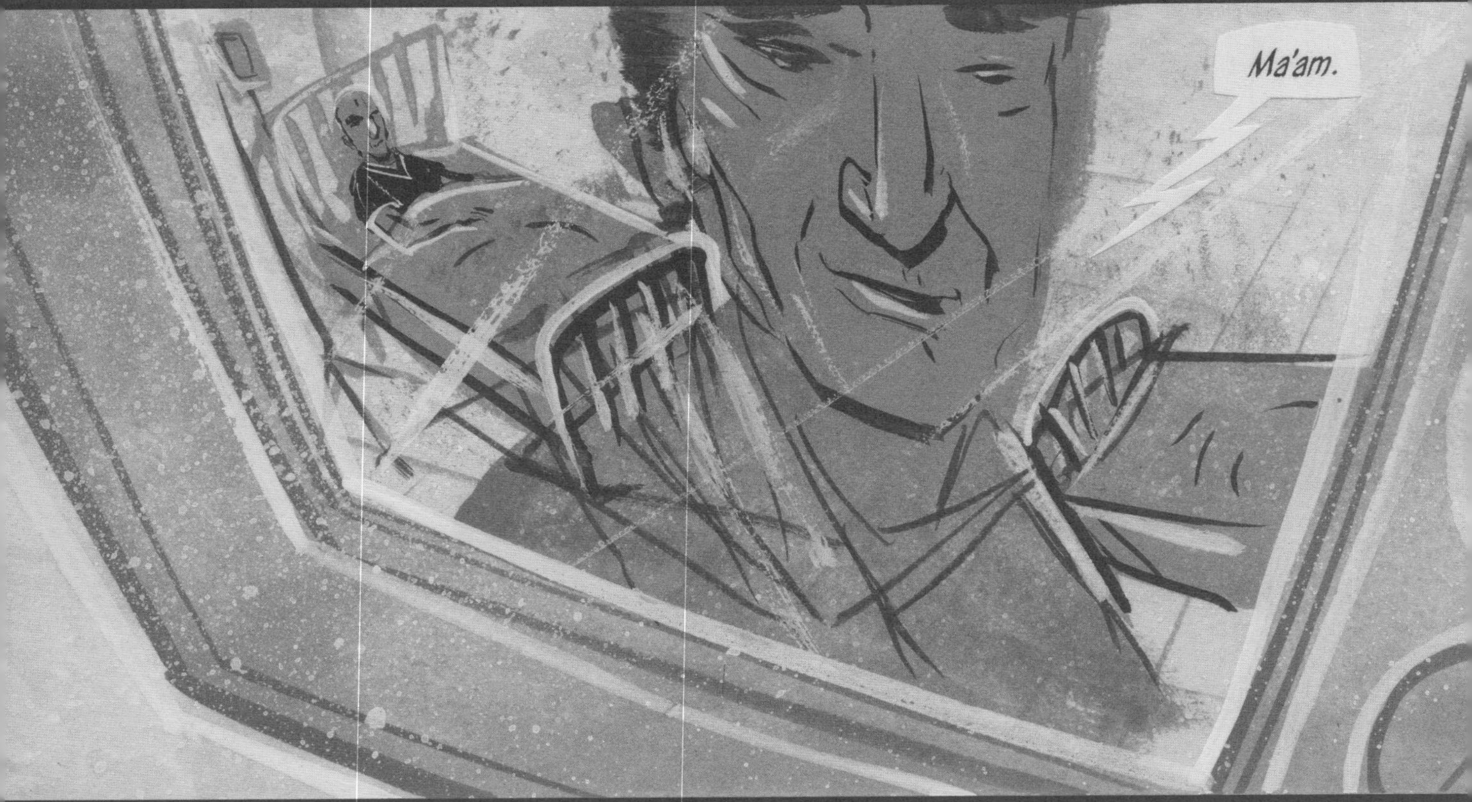
Ma'am.

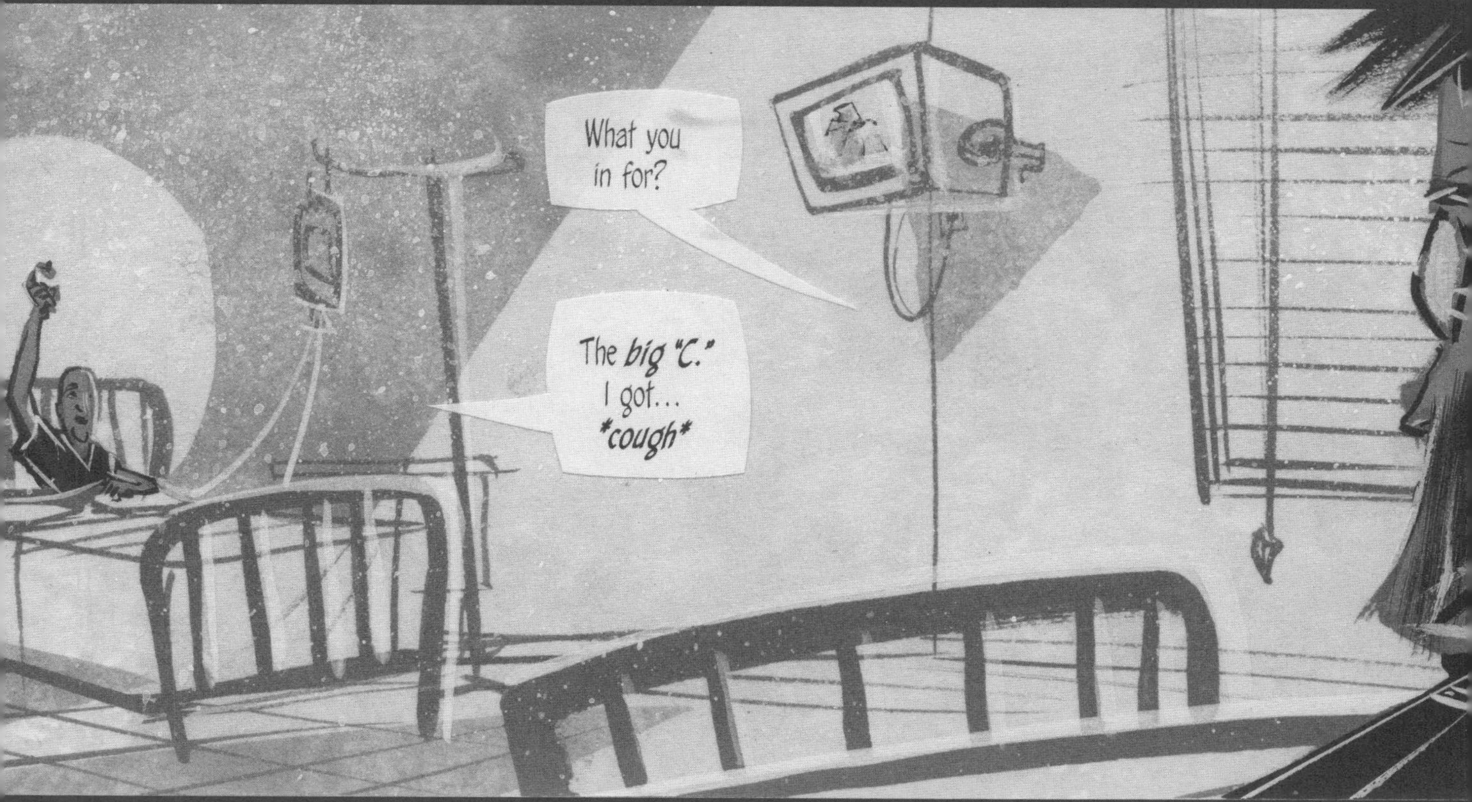
What you in for?
The *big "C."* I got... **cough**

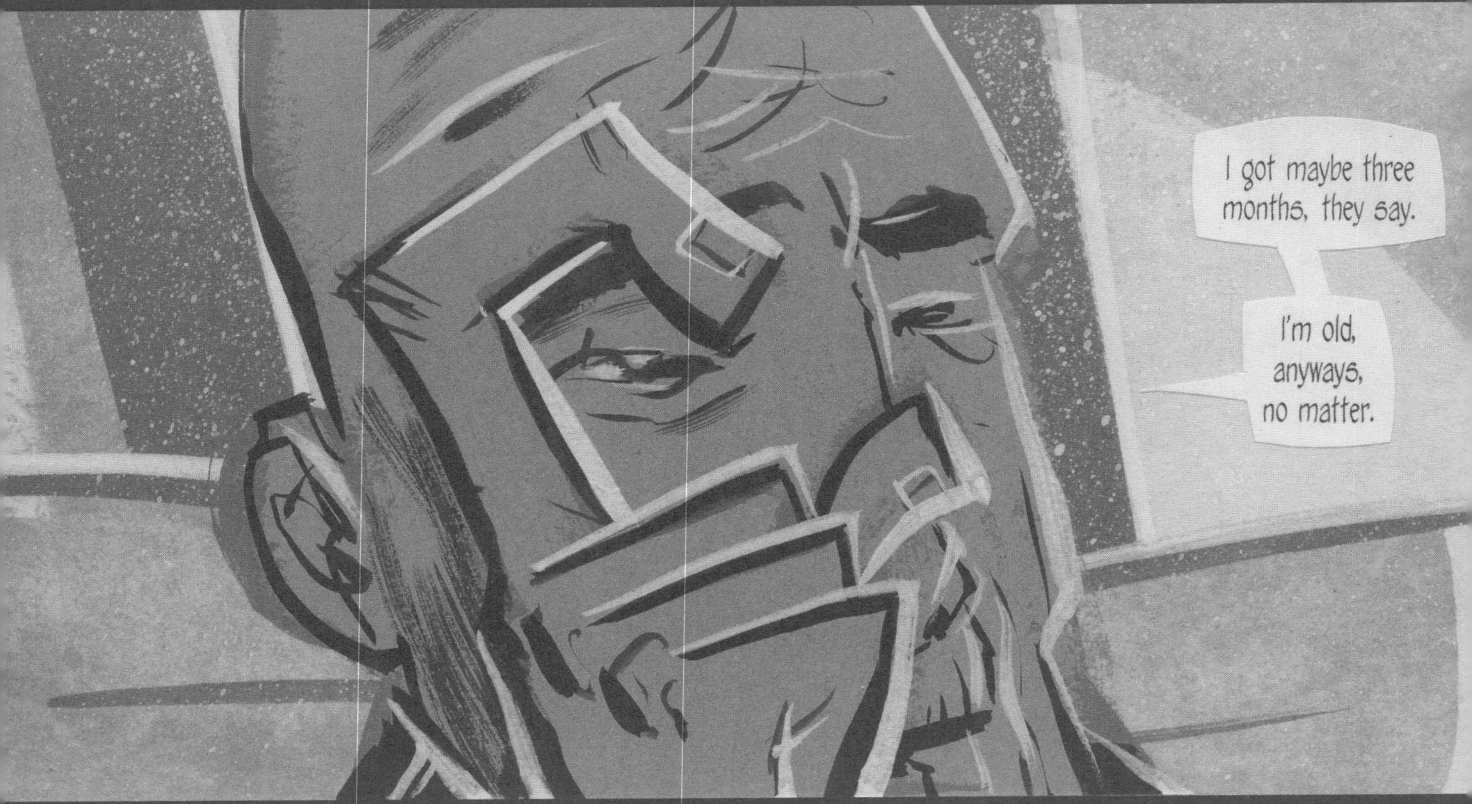
I got maybe three months, they say.
I'm old, anyways, no matter.

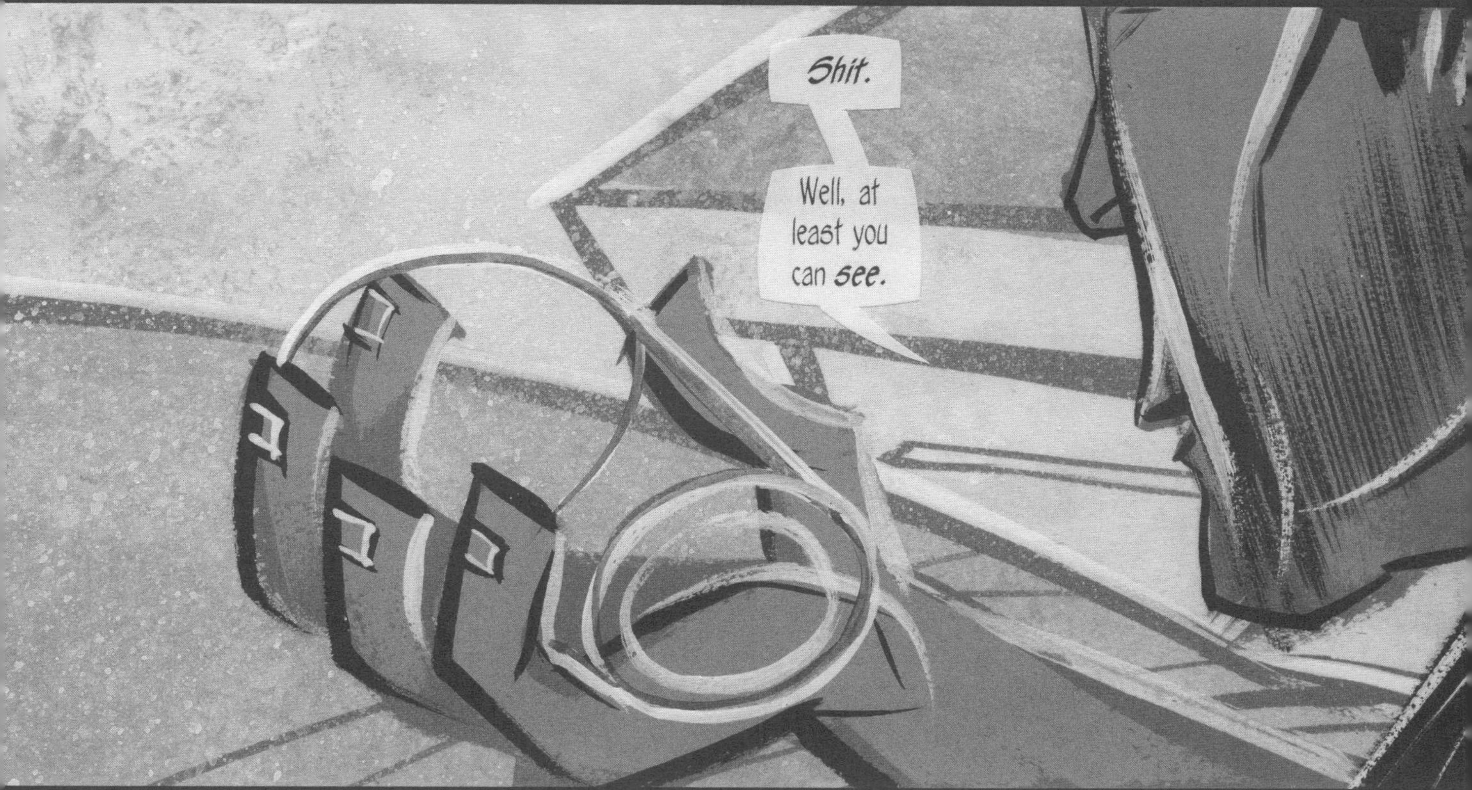
Shit.
Well, at least you can see.

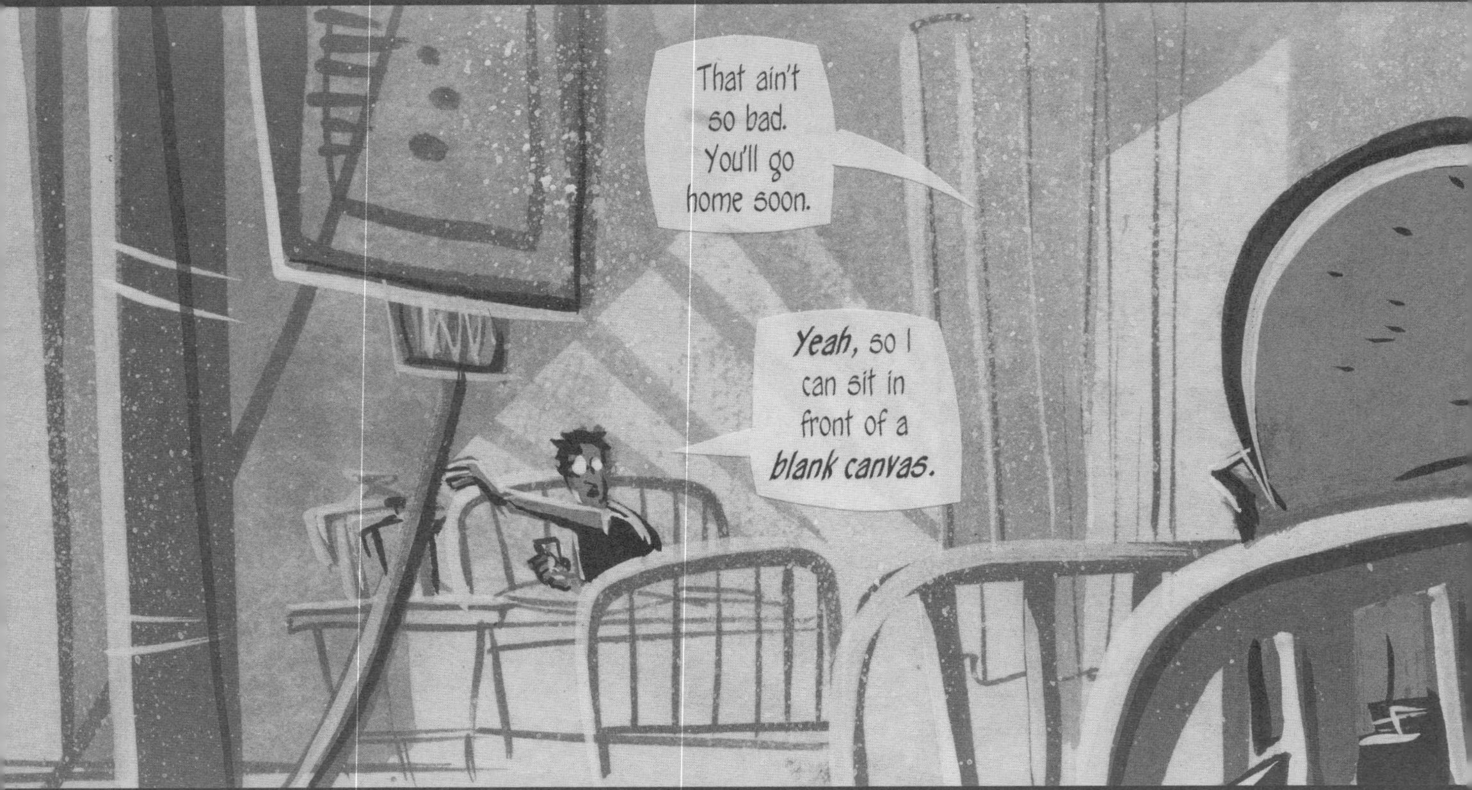
That ain't so bad. You'll go home soon.
Yeah, so I can sit in front of a *blank canvas.*

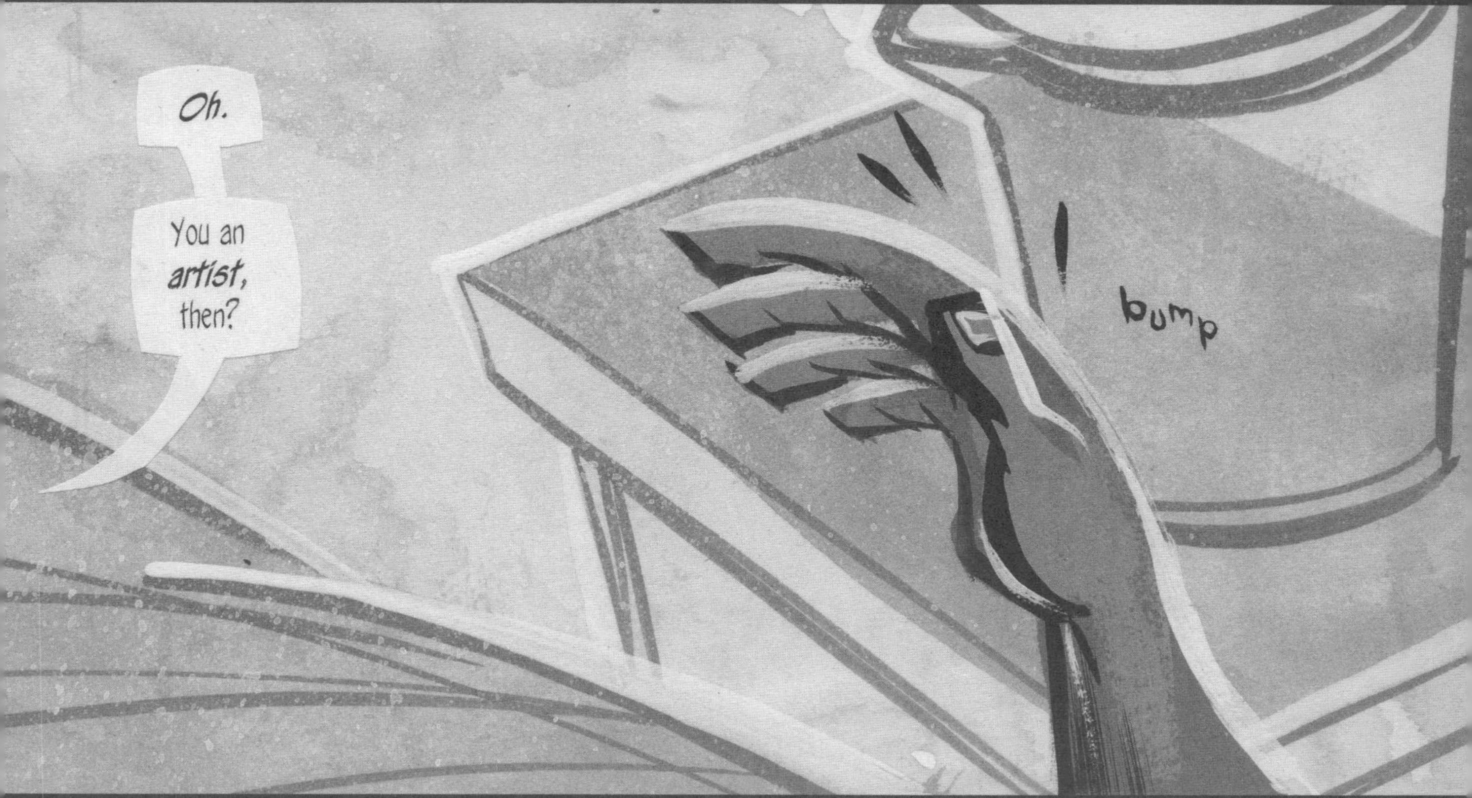
Oh.
You an *artist*, then?
bump

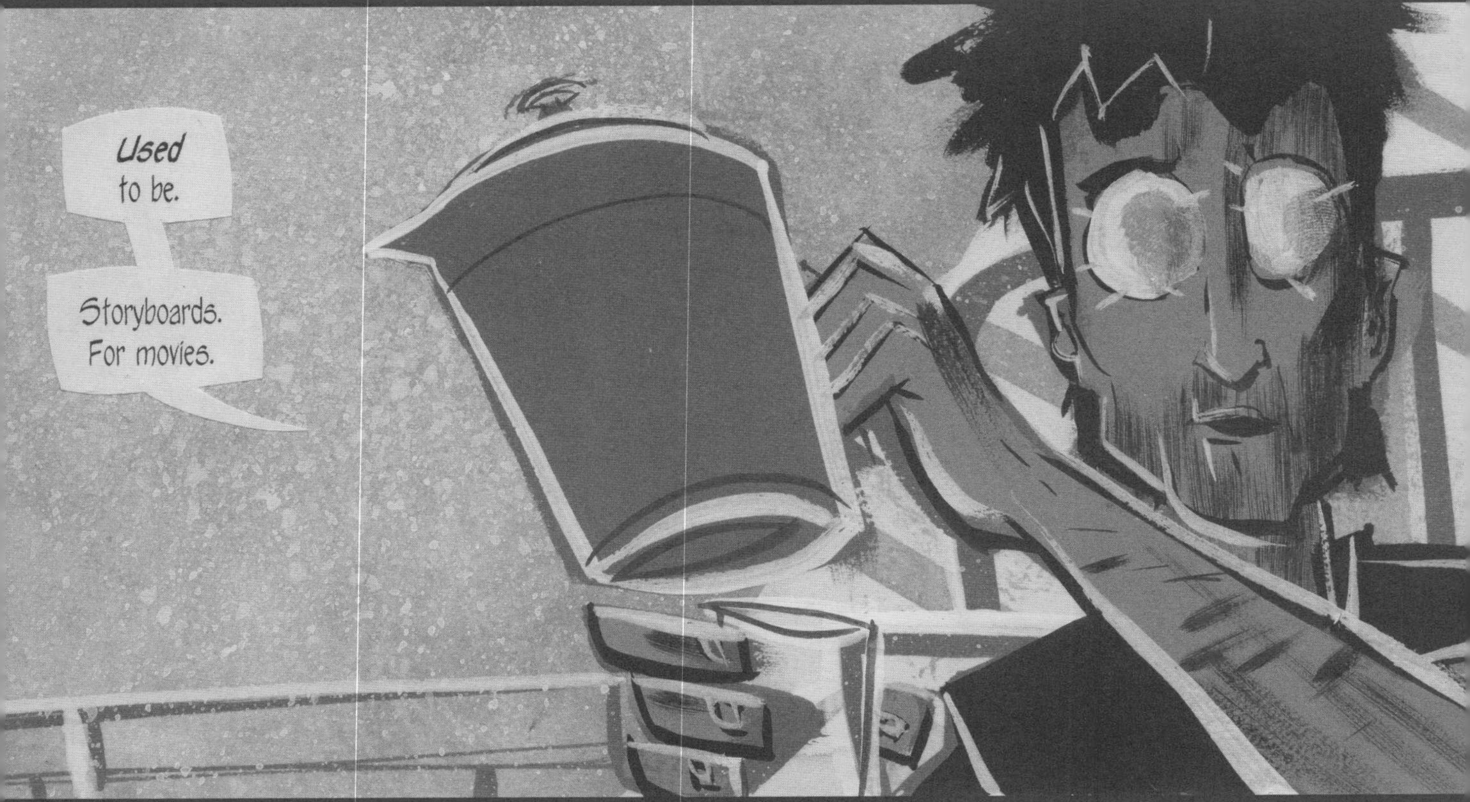
Used to be.
Storyboards. For movies.

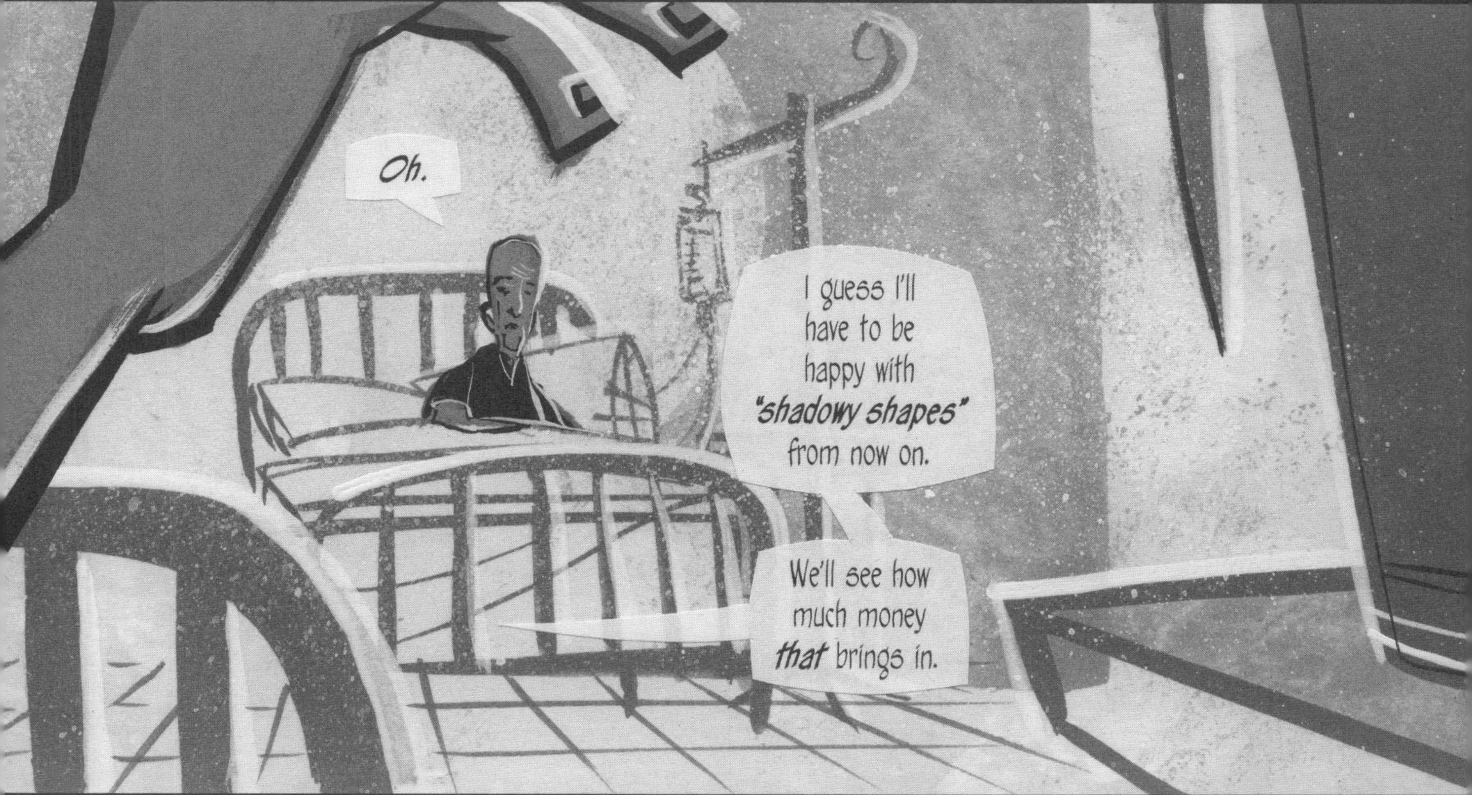
Oh.
I guess I'll have to be happy with *"shadowy shapes"* from now on.
We'll see how much money *that* brings in.

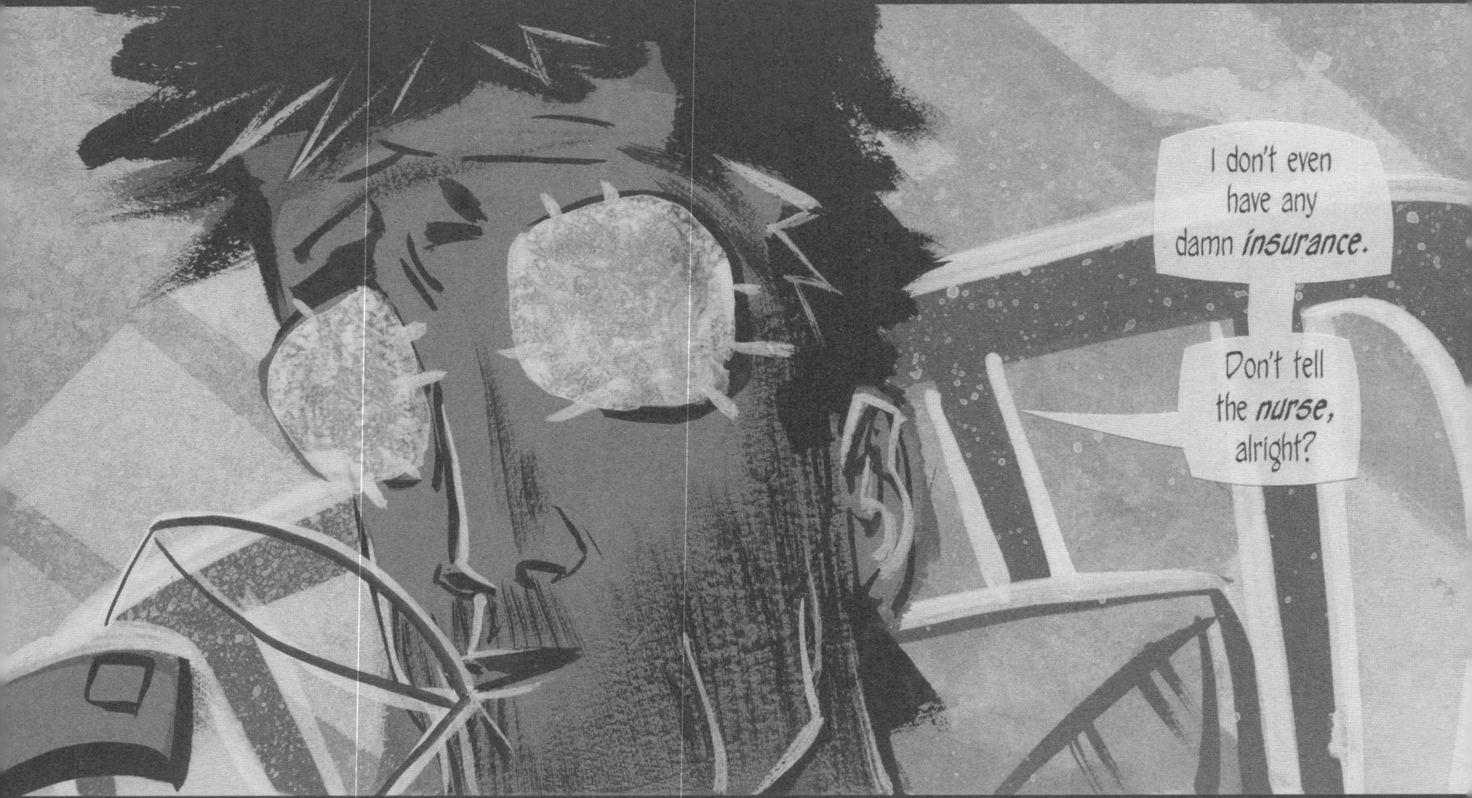
I don't even have any damn *insurance.*
Don't tell the *nurse,* alright?

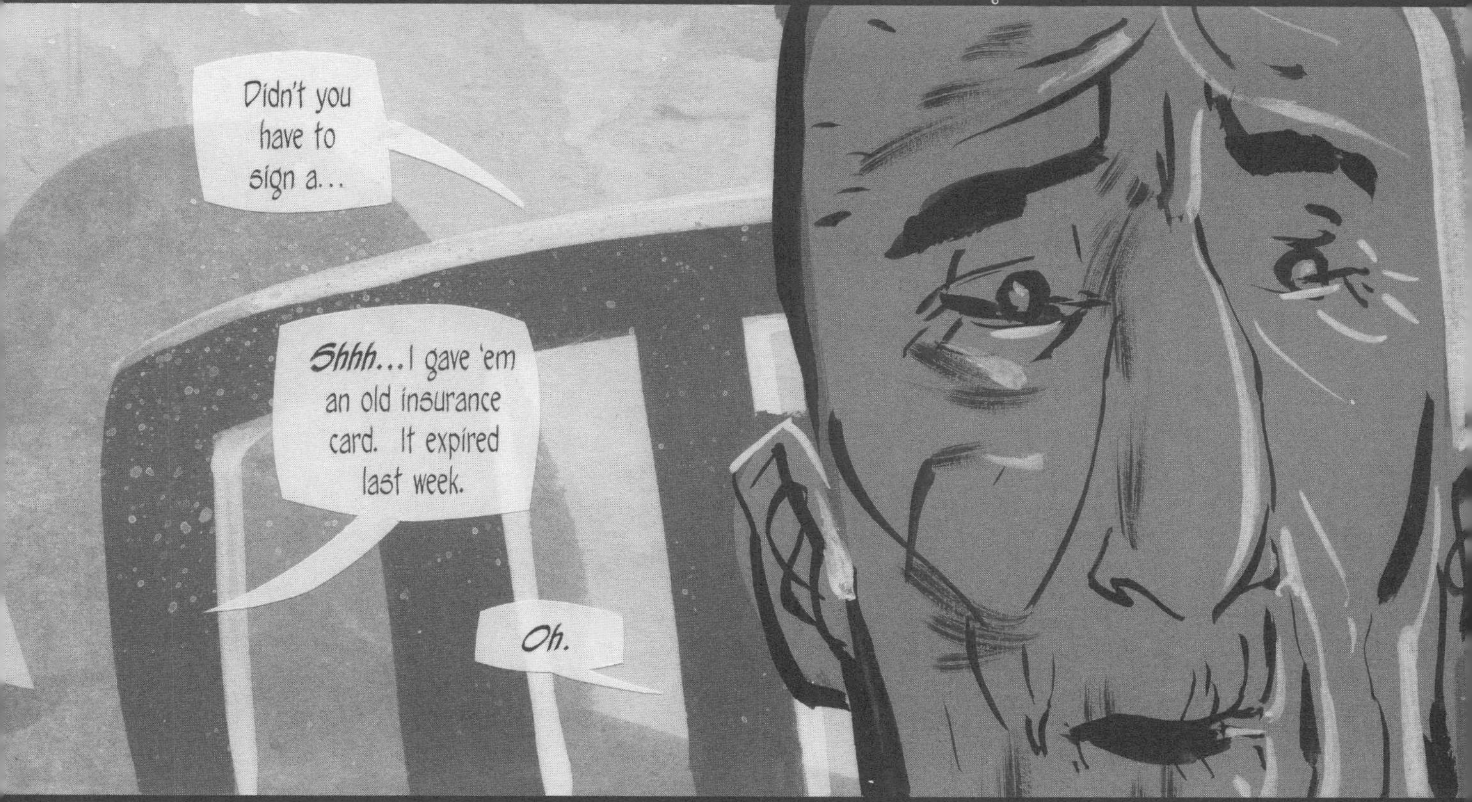
Didn't you have to sign a...
*Shhh...*I gave 'em an old insurance card. It expired last week.
Oh.

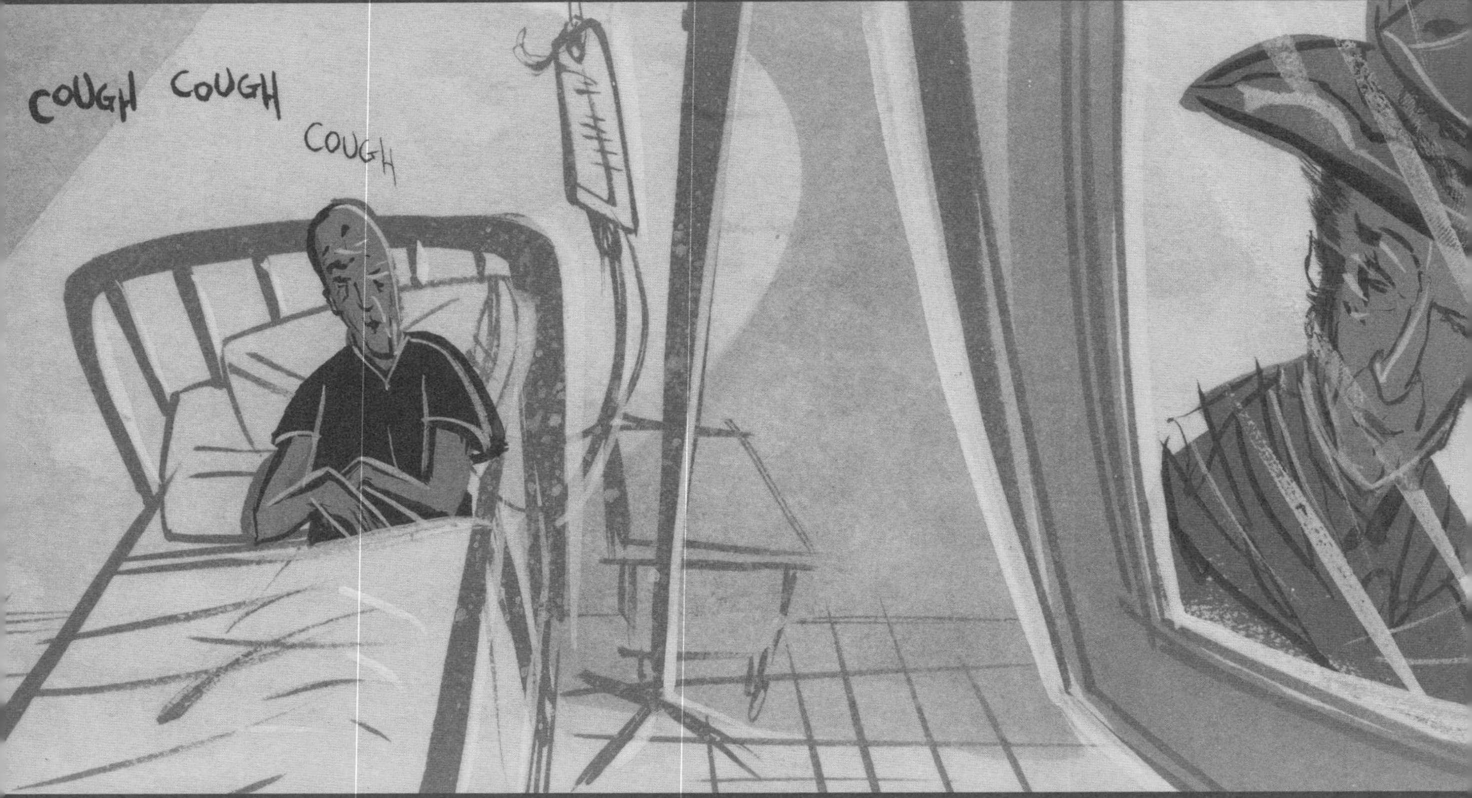
COUGH COUGH
COUGH

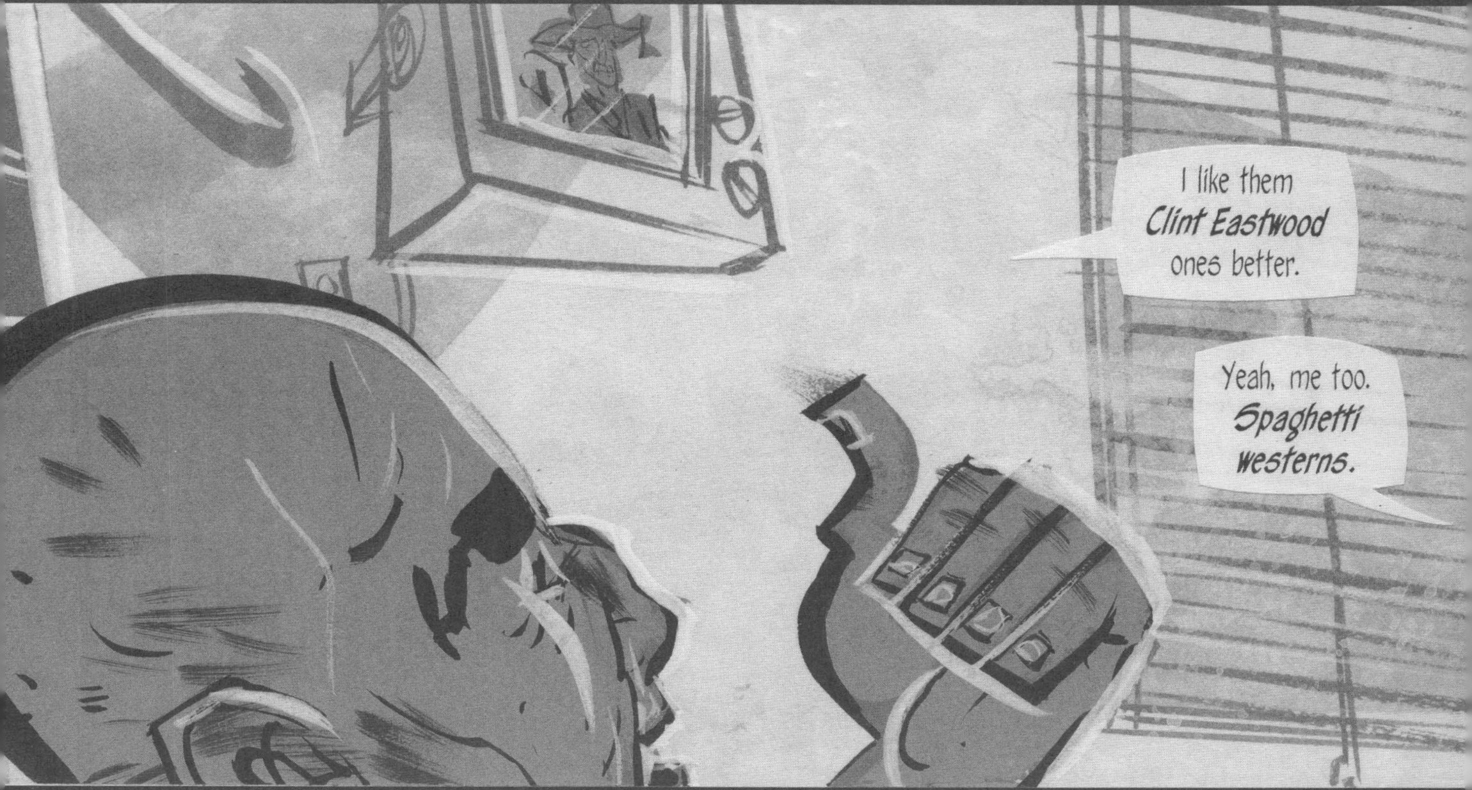
I like them *Clint Eastwood* ones better.
Yeah, me too. *Spaghetti westerns.*

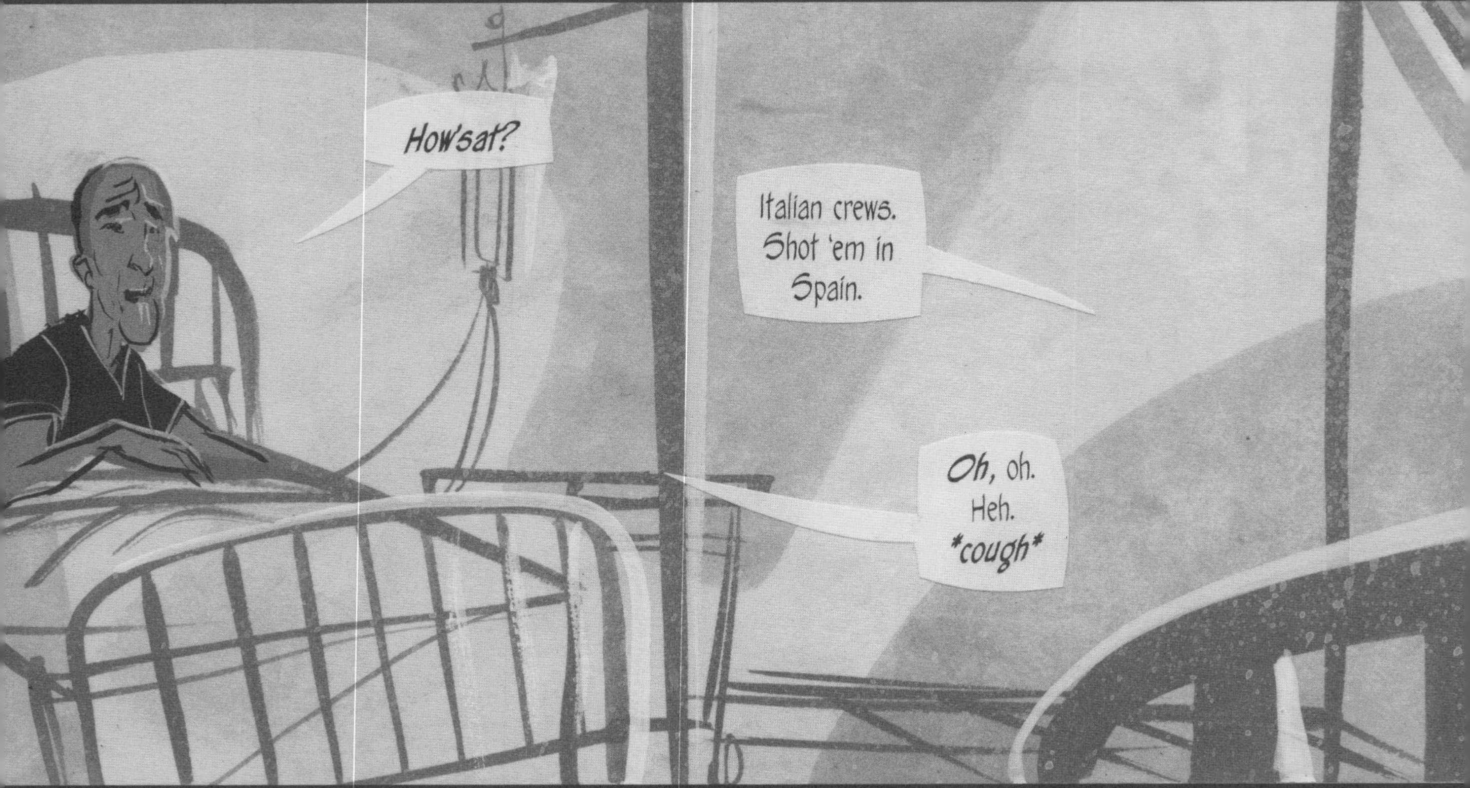
How'sat?
Italian crews. Shot 'em in Spain.
Oh, oh. Heh. *cough*

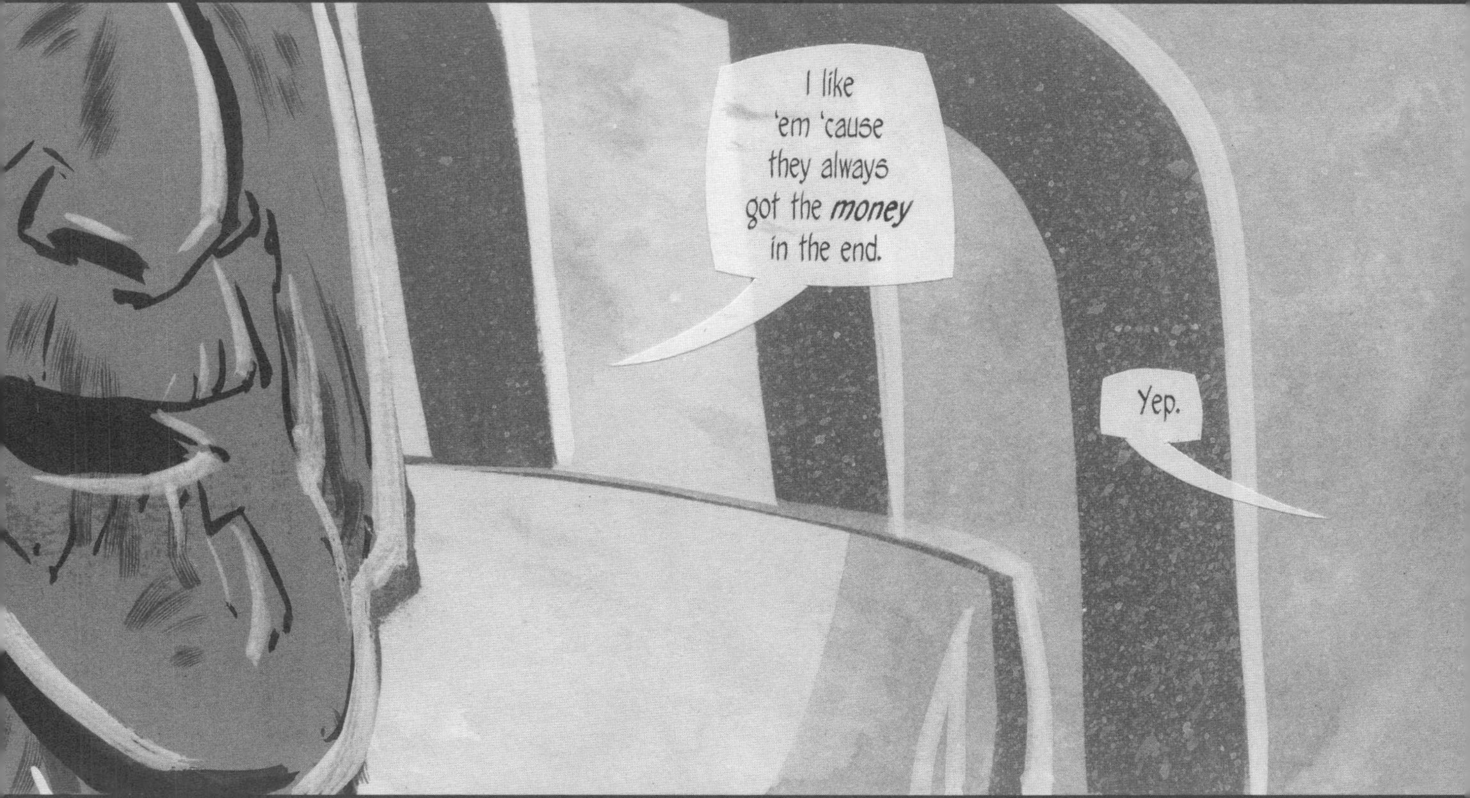
I like 'em 'cause they always got the *money* in the end.
Yep.

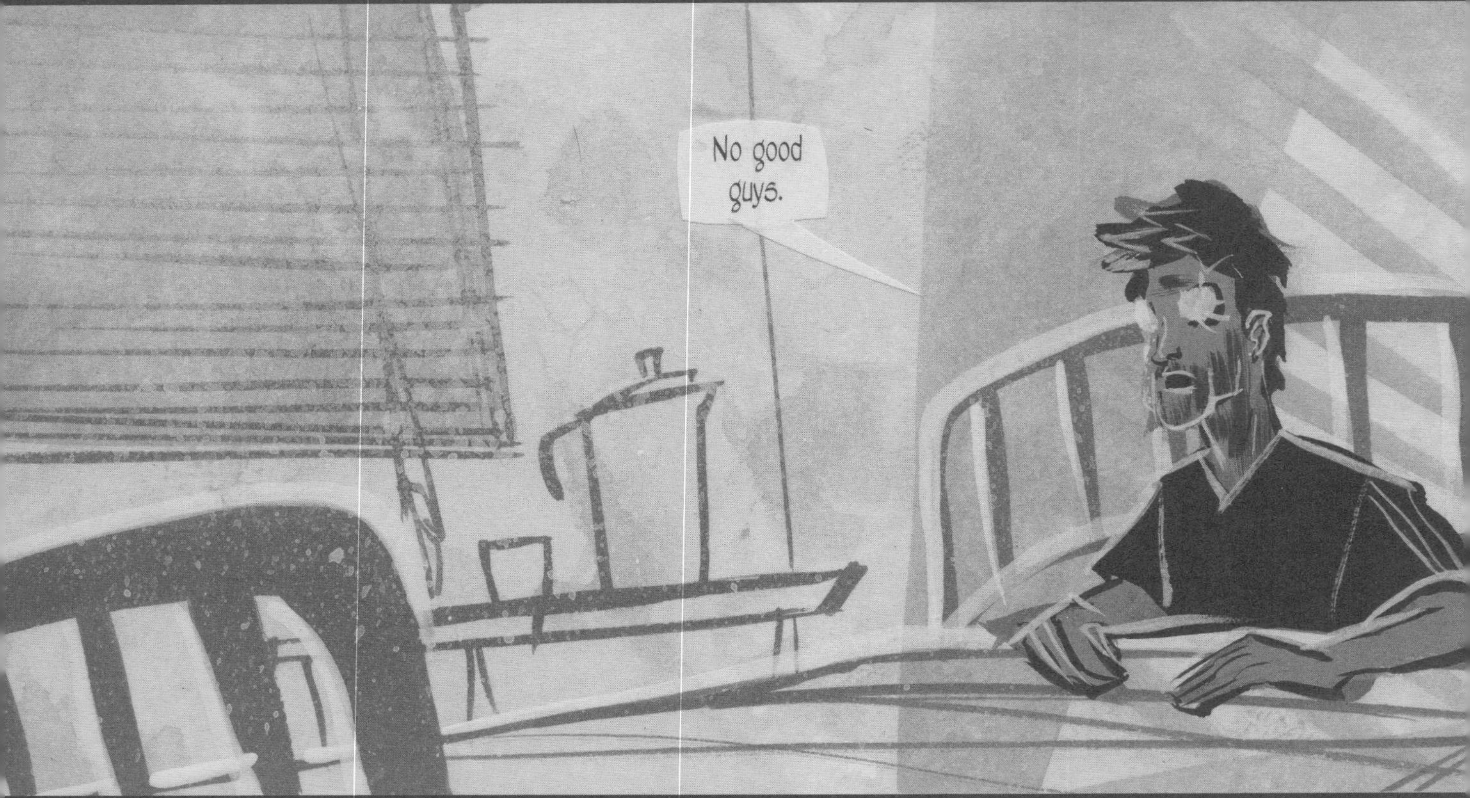
No good guys.

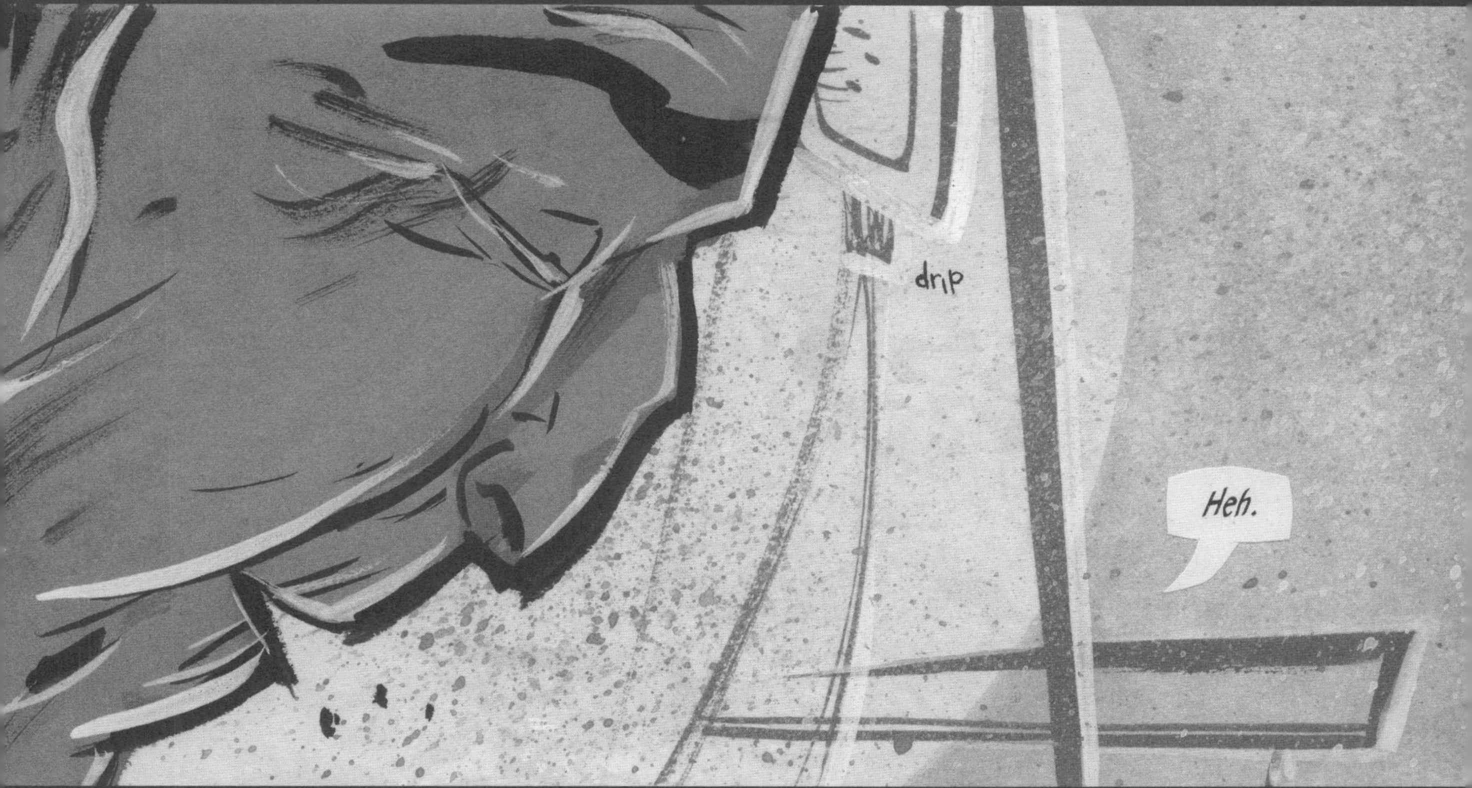
drip
Heh.

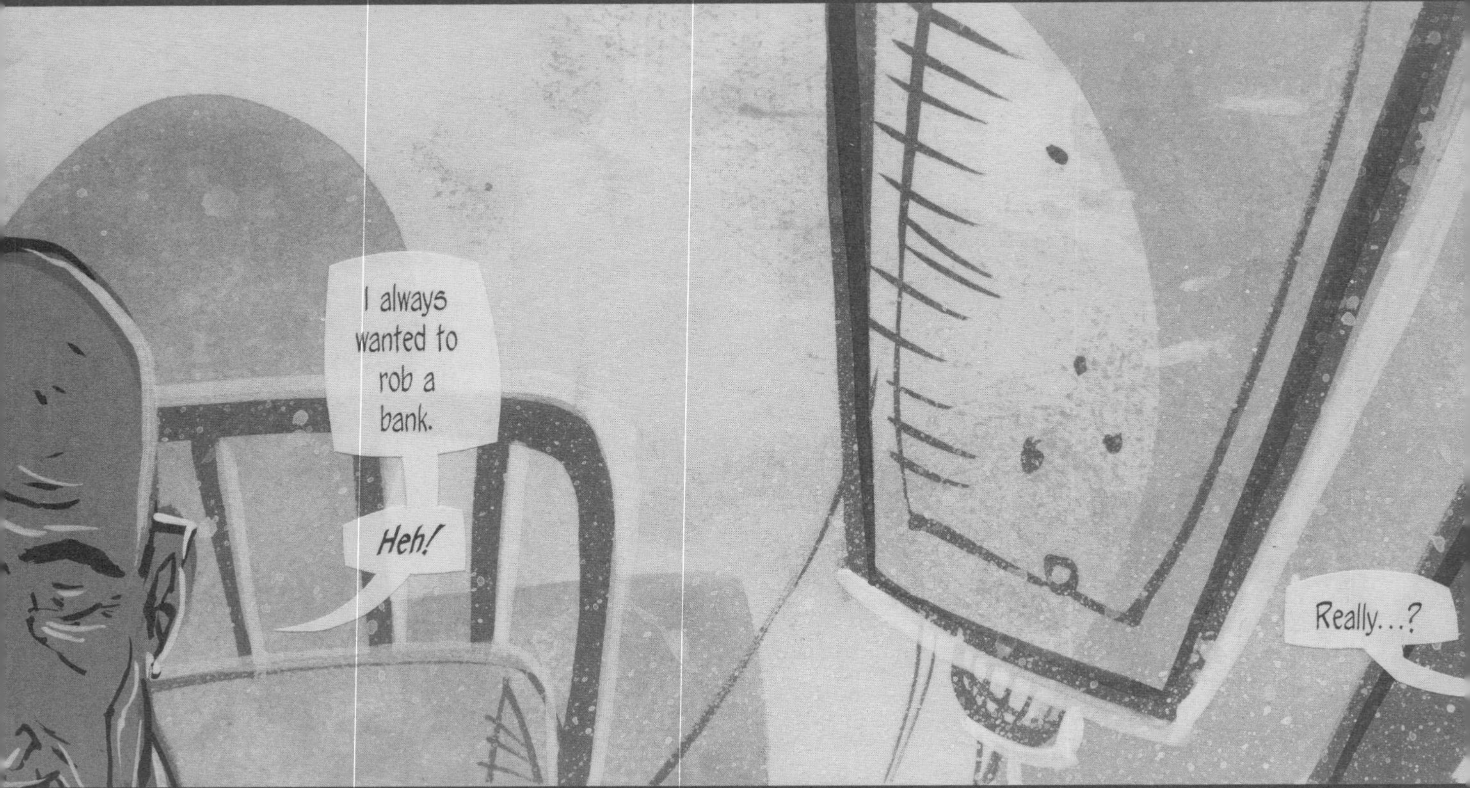
I always wanted to rob a bank.
Heh!
Really...?

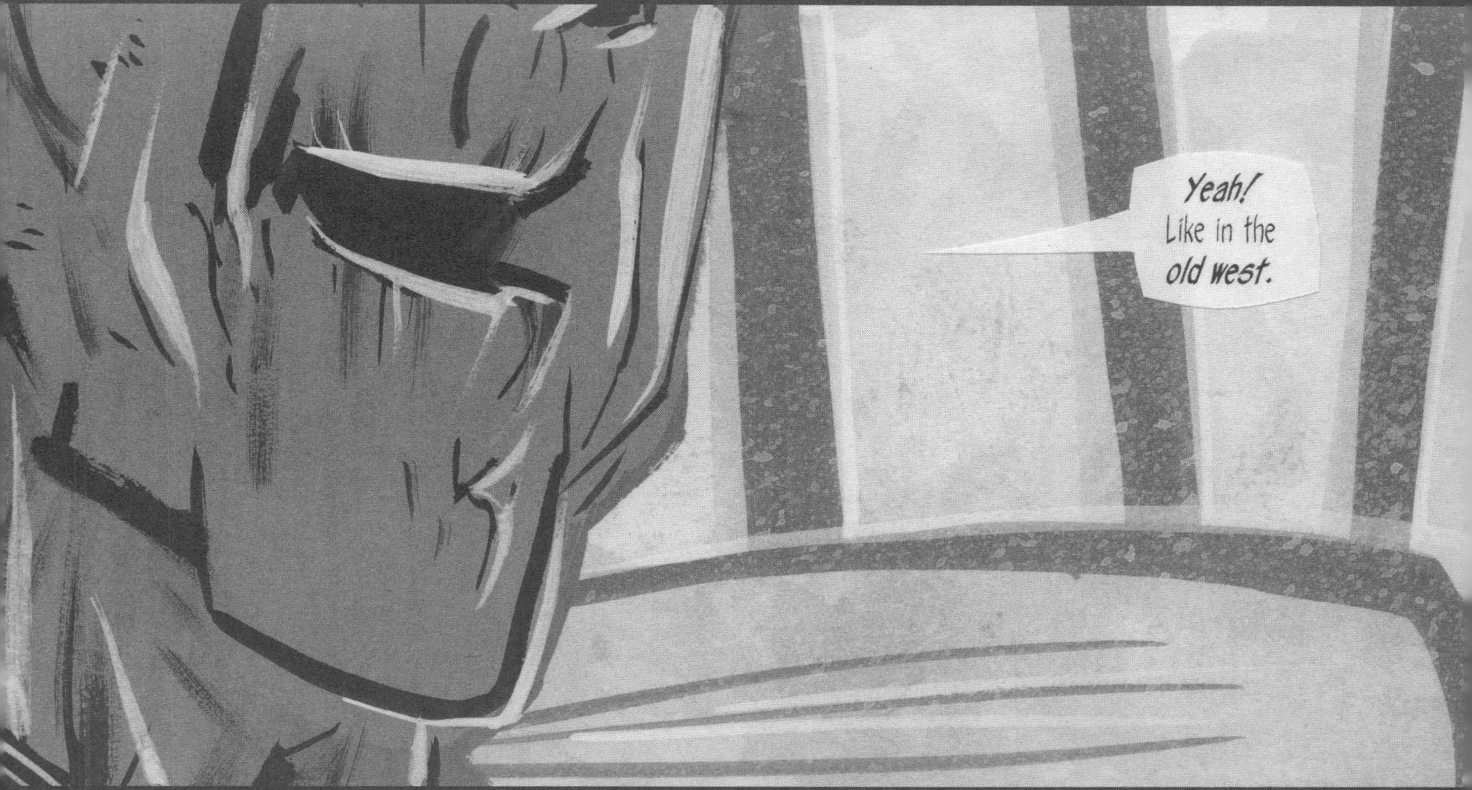
Yeah! Like in the old west.

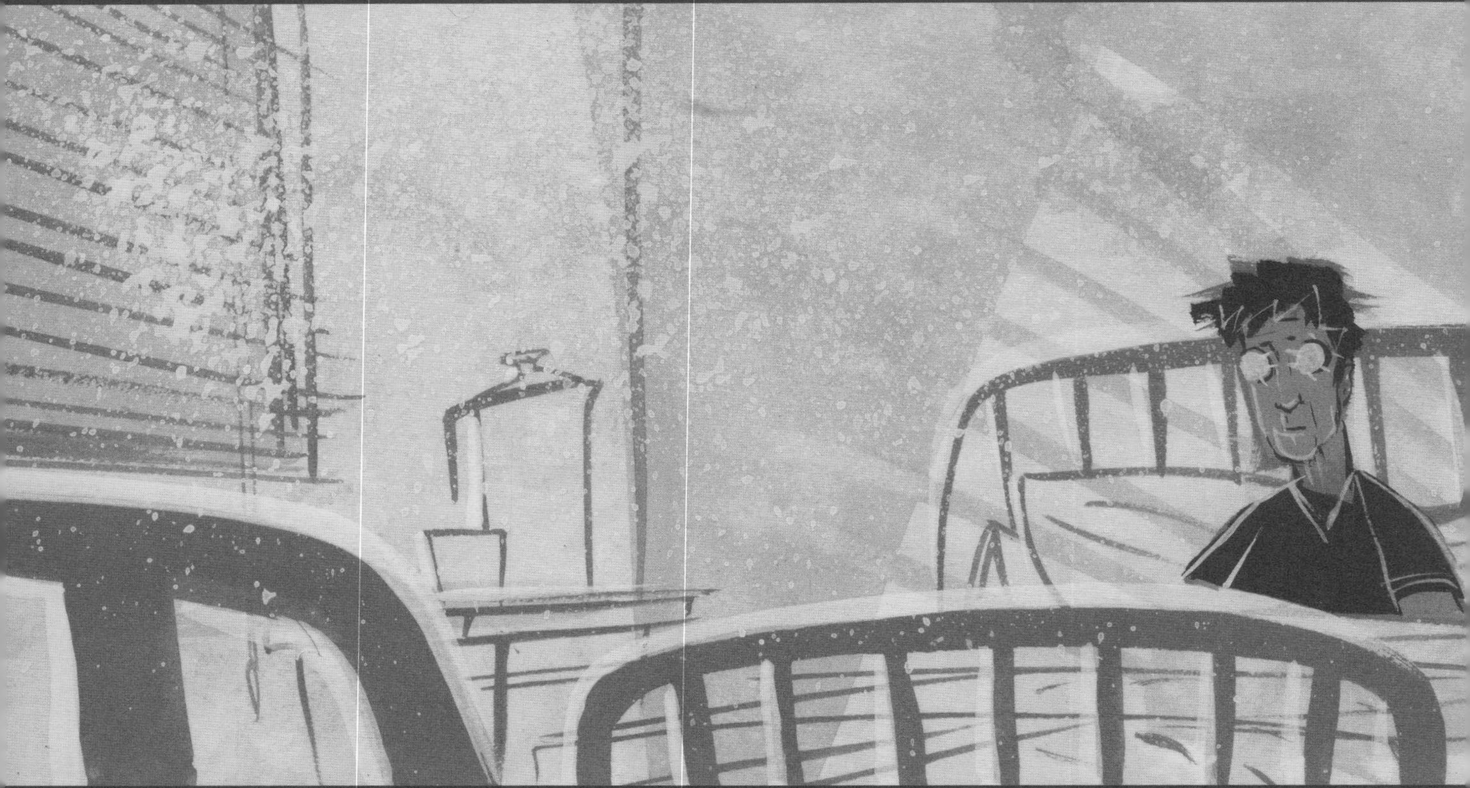

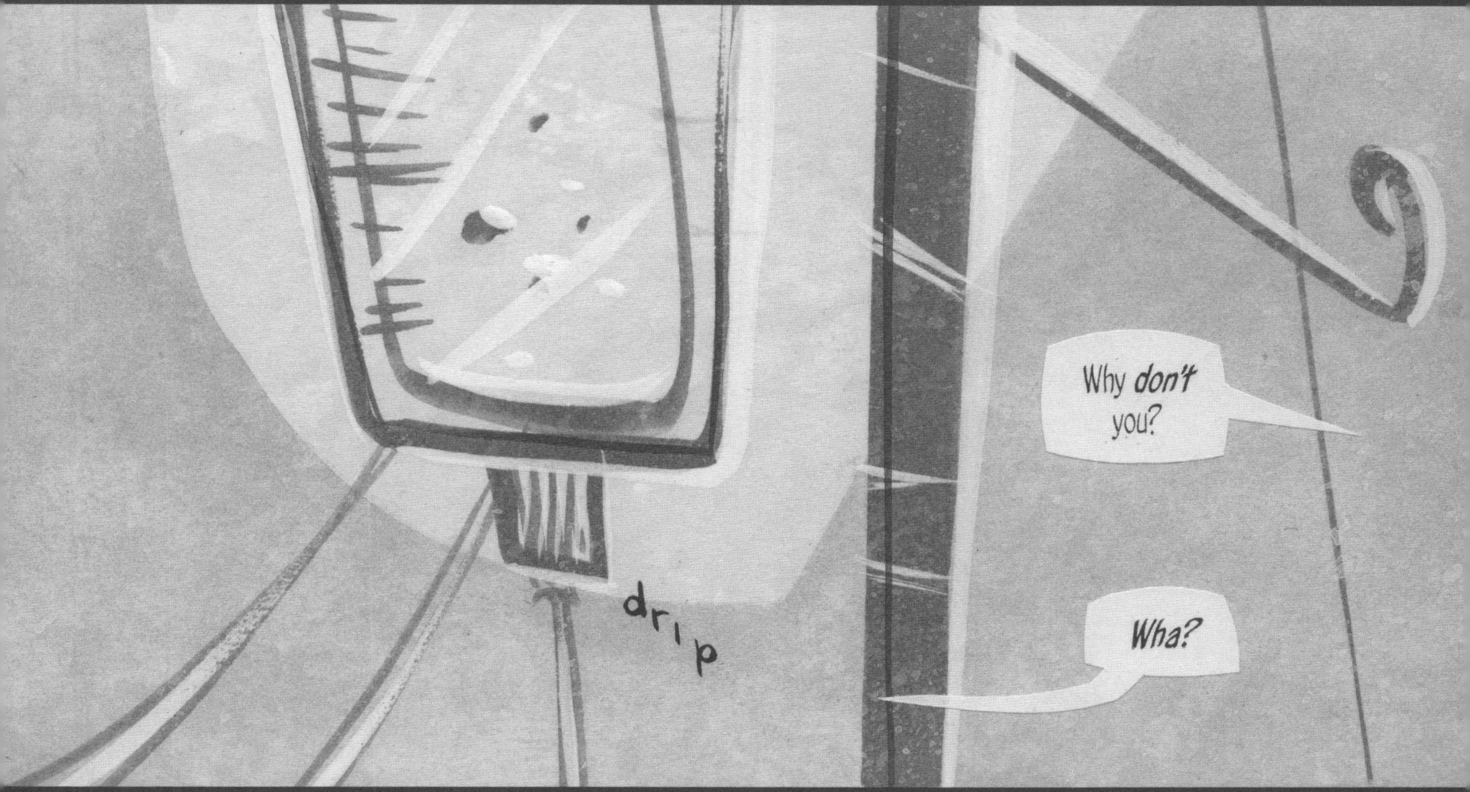
drip
Why *don't* you?
Wha?

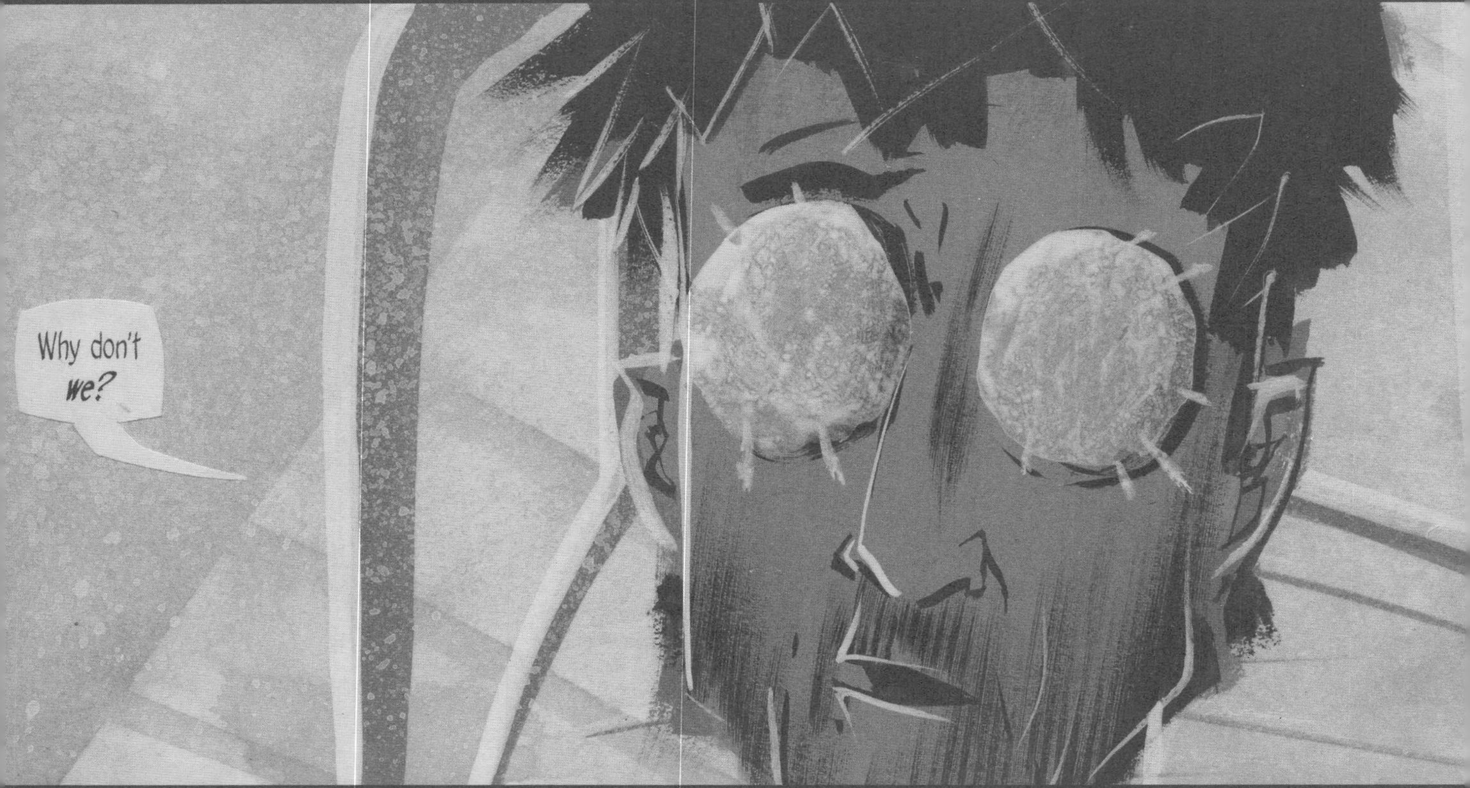
Why don't we?

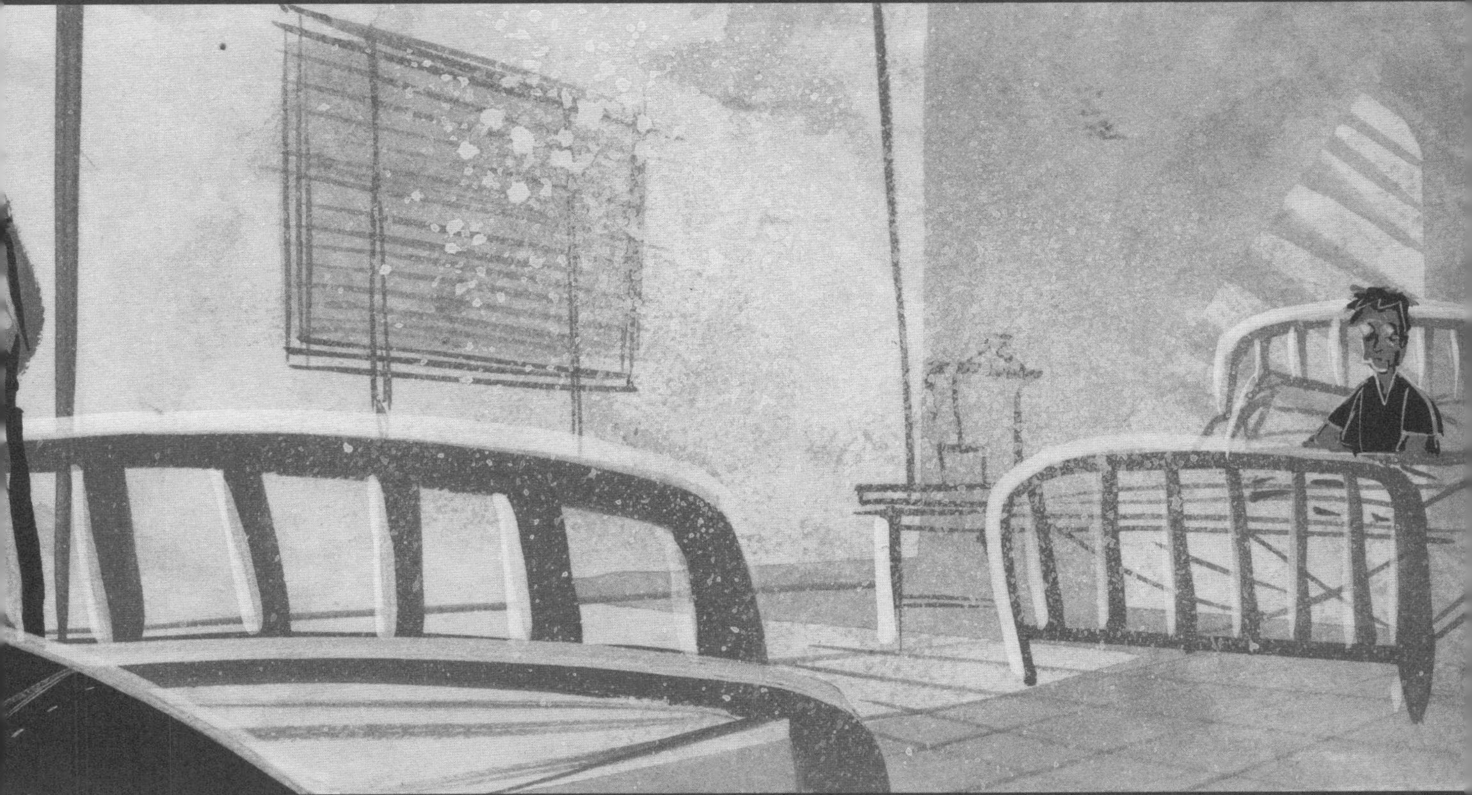

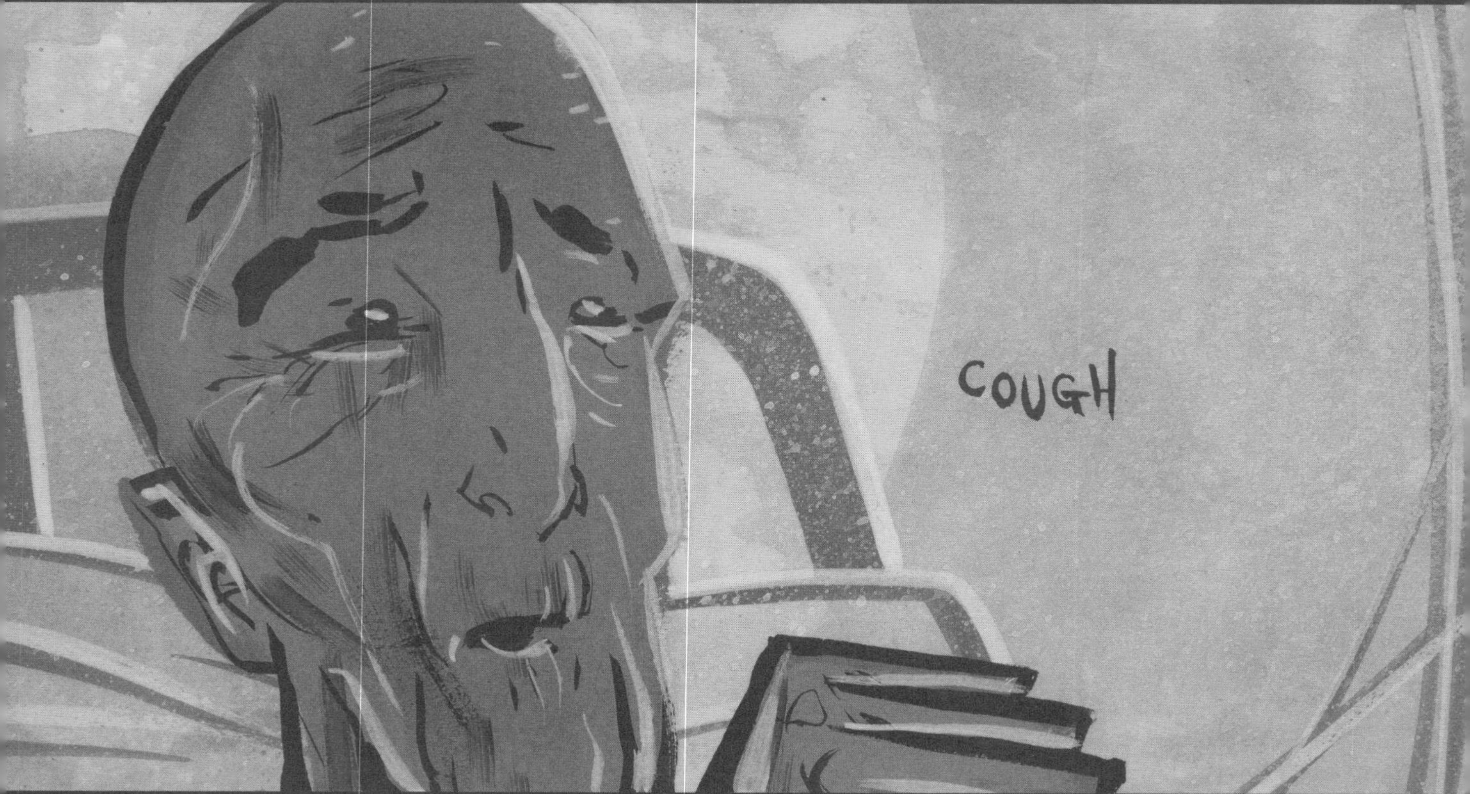
COUGH

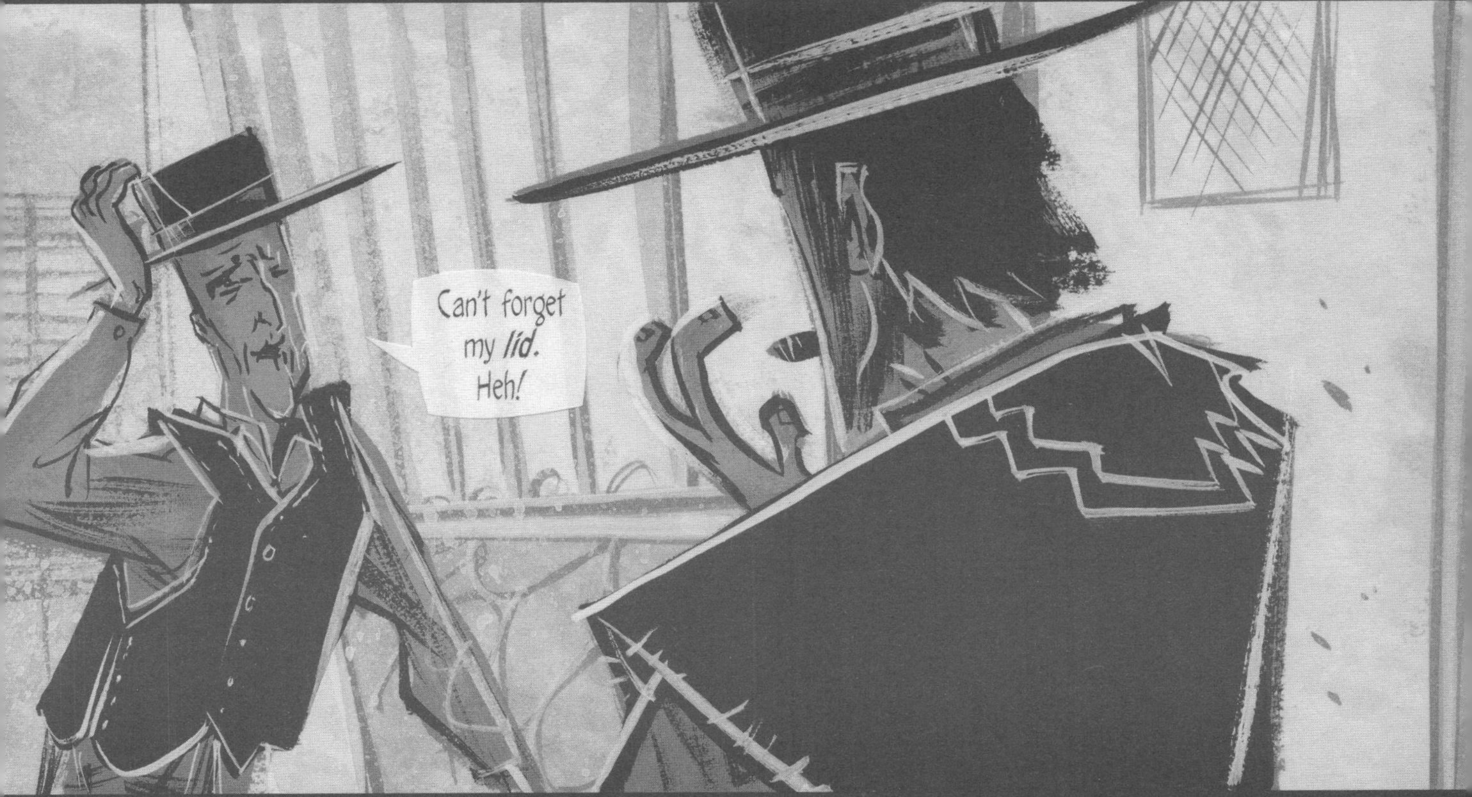
Can't forget my *lid*. Heh!

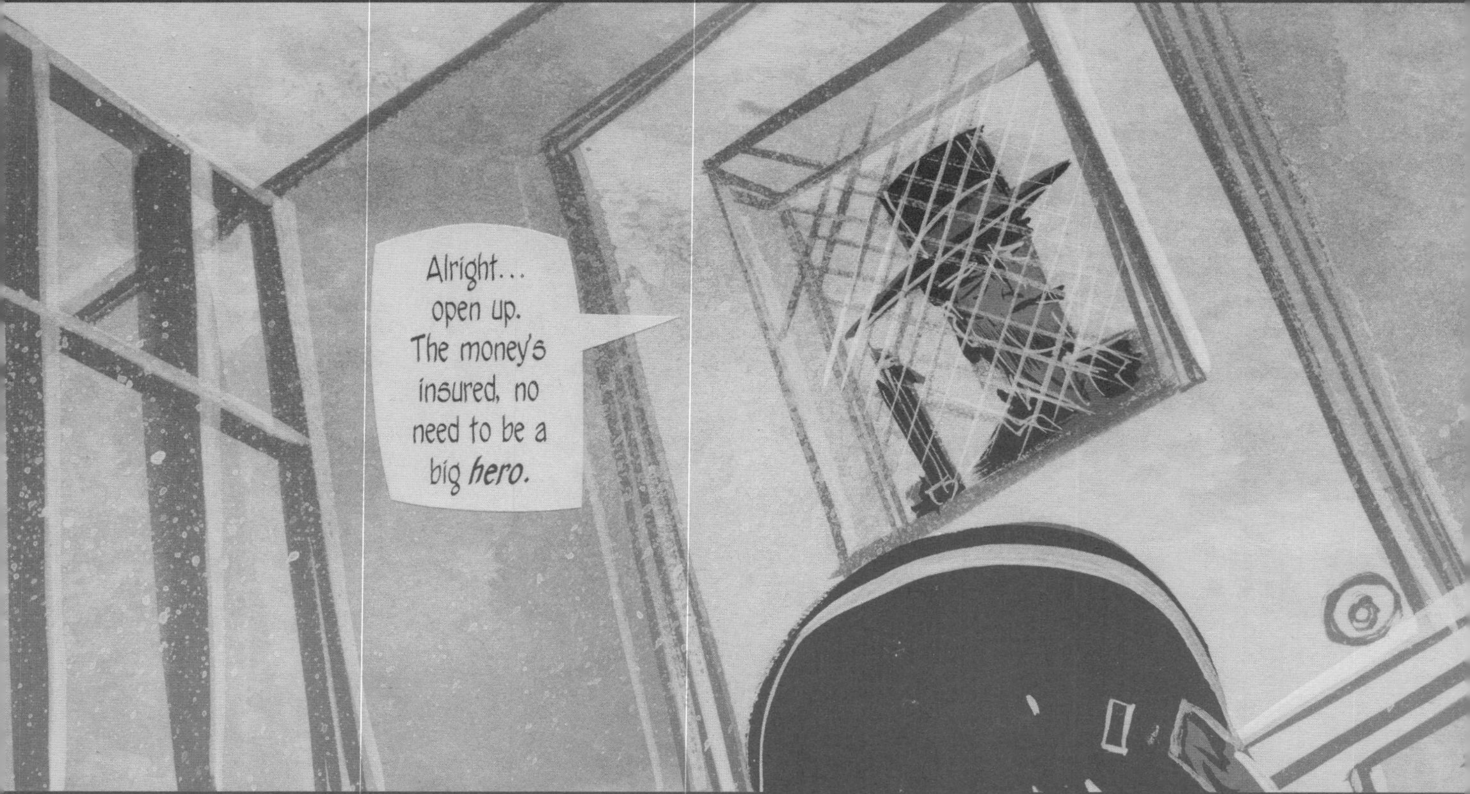
Alright... open up. The money's insured, no need to be a big *hero.*

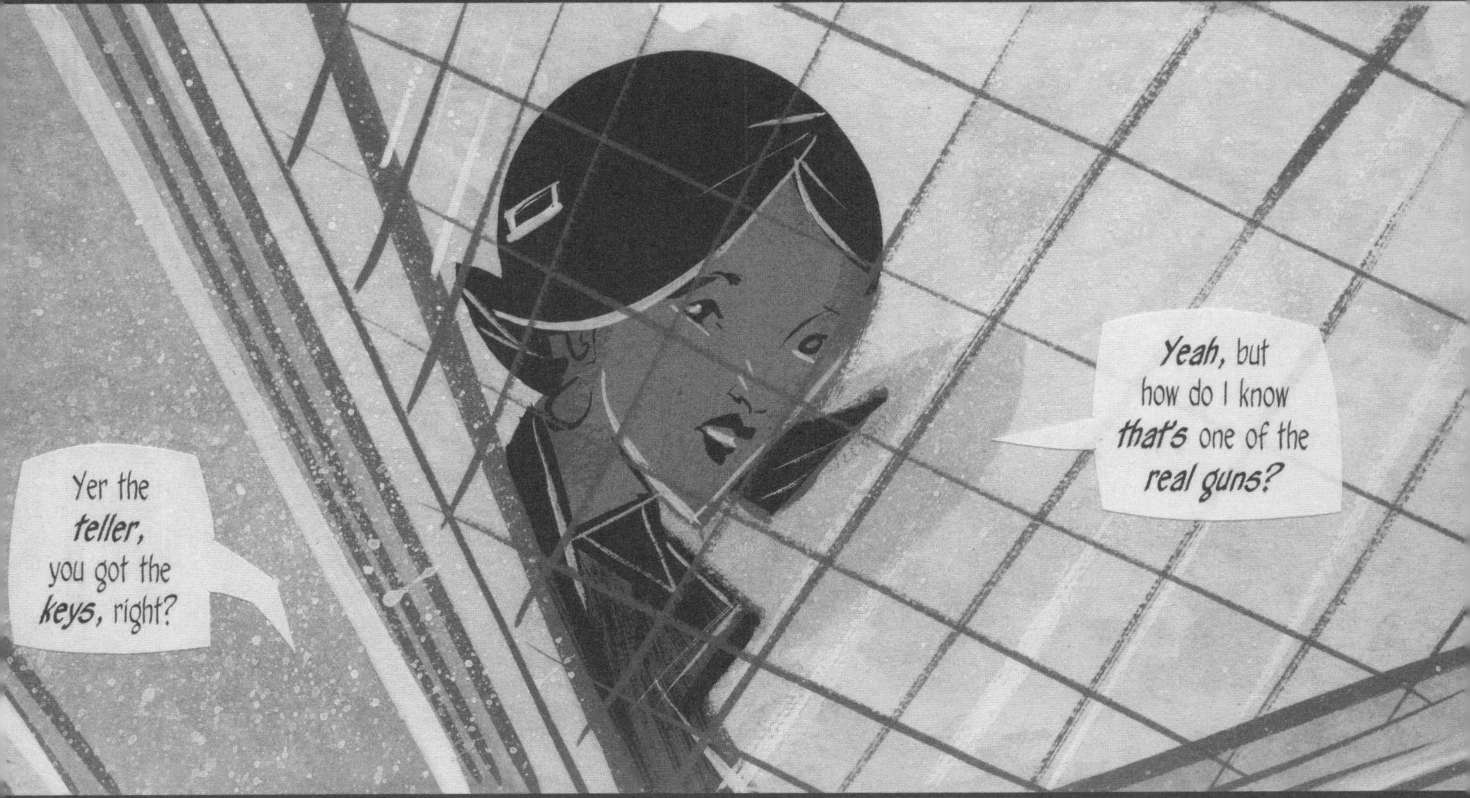
Yer the *teller*, you got the *keys*, right?
Yeah, but how do I know *that's* one of the *real guns?*

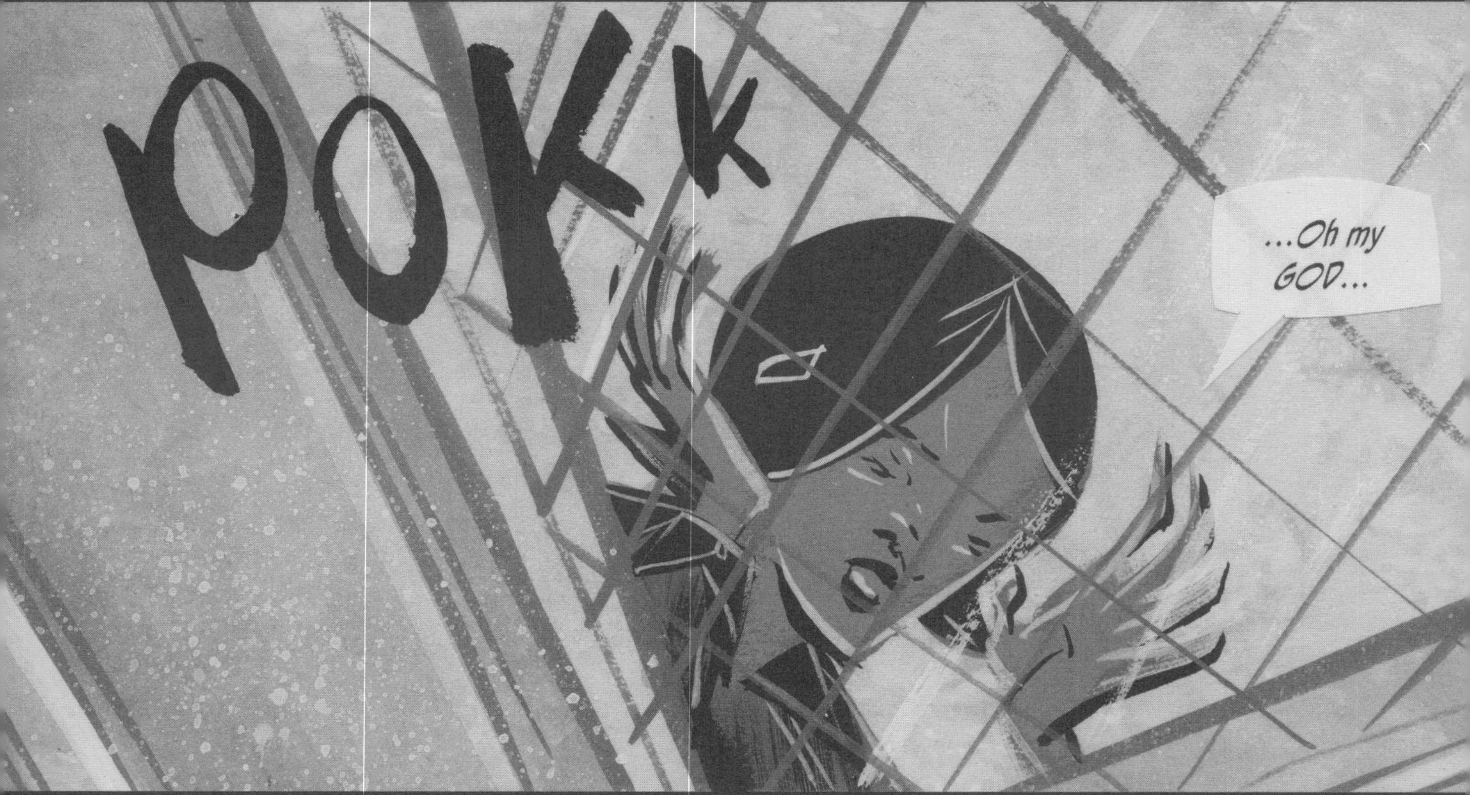
POKK
...Oh my GOD...

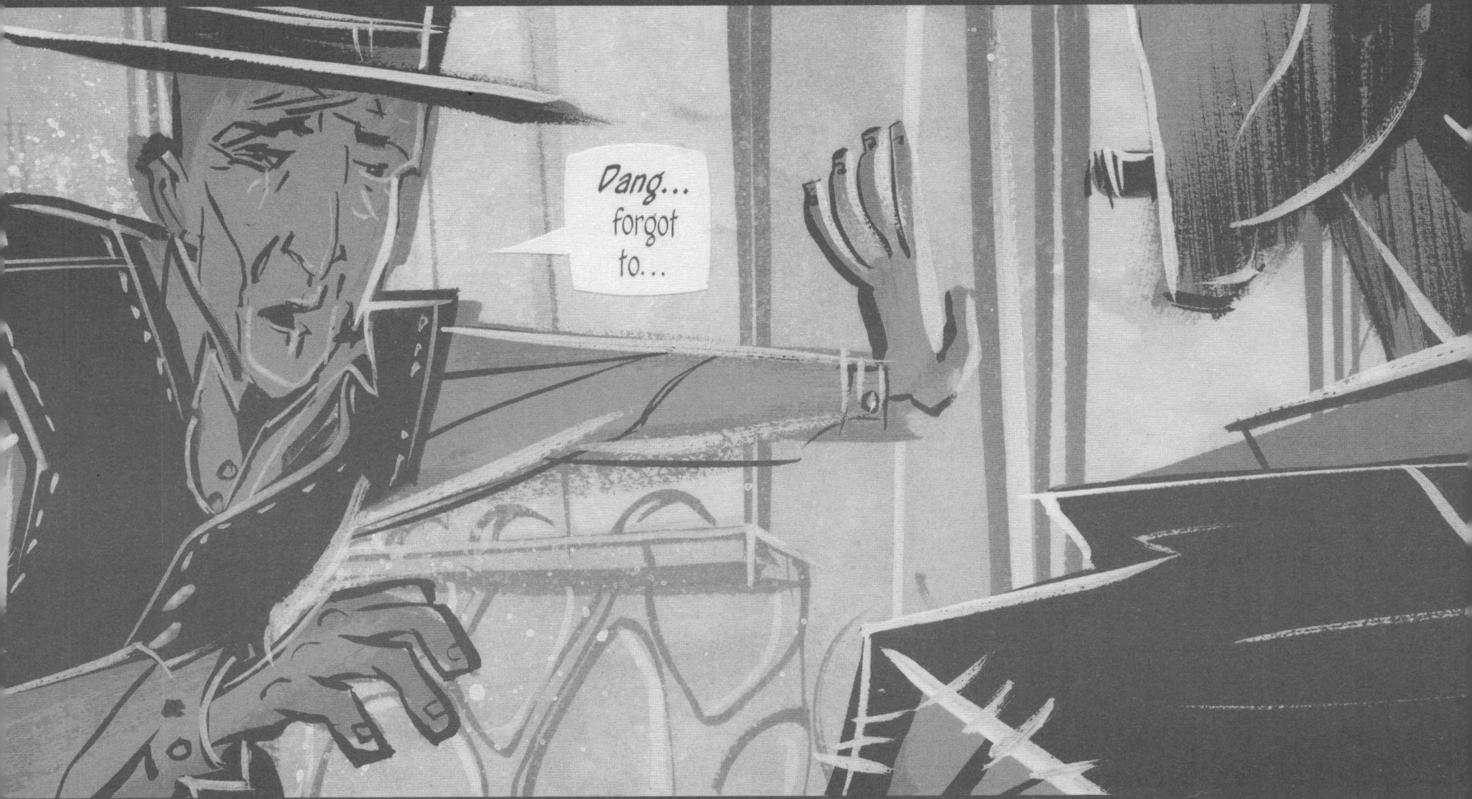
Dang... forgot to...

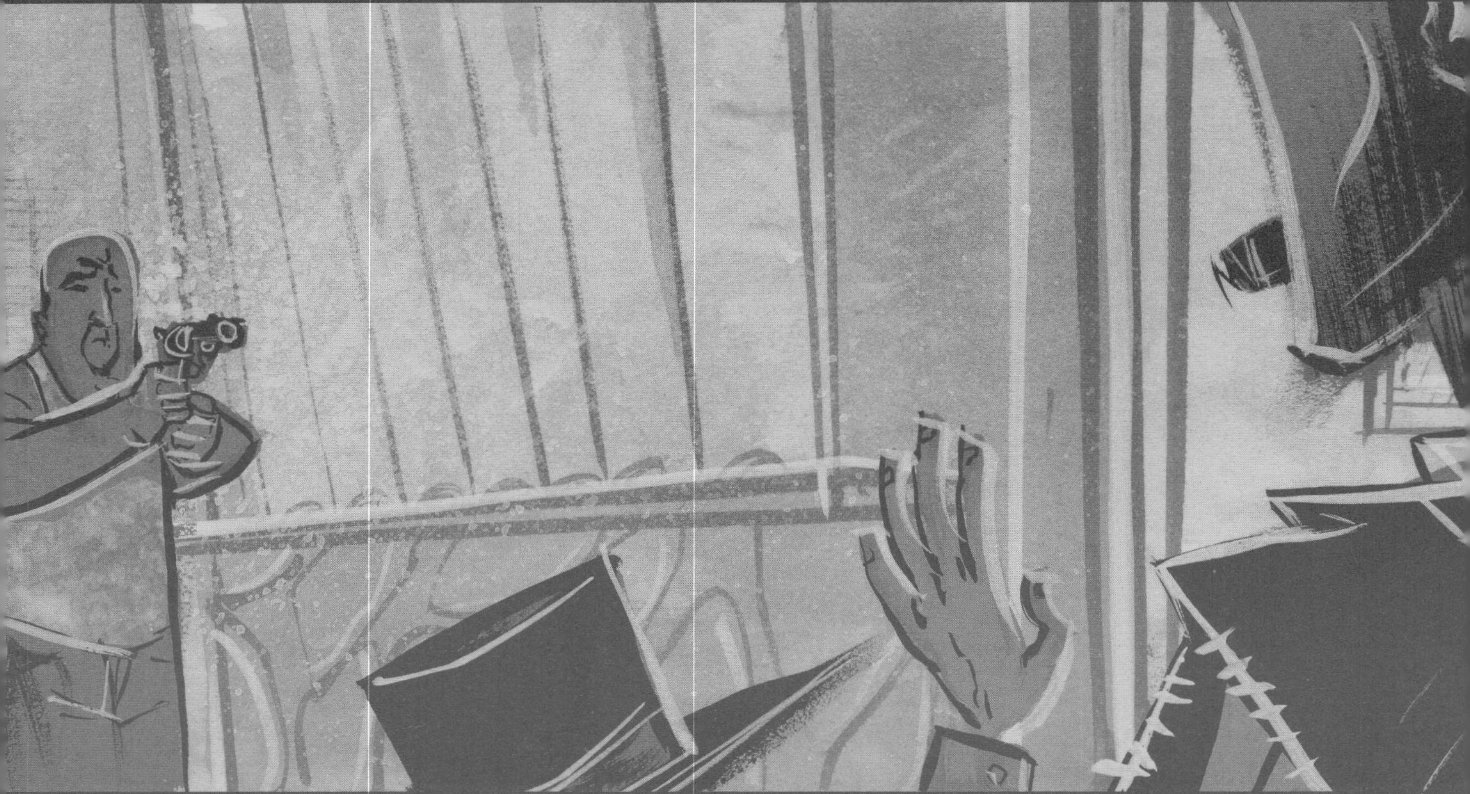

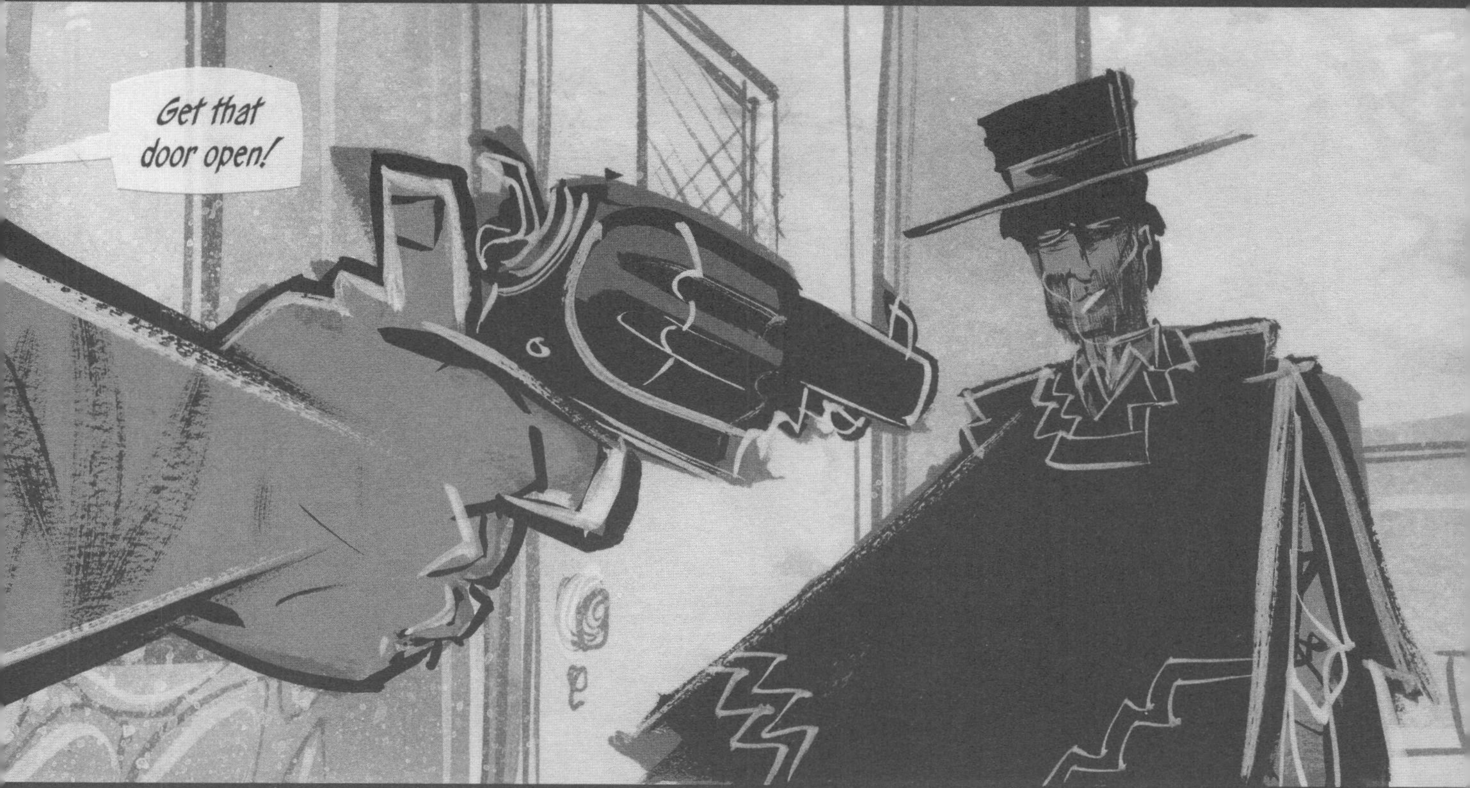
Get that door open!

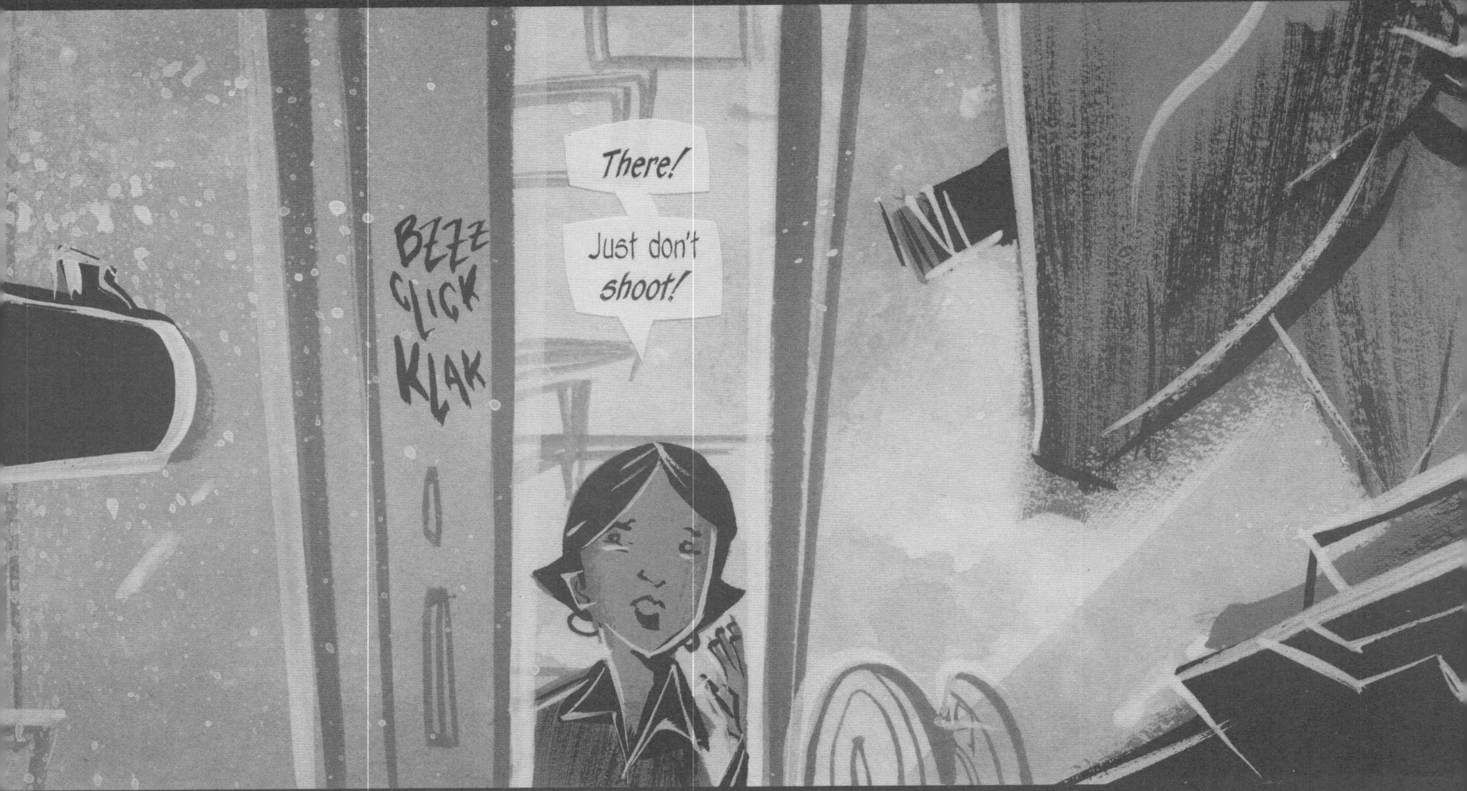
BZZZ
CLICK
KLAK
There!
Just don't shoot!

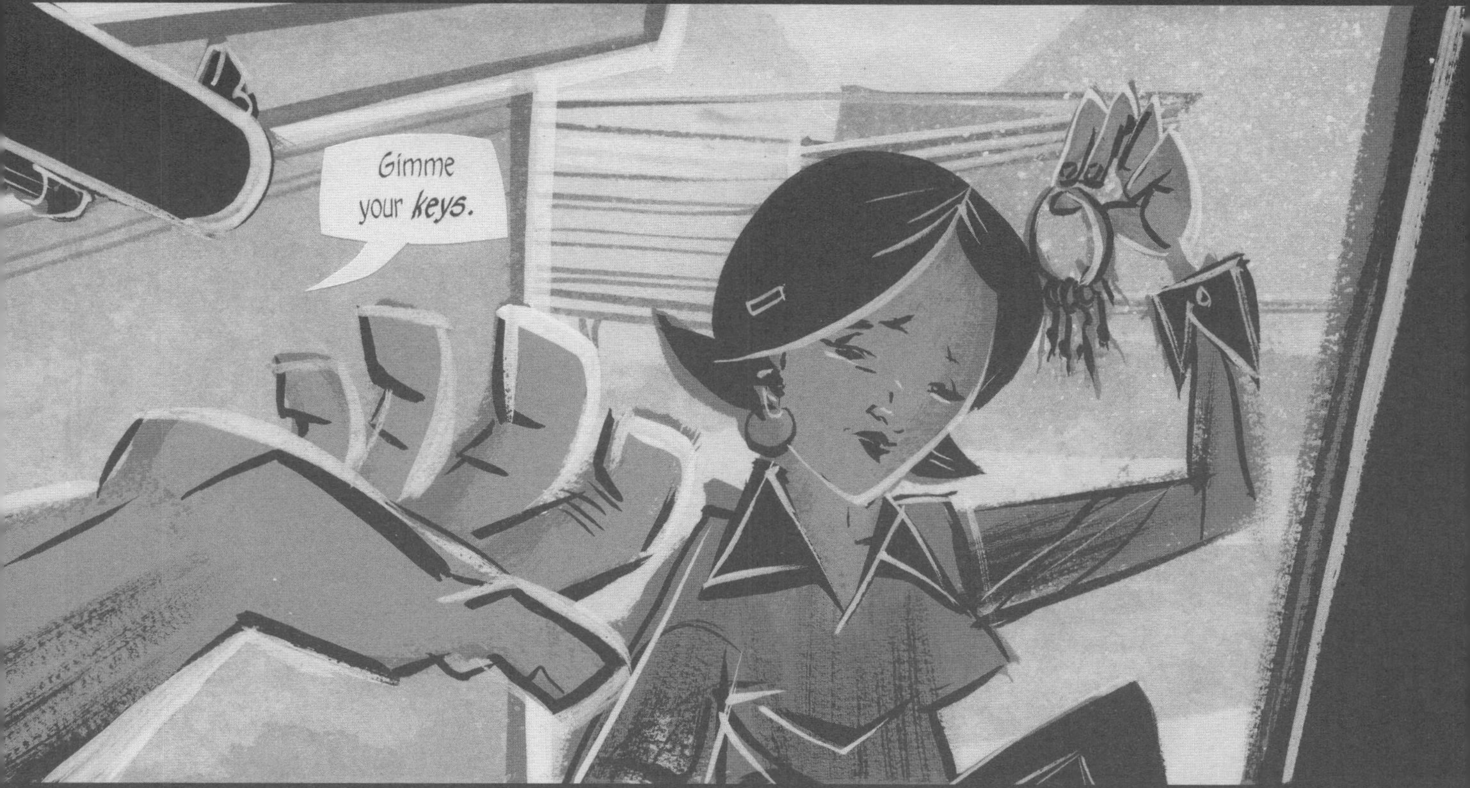
Gimme your *keys*.

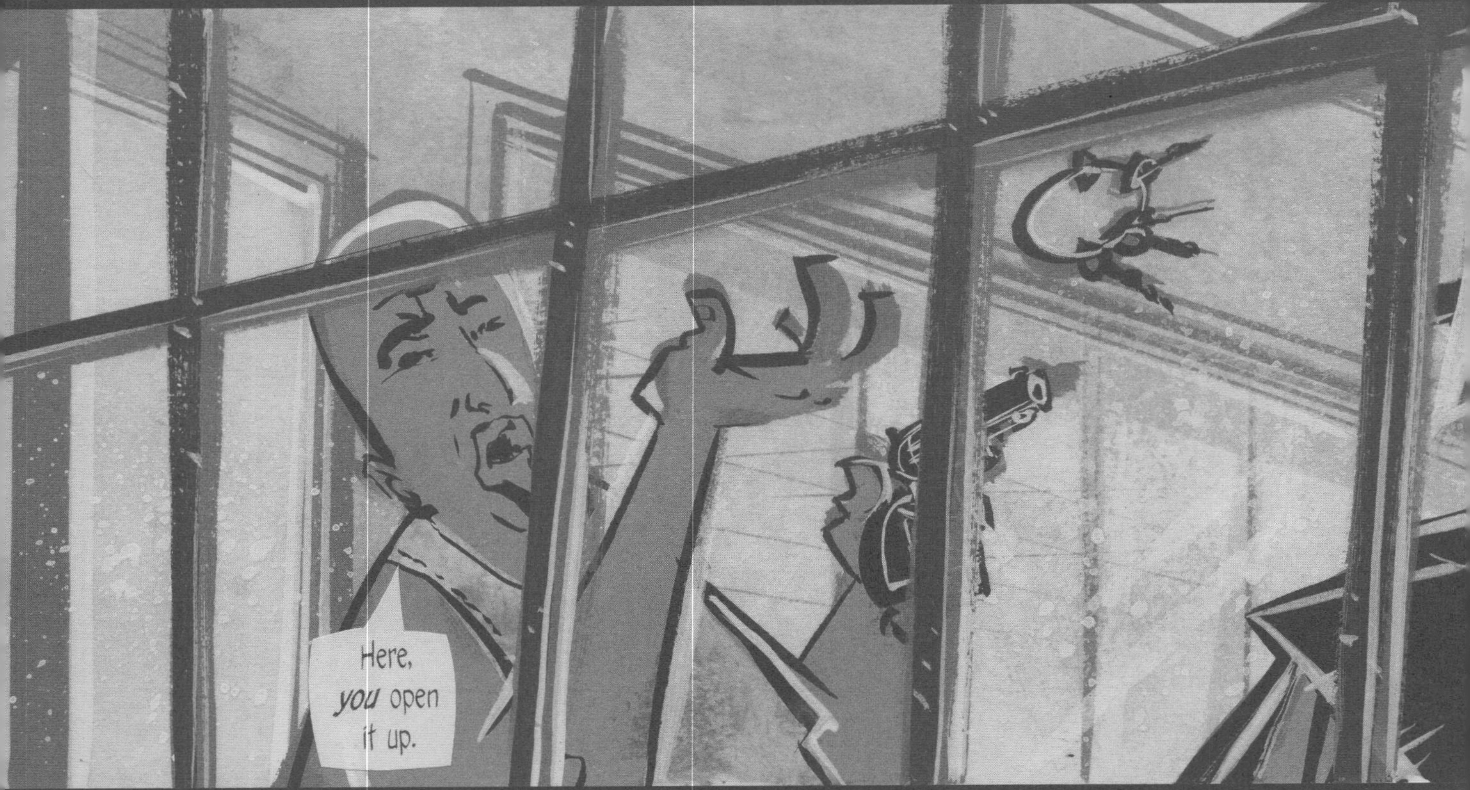
Here, *you* open it up.

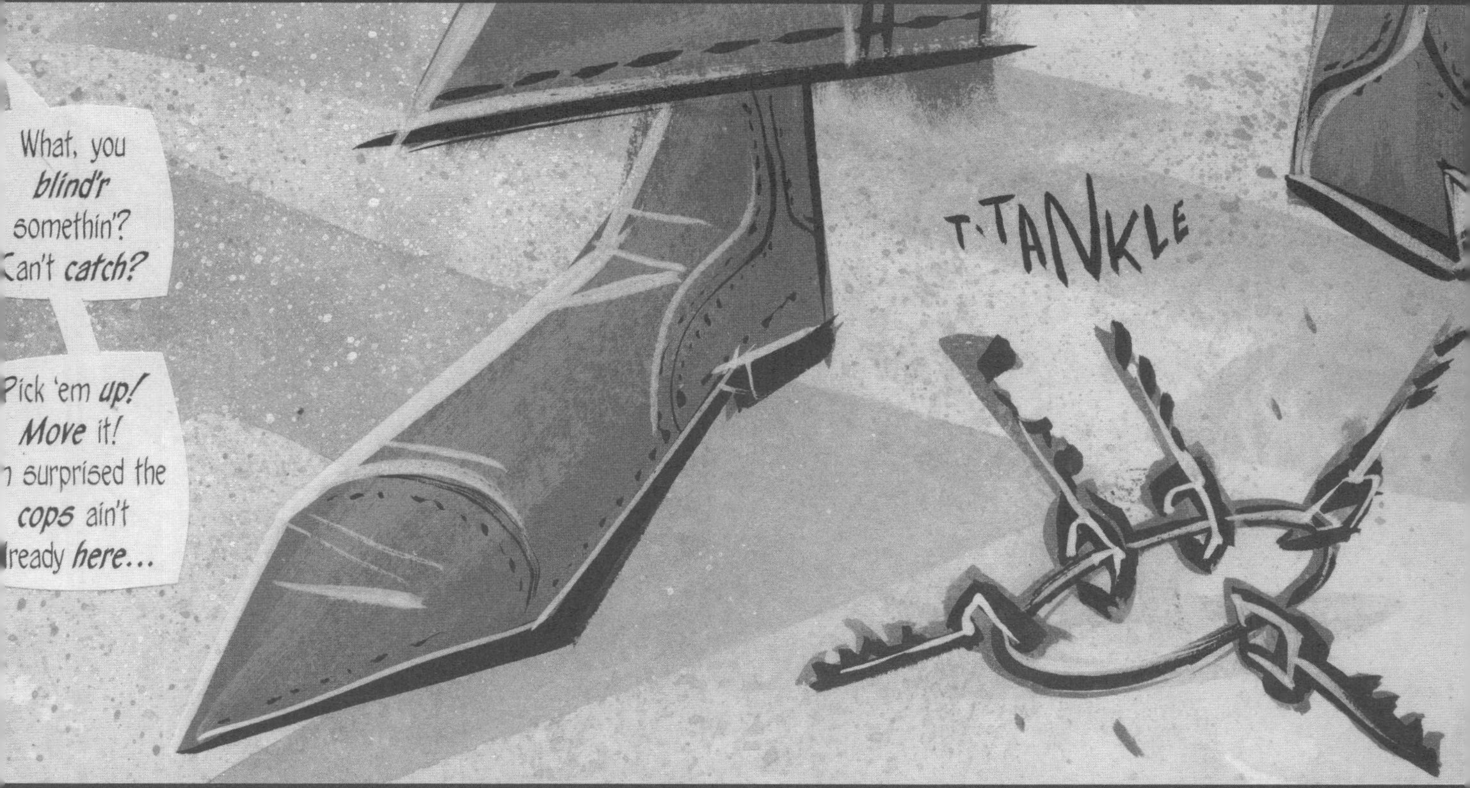
What, you *blind'r* somethin'? Can't *catch?*
Pick 'em *up!* *Move* it! n surprised the *cops* ain't lready *here...*
T-TANKLE

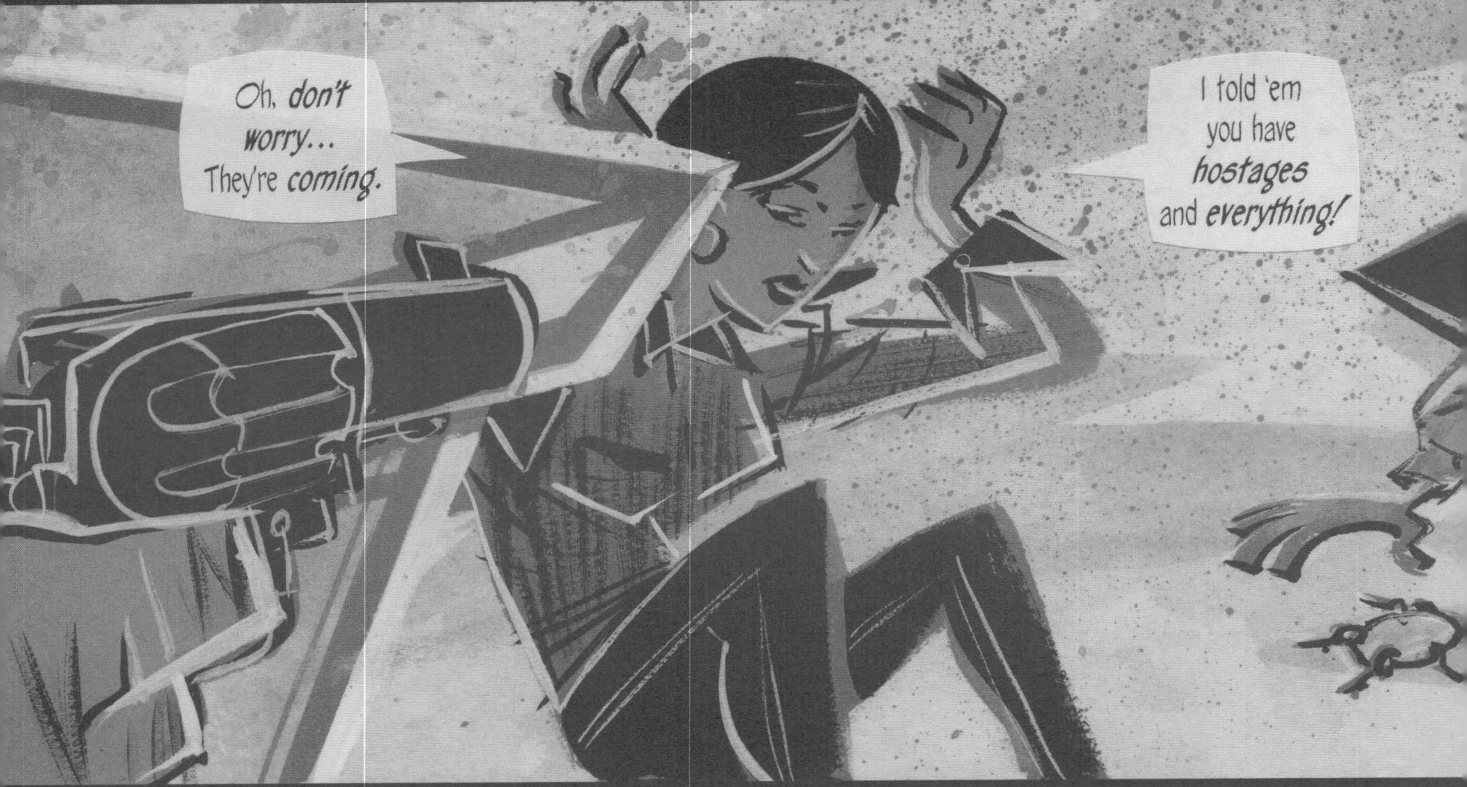
Oh, don't worry... They're coming.
I told 'em you have hostages and everything!

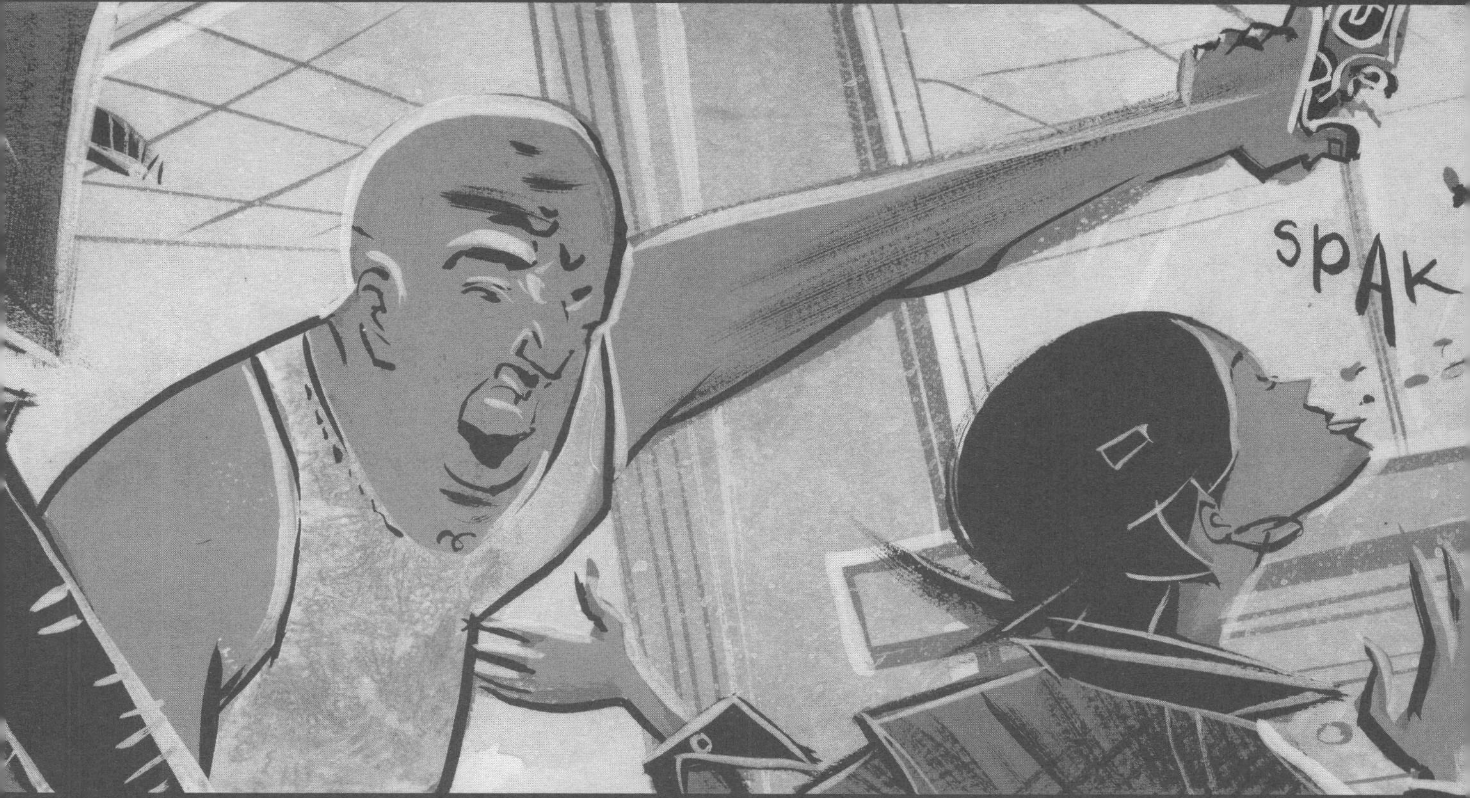
SPAK

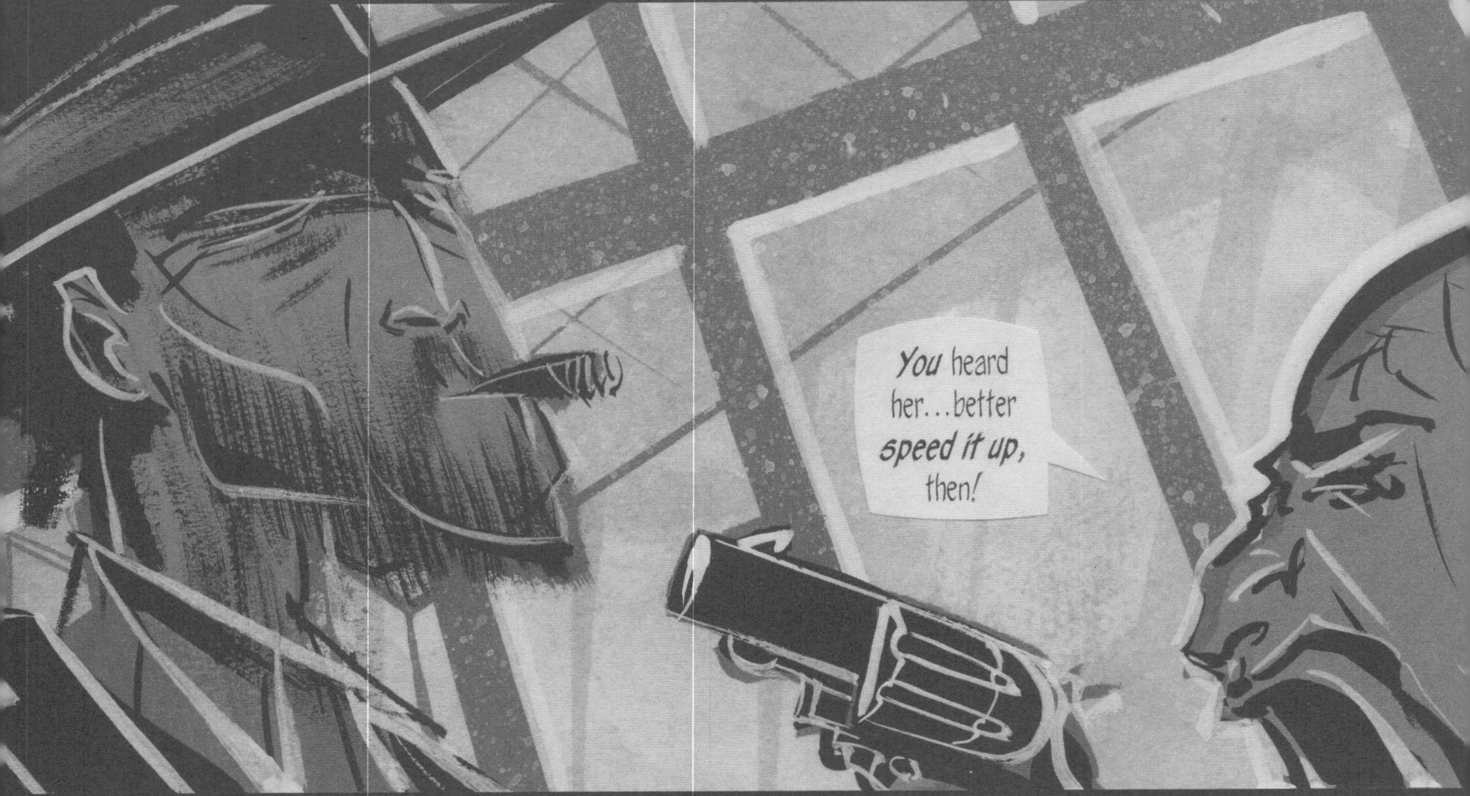
You heard her...better *speed it up,* then!

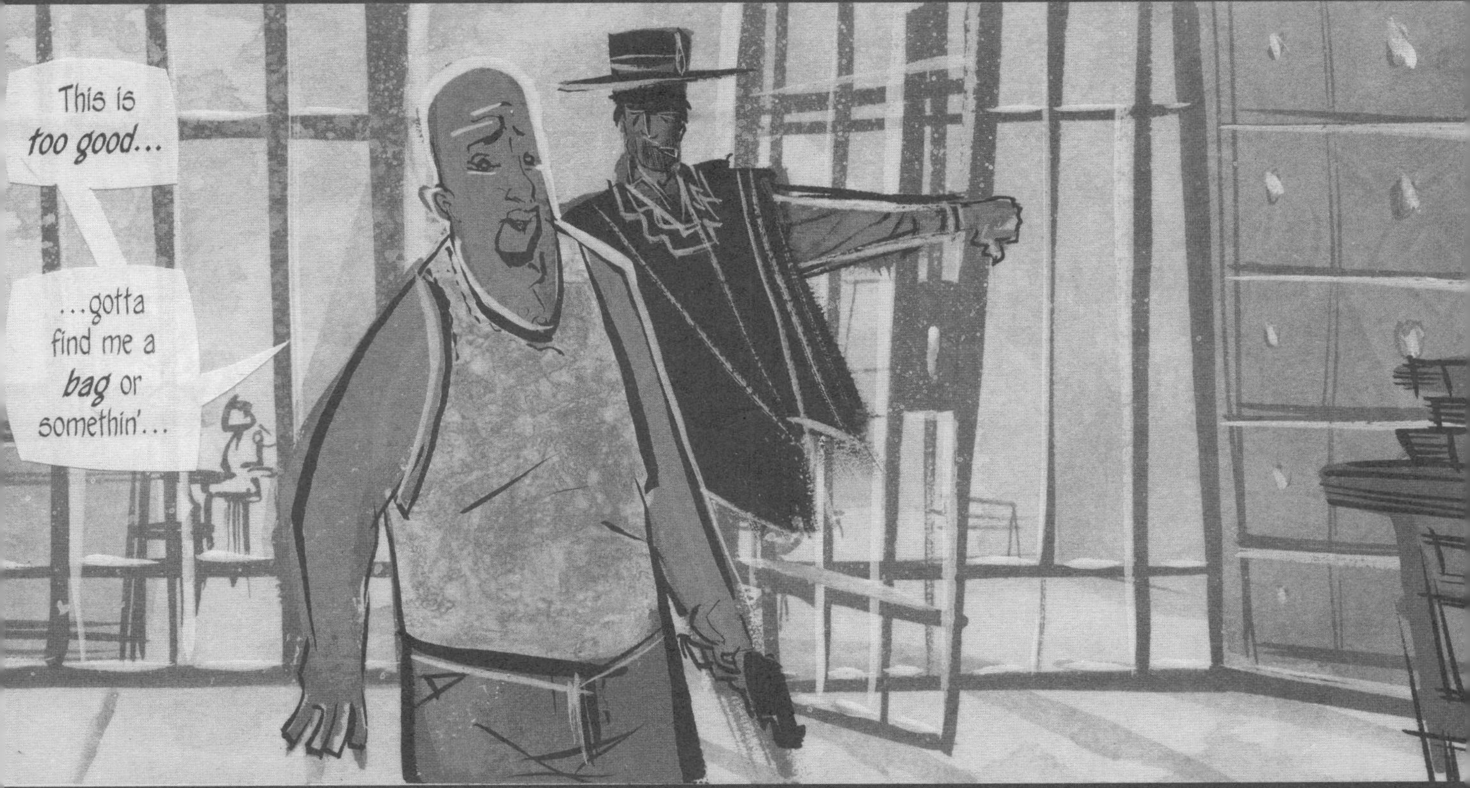
This is *too good*...
...gotta find me a *bag* or somethin'...

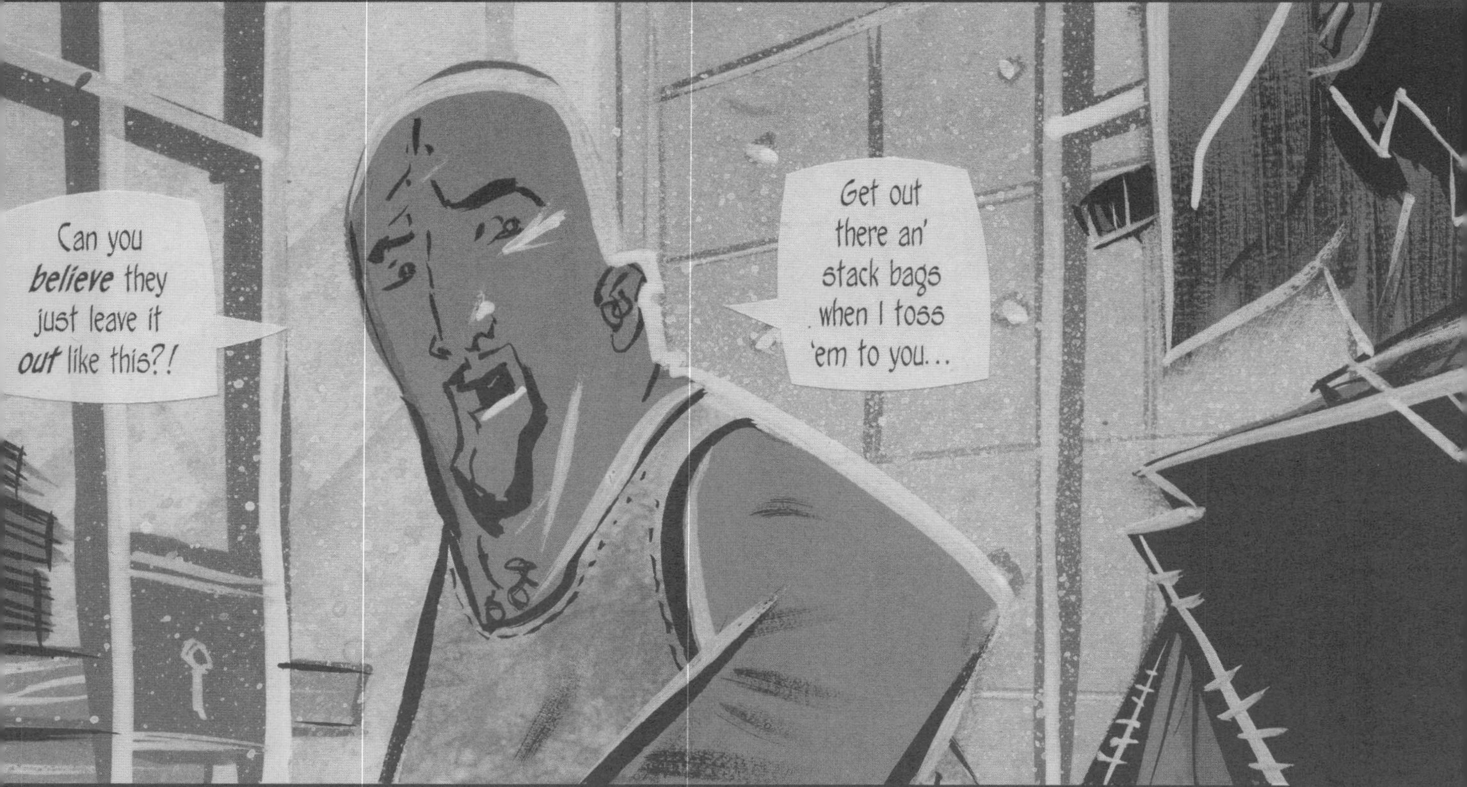
Can you believe they just leave it out like this?!
Get out there an' stack bags when I toss 'em to you...

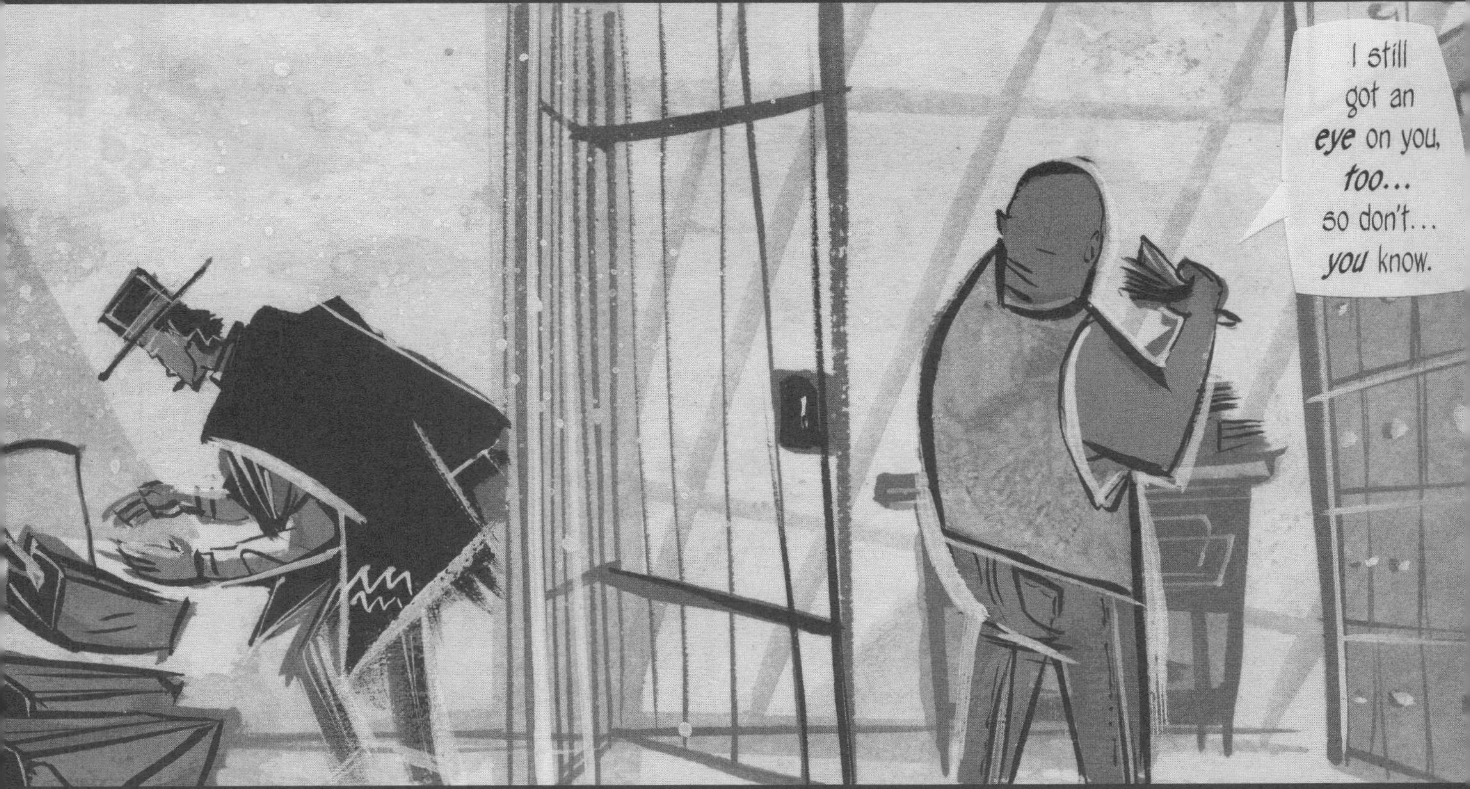
I still got an *eye* on you, *too...* so don't... *you* know.

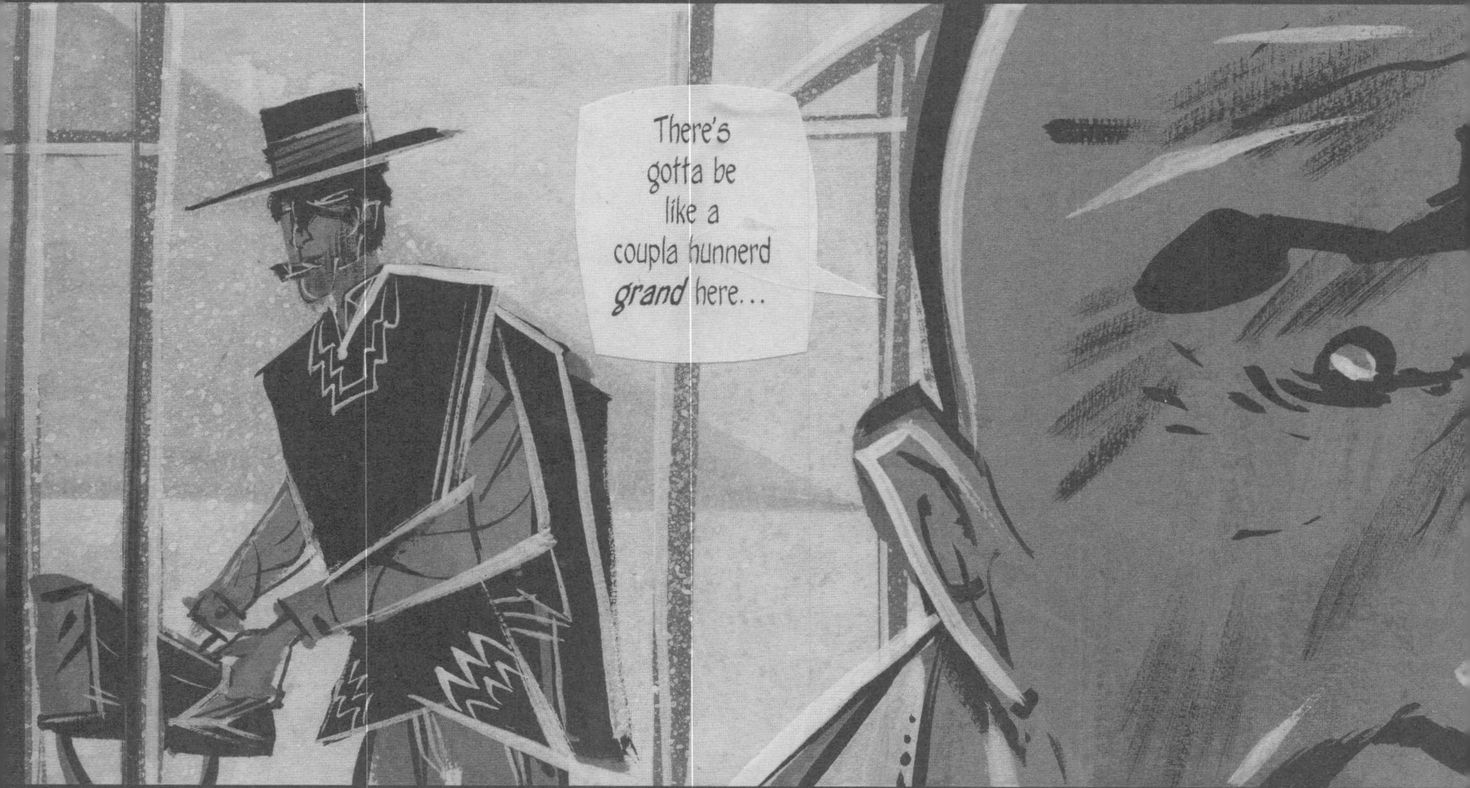
There's gotta be like a coupla hunnerd *grand* here...

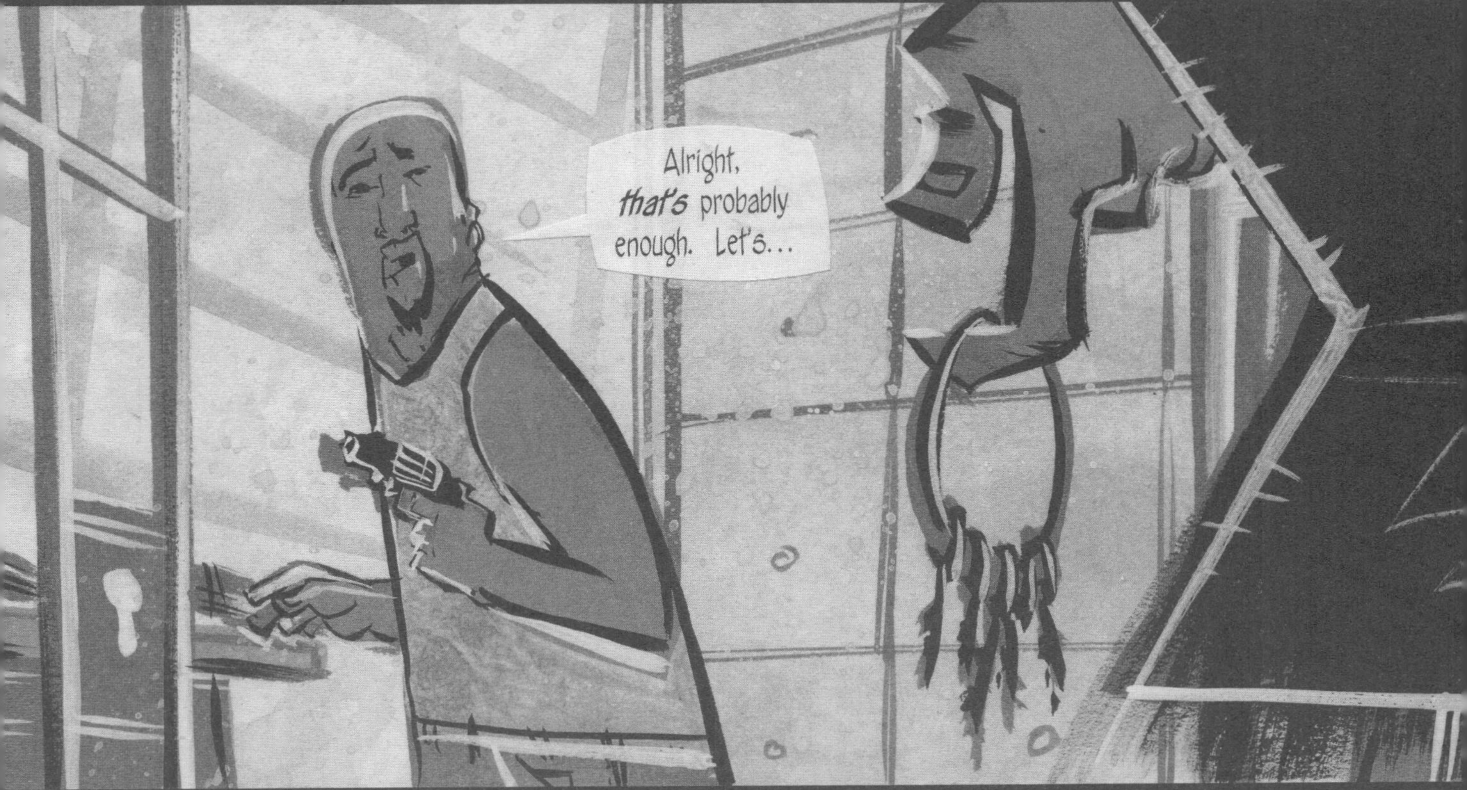
Alright, *that's* probably enough. Let's...

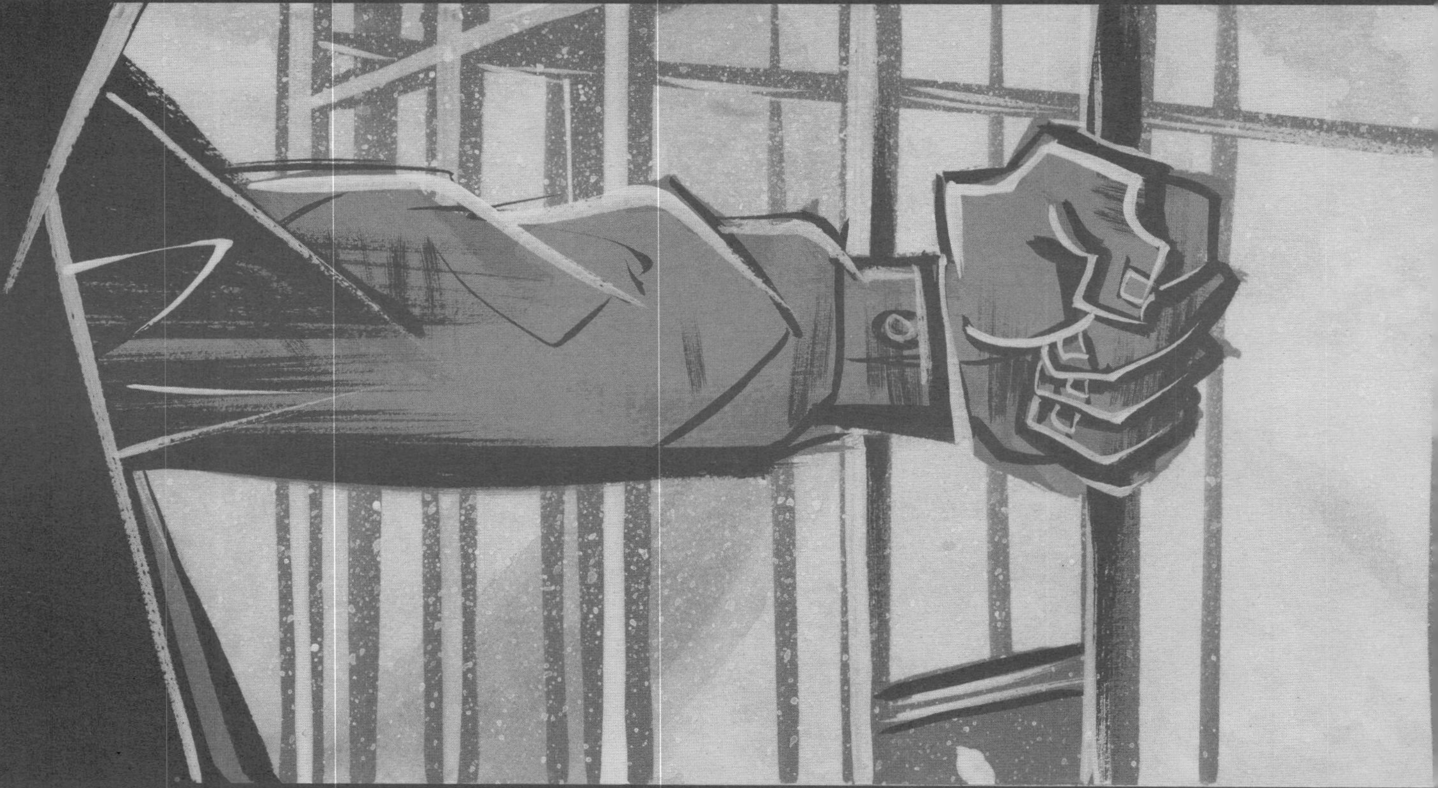

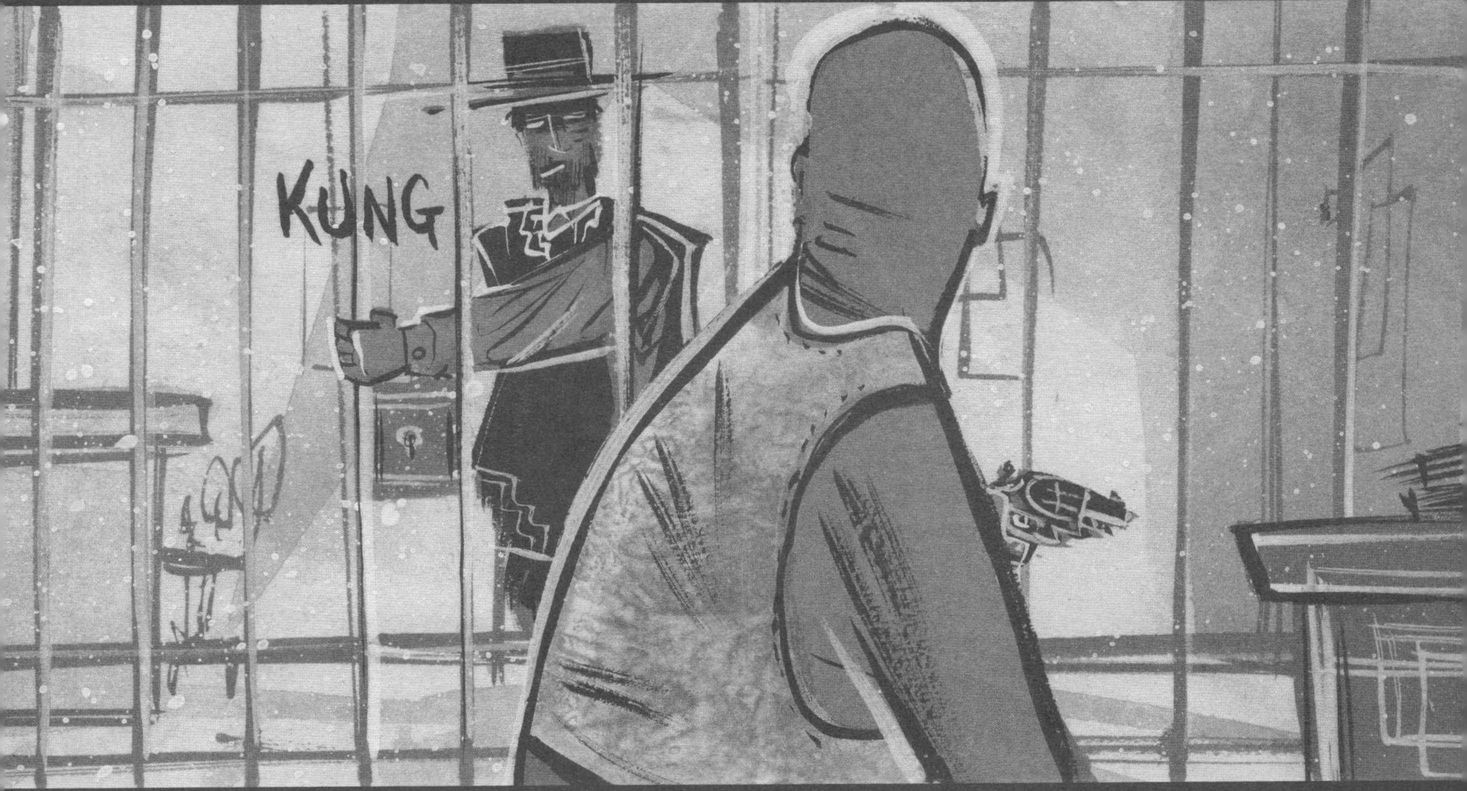
KUNG

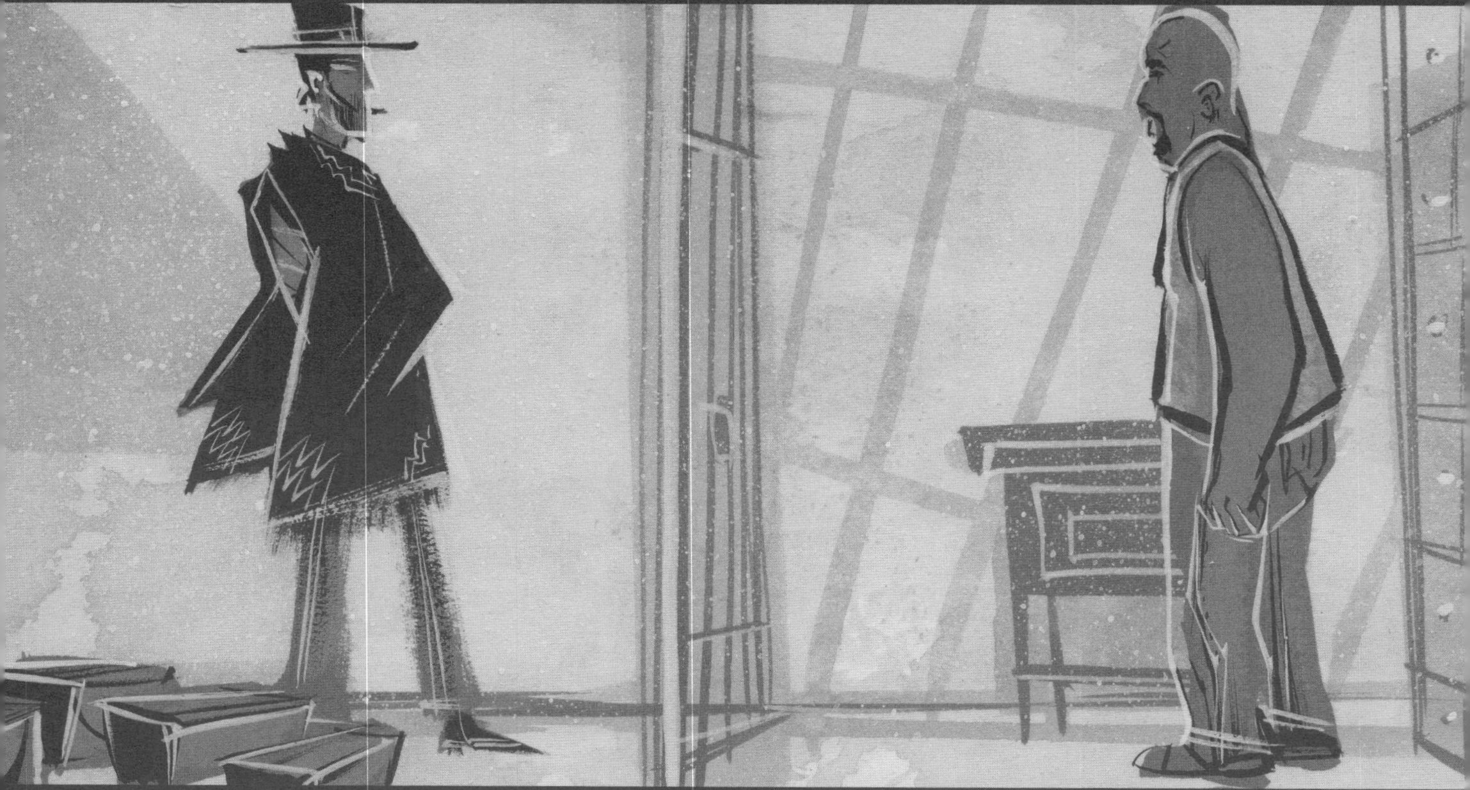

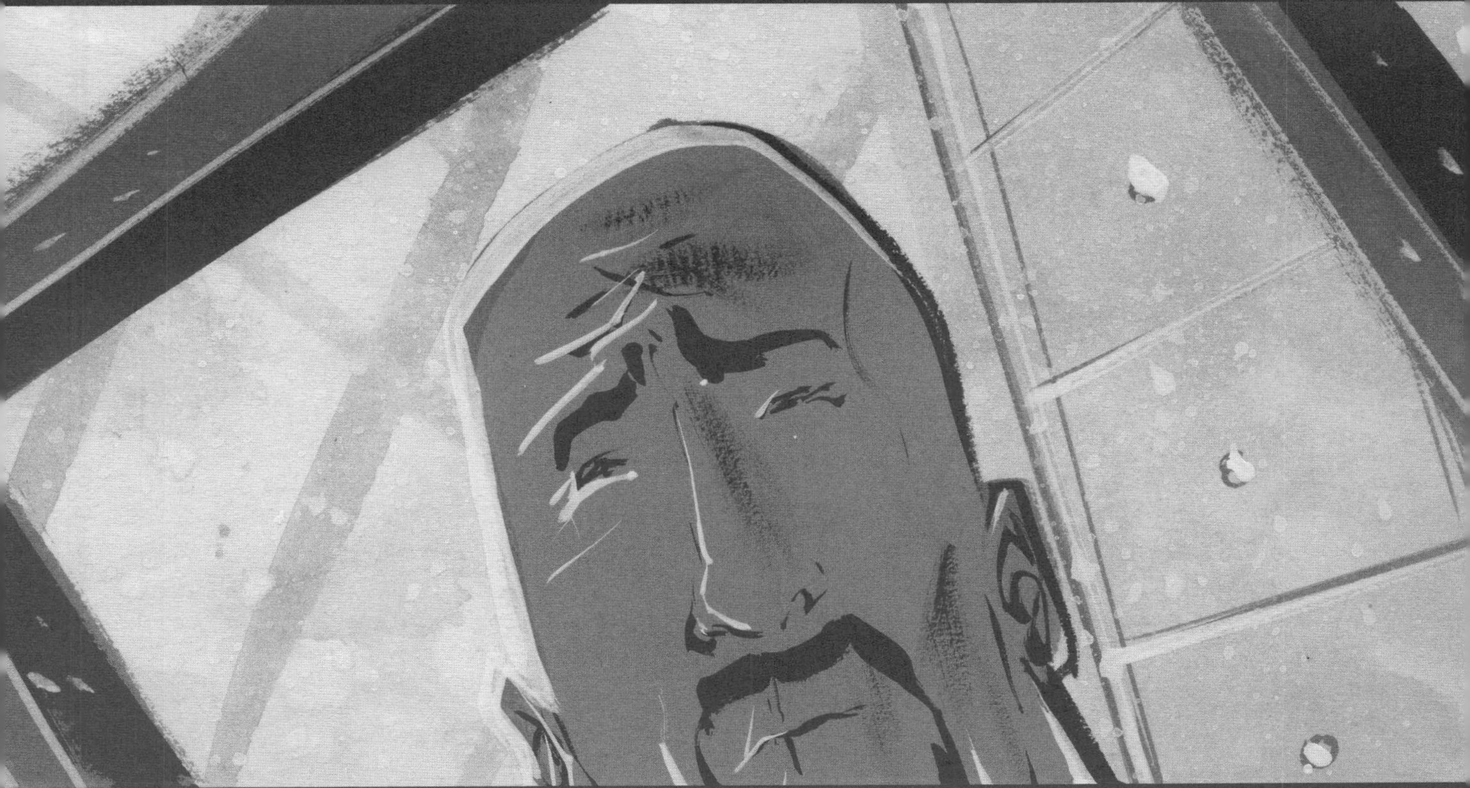

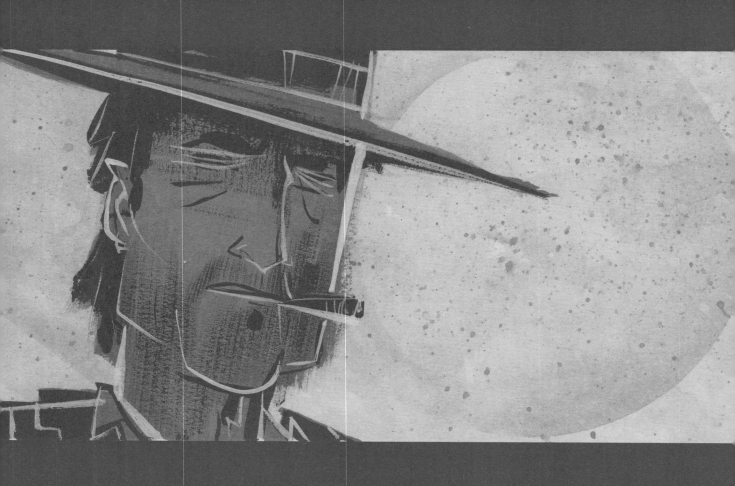

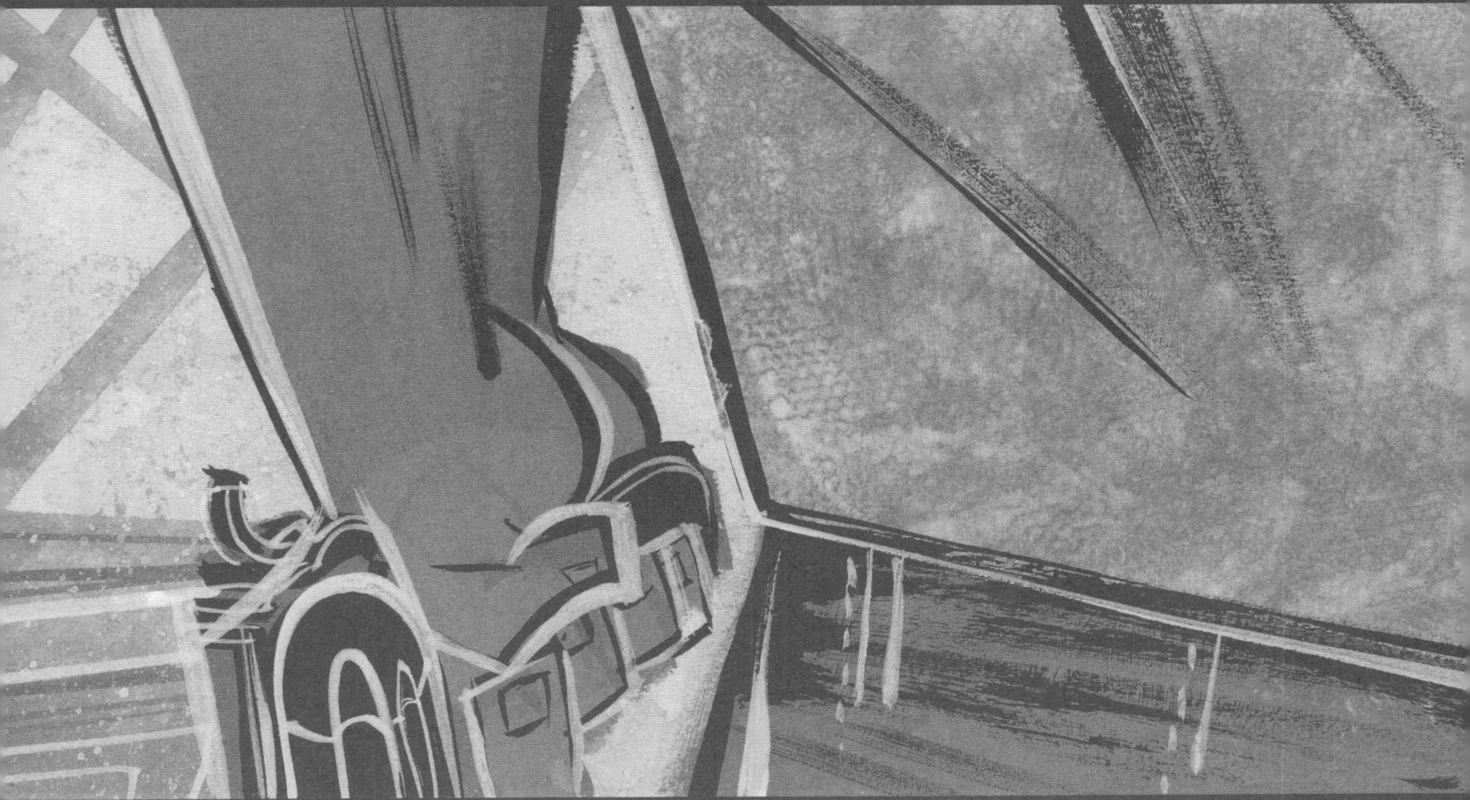

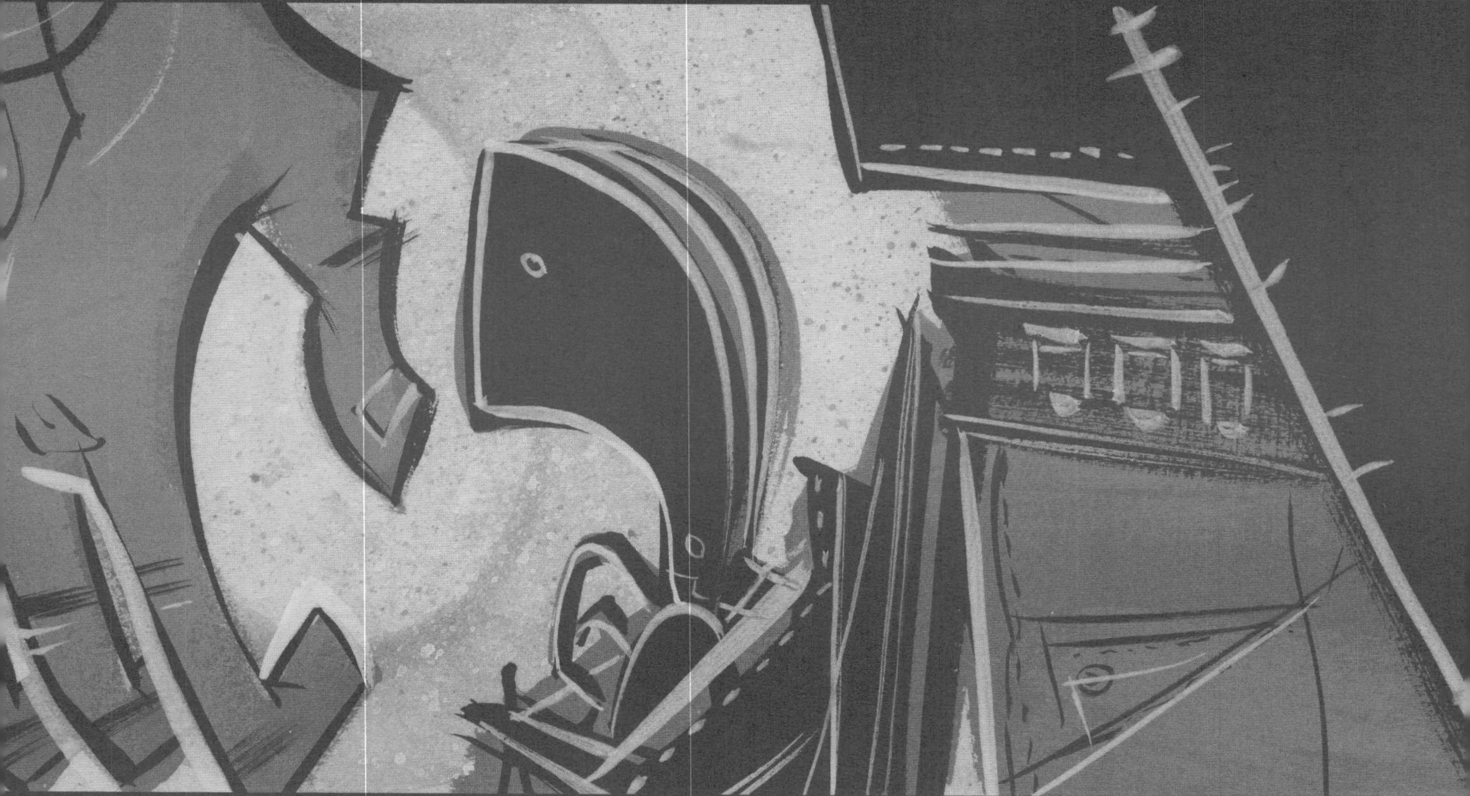

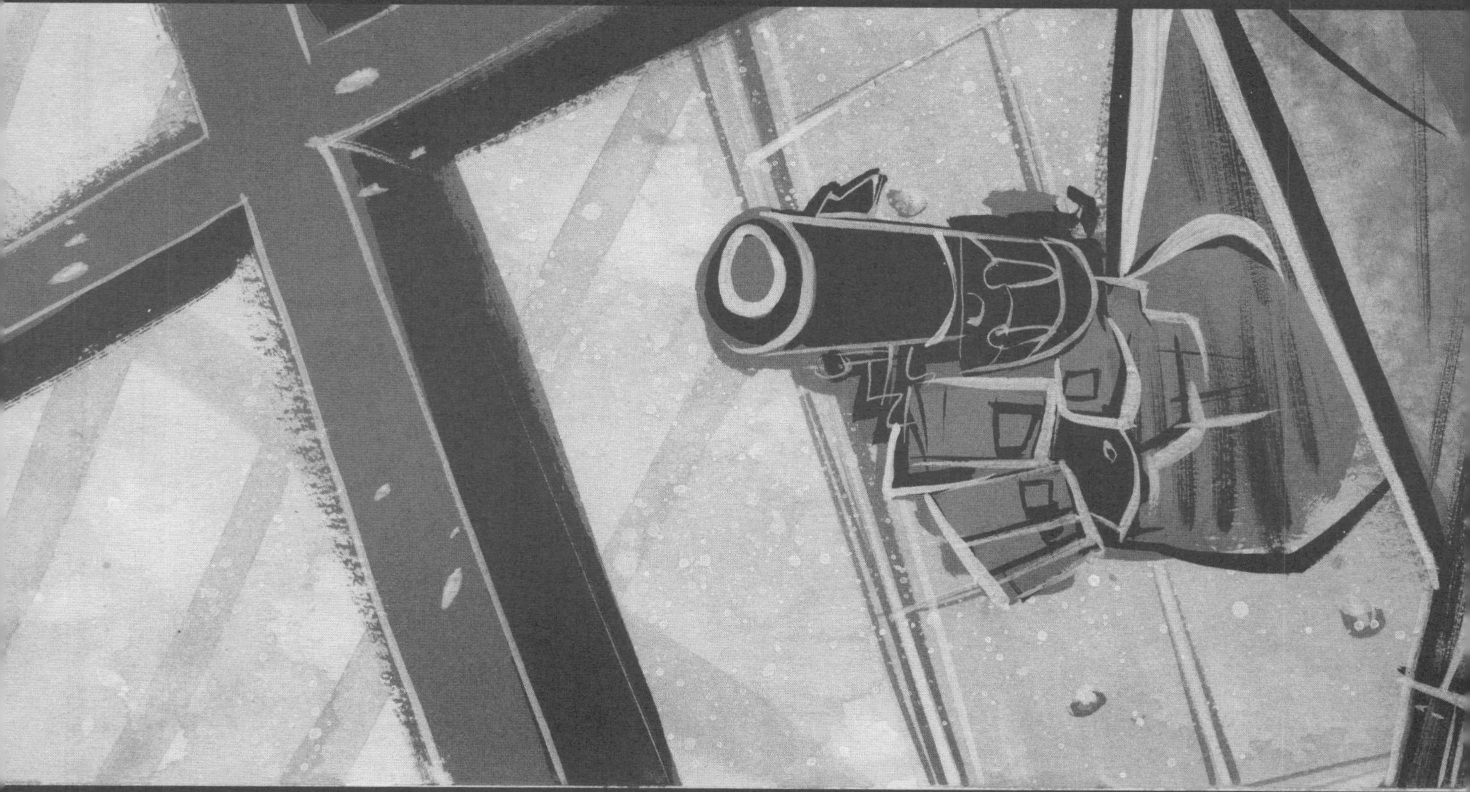

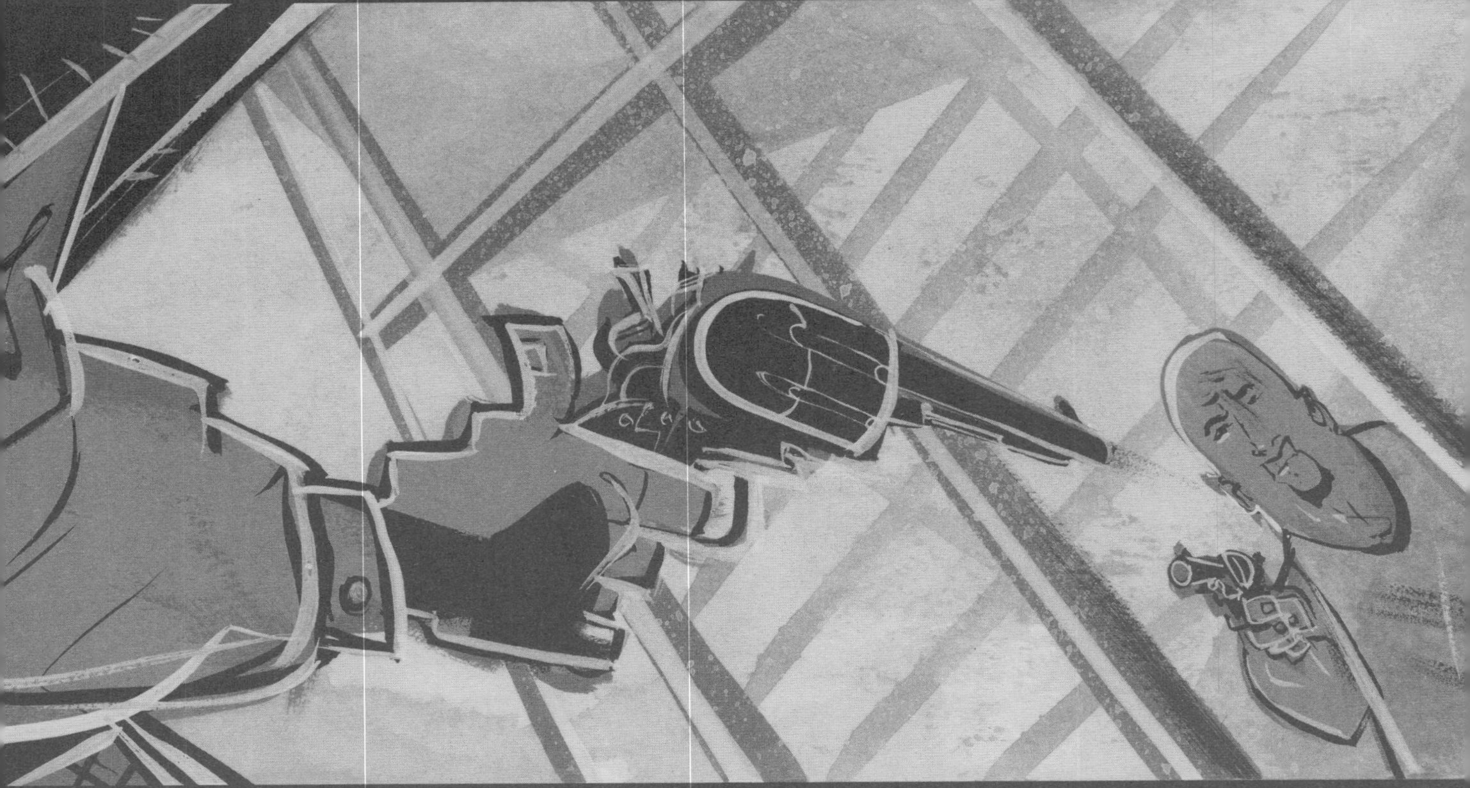

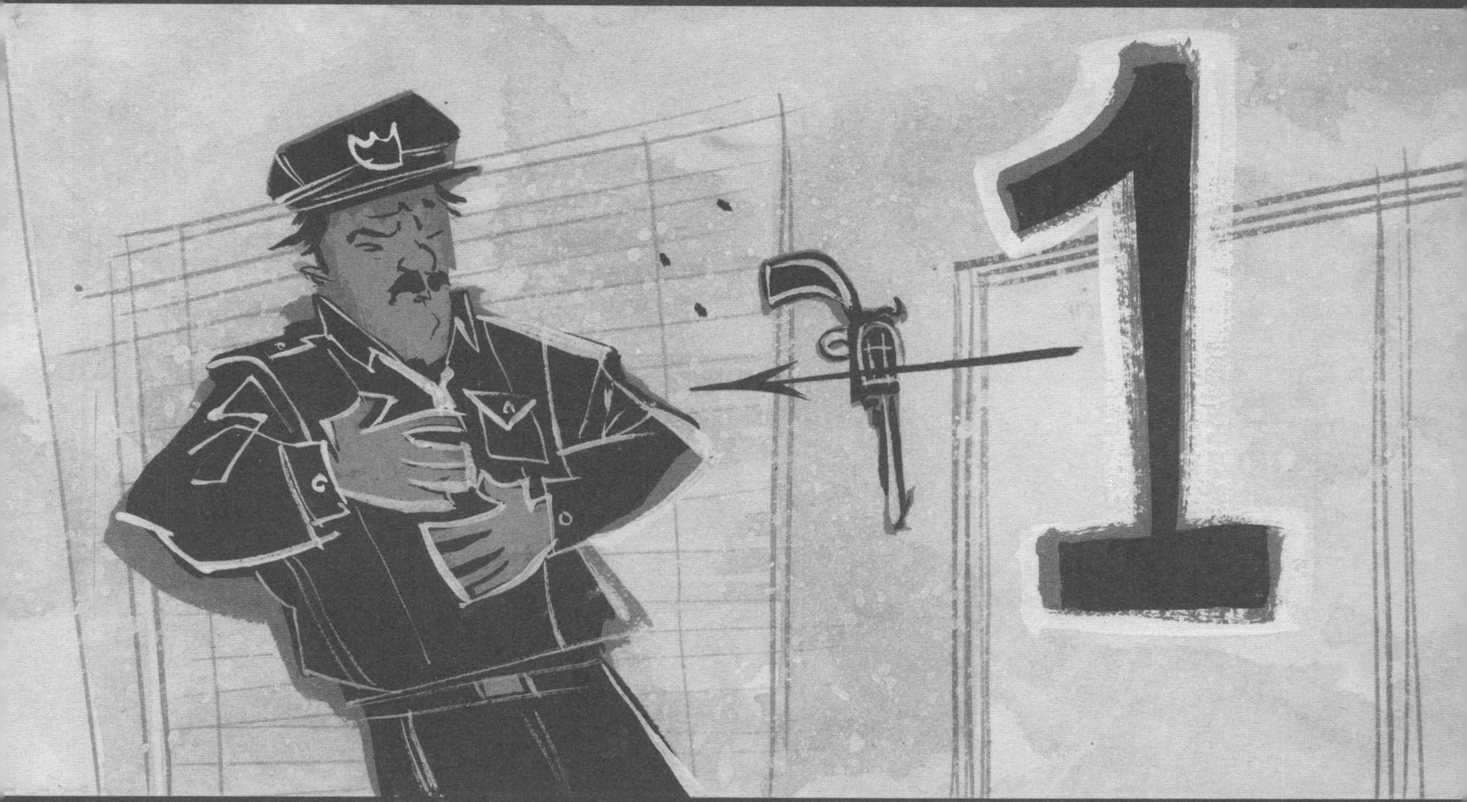
1

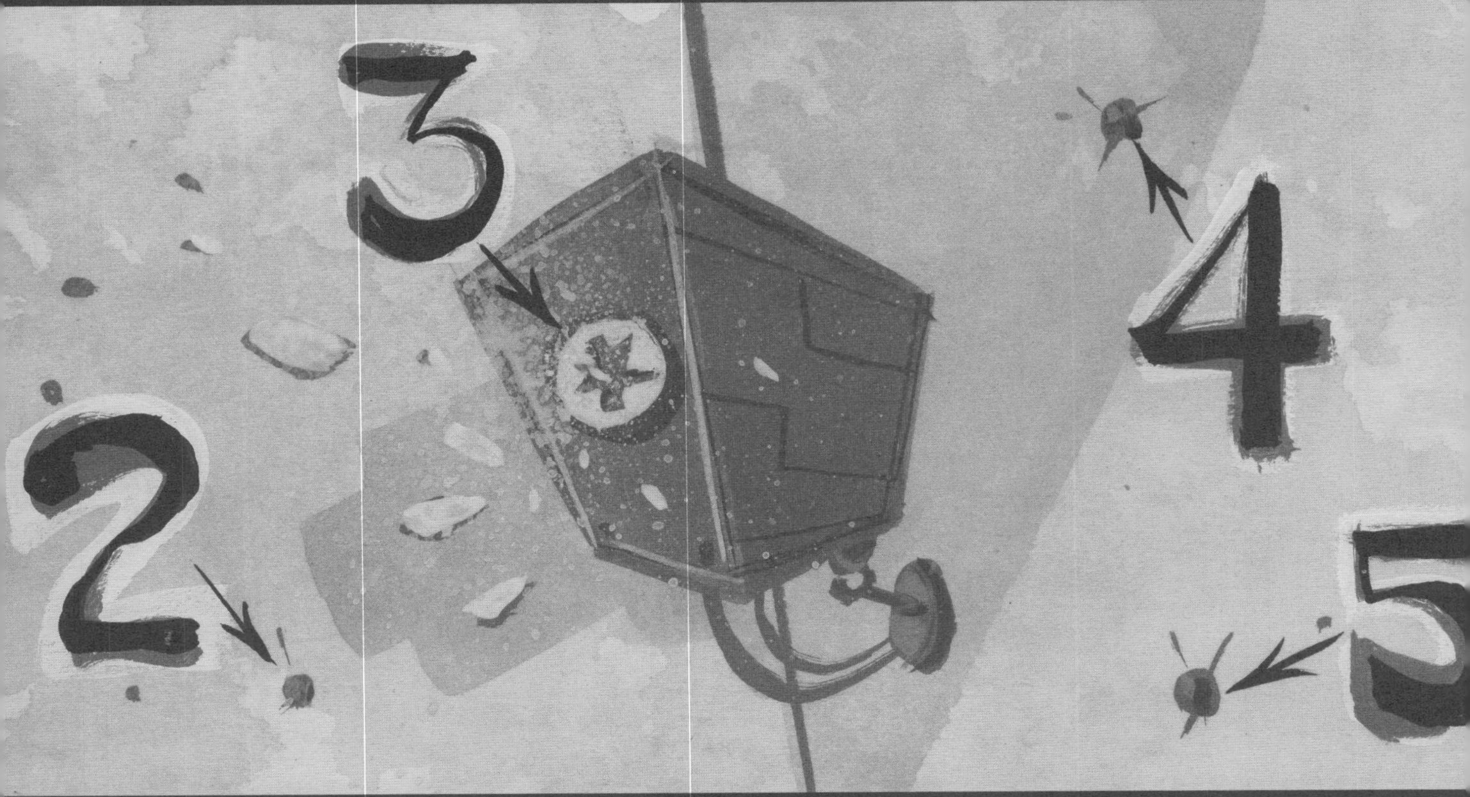

2
3
4
5

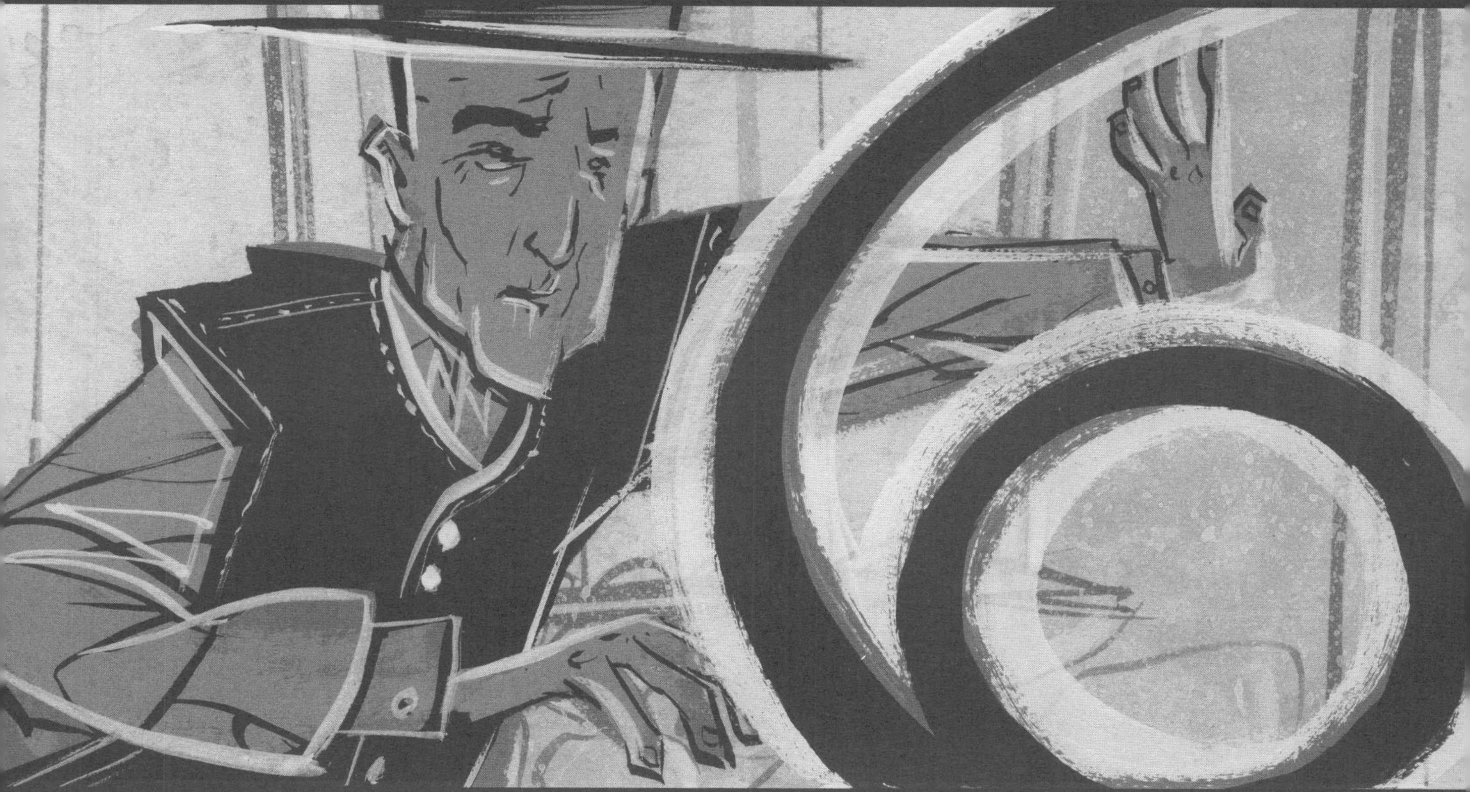

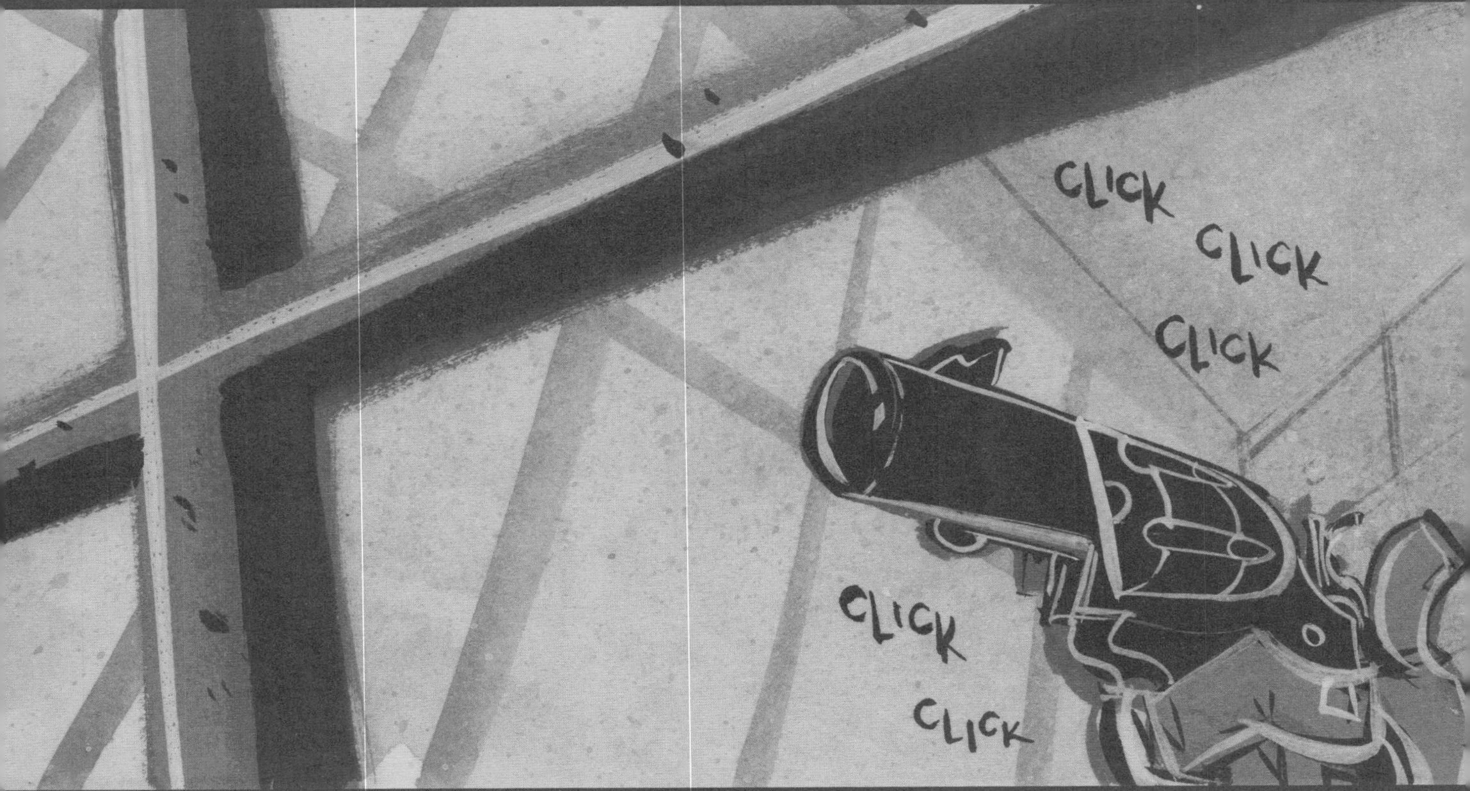
CLICK
CLICK
CLICK
CLICK
CLICK

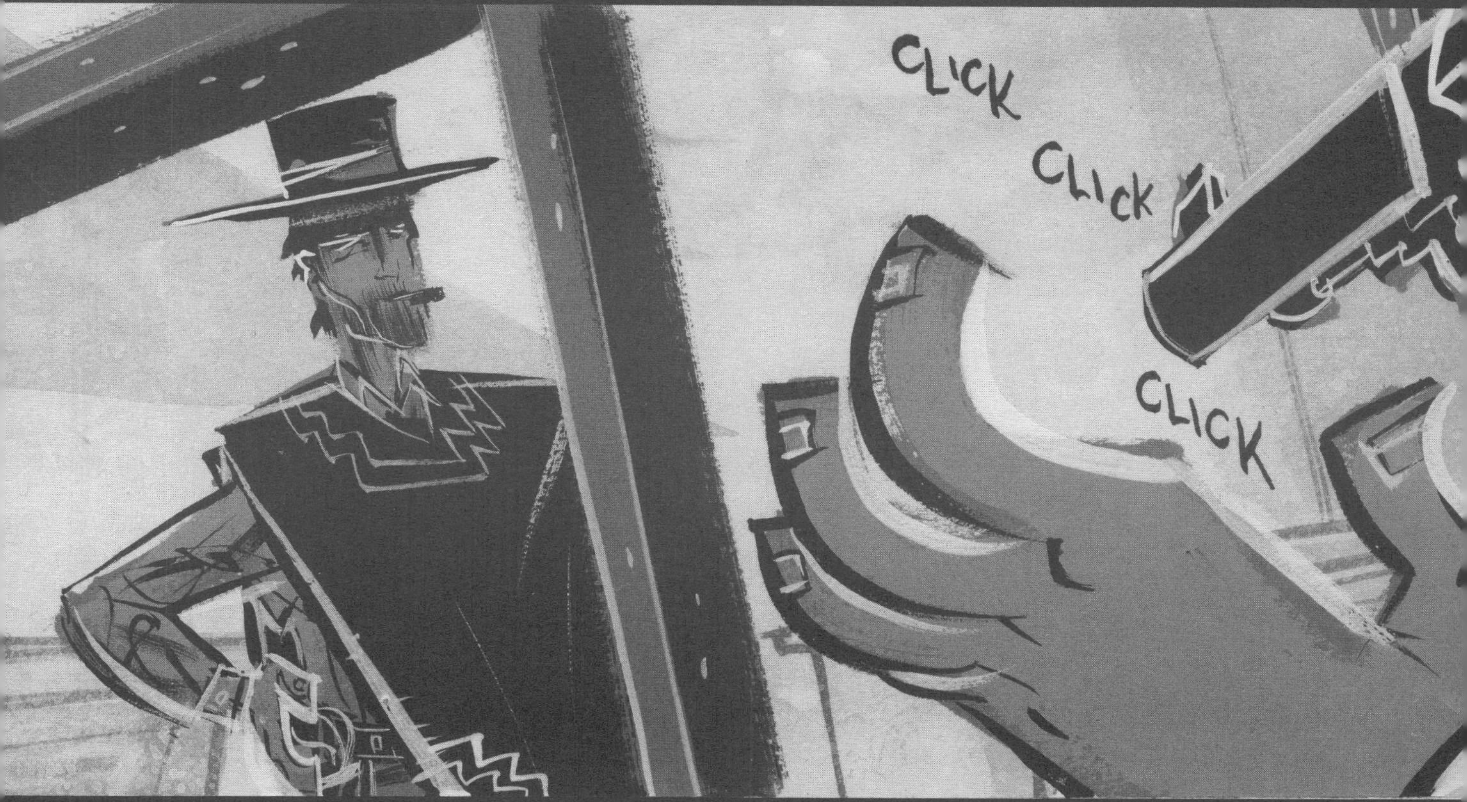
CLICK
CLICK
CLICK

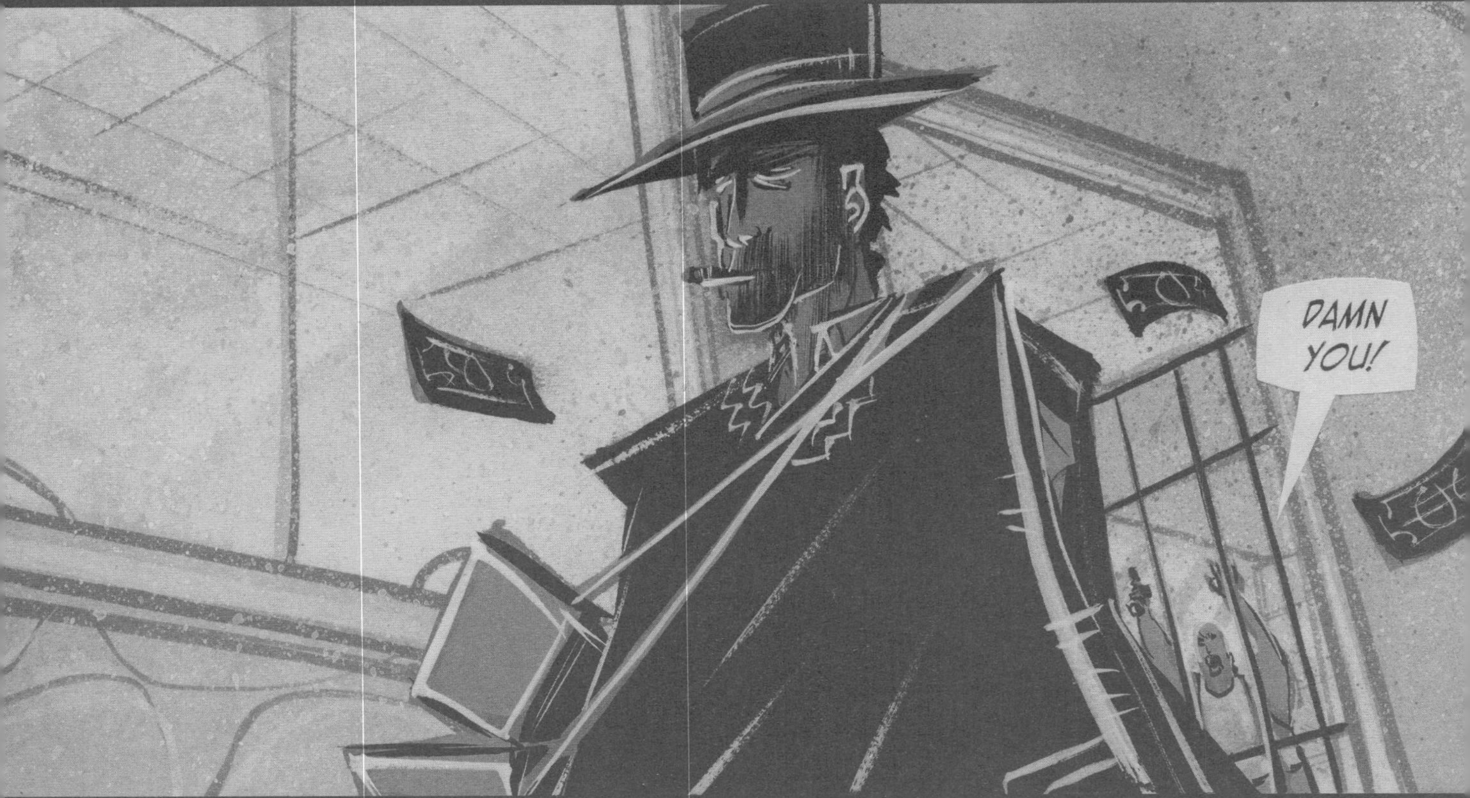
DAMN YOU!

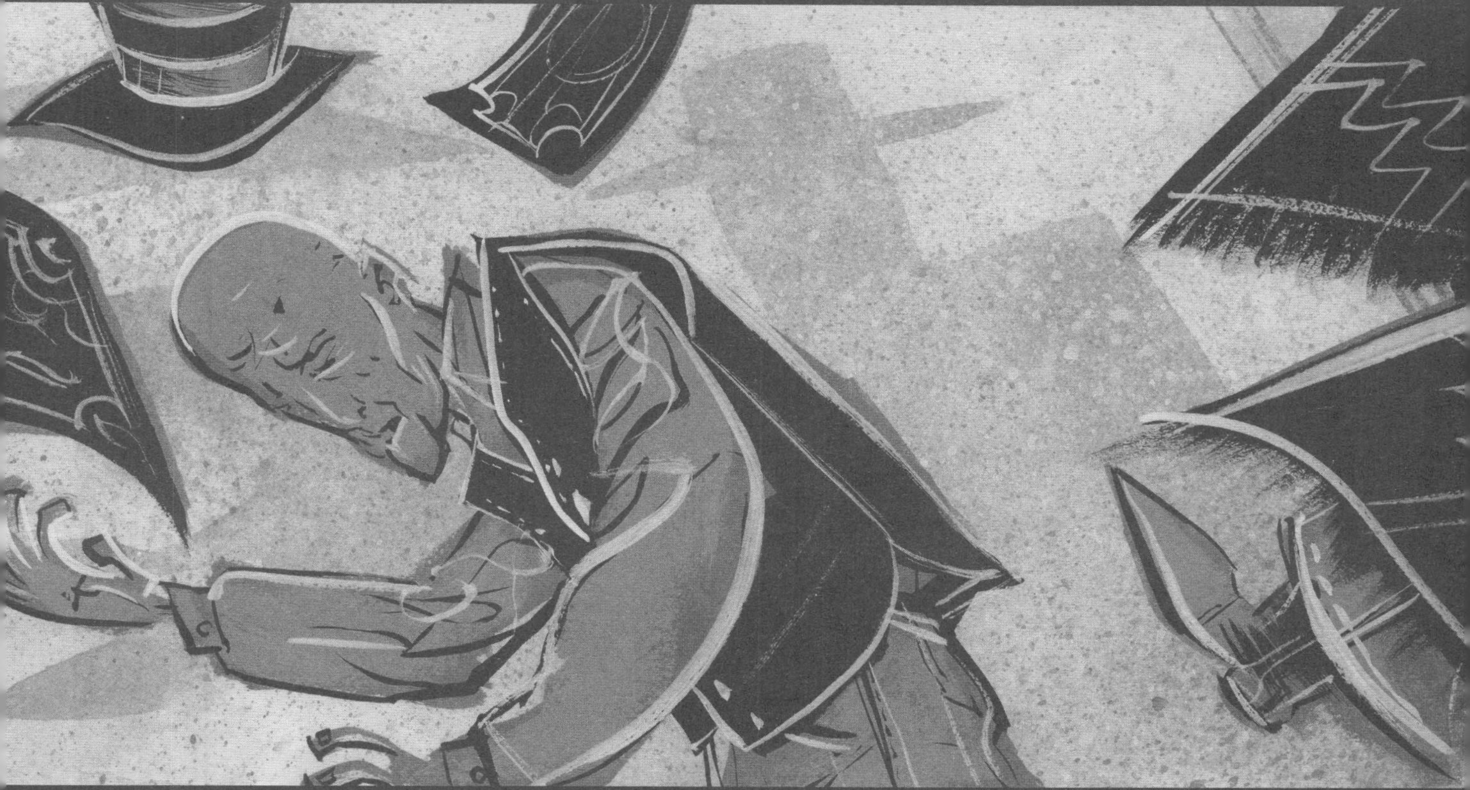

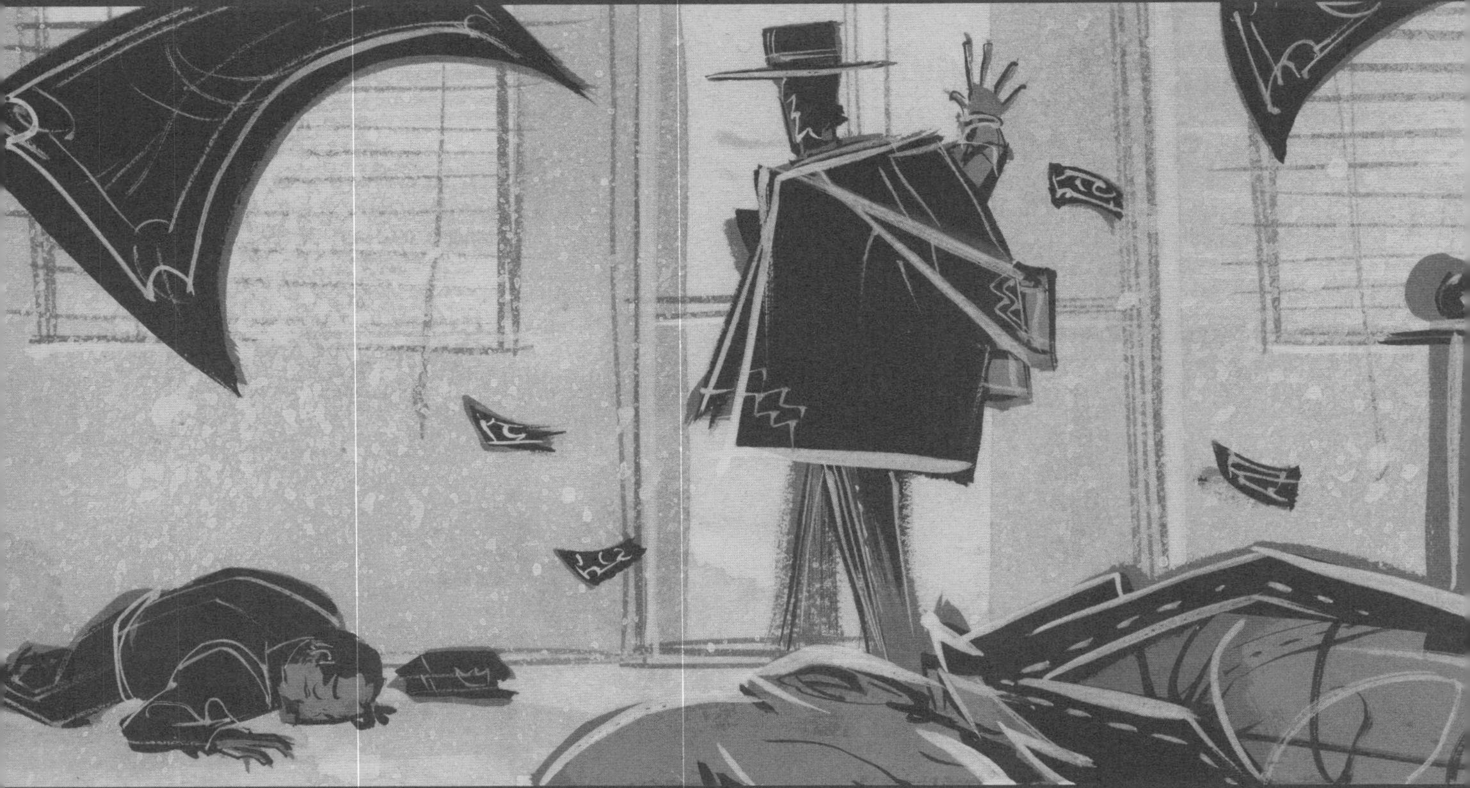

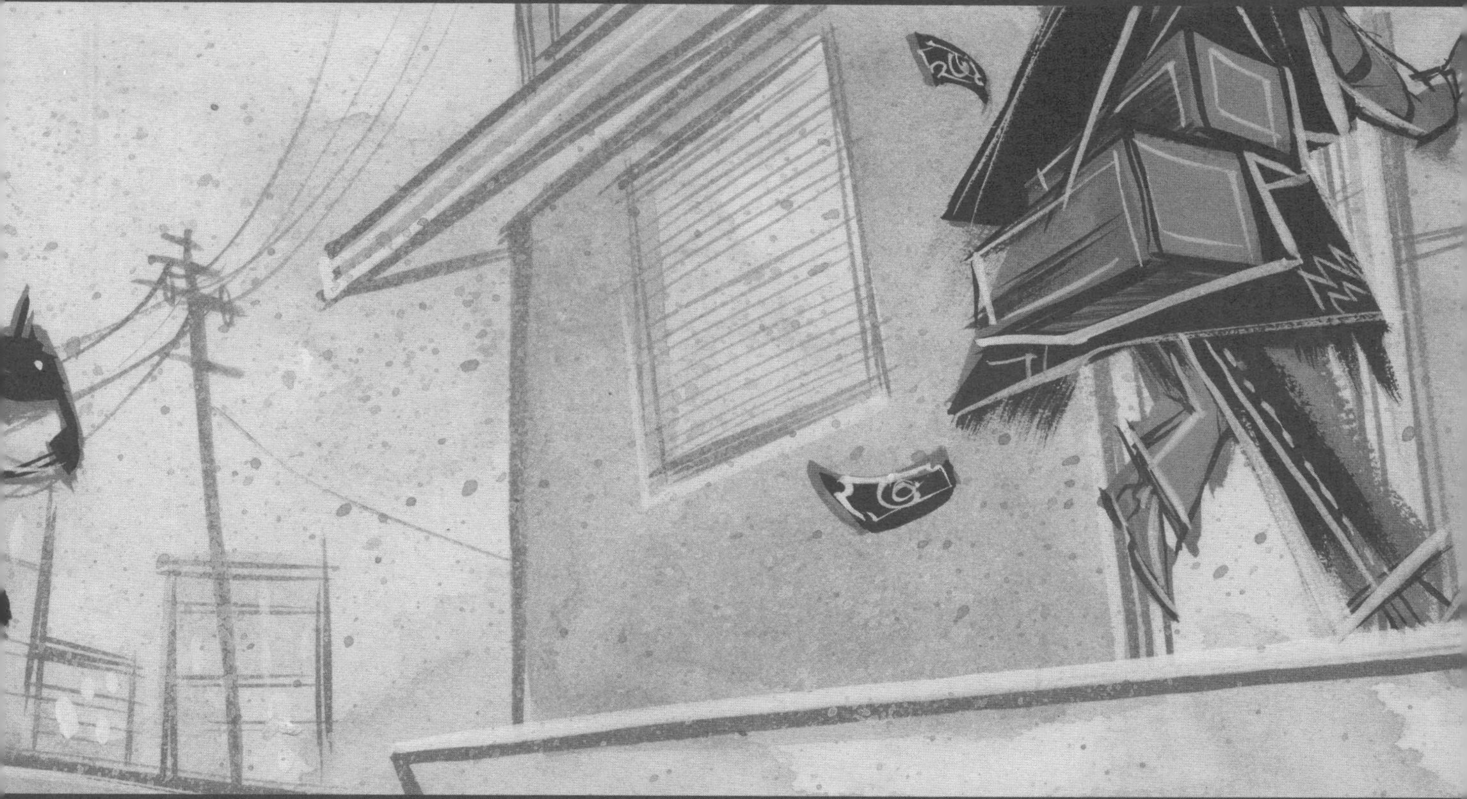

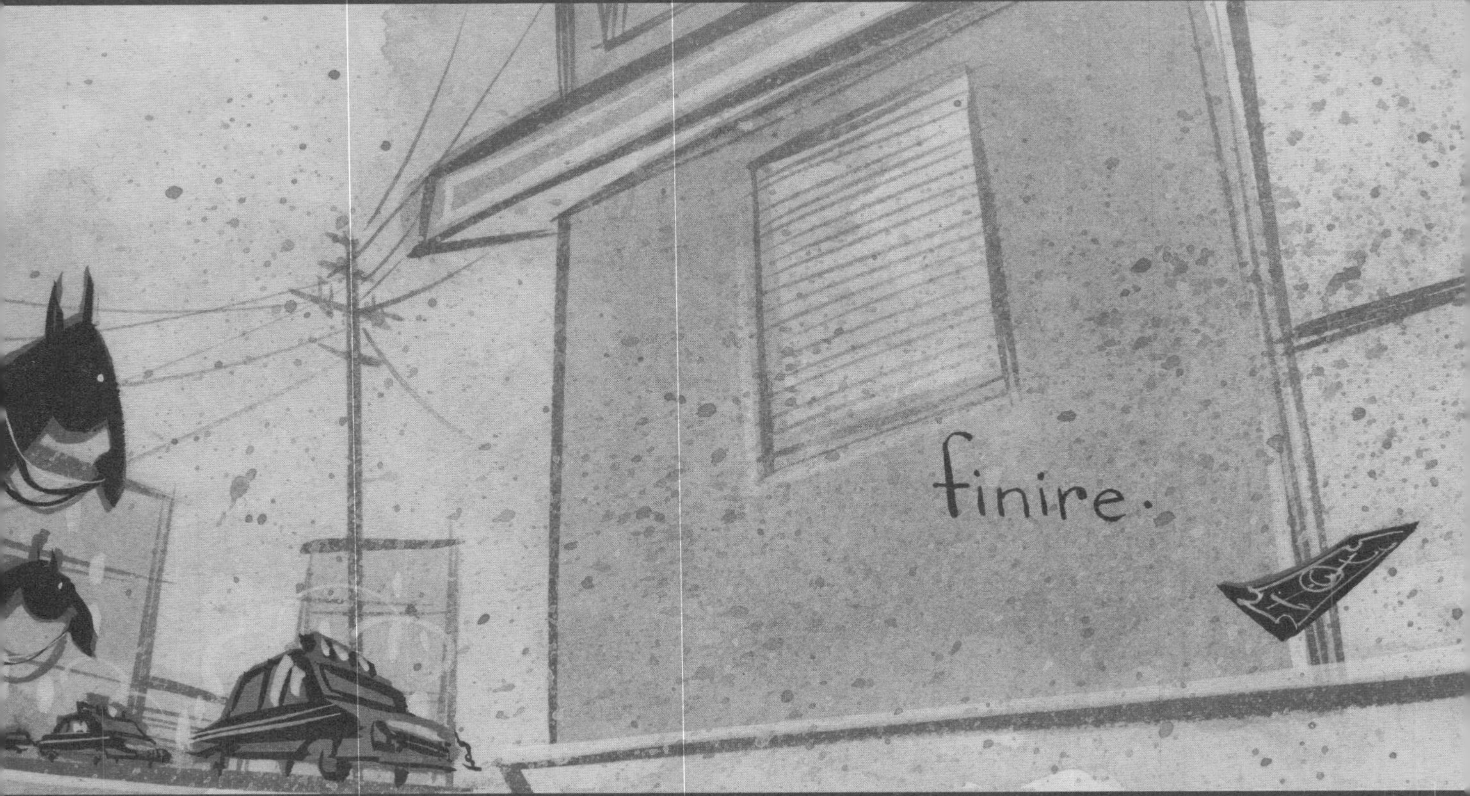
finire.